Praise for *Letters to the Chief*

Letters to the Chief offers a look at the character of life—and the characters—of a small, Midwestern town through the innocent eyes of a young girl. The stories she tells are so much fun that they might seem too good to be true, but know this: in the letters she wrote to the native man she knew as the chief, Judi Lifton is telling the stories of a very real place. Although now greatly changed by the modern world, her hometown still retains much of the spirit she celebrates in *Letters to the Chief*.

Tom Cherveny, Regional Reporter, *West Central Tribune*

Judi Lifton's *Letters to the Chief* is a charming story told in a series of letters to the remarkable Chief White Feather, a descendant of Sitting Bull. The historical Chief White Feather was a renowned preacher, opera singer and evangelist. As a friend of the family, the author met him as a young girl and made him her spiritual guide. Fact and fancy coexist to their mutual benefit as the author writes the chief long letters full of warm, human tales of her childhood in the small Minnesota town of Parker Falls. Reminiscent of *Anne of Green Gables* for its richly rendered setting and large cast of engaging characters as seen through the eyes of a young girl, *Letters to the Chief* is a beautiful melding of memory and imagination by a talented writer.

Patricia Averbach, author of *Painting Bridges and Resurrecting Rain*

A remarkable memoir of a young girl's life in small town America. Every chapter is a short story that is nostalgic and filled with detail. This beautiful story will have you visualizing life in the 1950s and imagining yourself living alongside the author. Five Stars!

Colleen Baldrica, multi-award winning author/presenter, *Tree Spirited Woman*

LETTERS TO THE CHIEF

JUDI LIFTON

Wisdom
Editions

Minneapolis

Wisdom
Editions

Minneapolis

FIRST EDITION FEBRUARY 2020

For information, write to Calumet Editions,
6800 France Avenue South, Suite 370, Edina, MN 55435

Printed in the United States of America.
10 9 8 7 6 5 4 3 2 1

Cover and interior design: Gary Lindberg

Front cover drawing of the Chief and the author used by permission of the artist, Peg Asensio.

ISBN: 978-1-950743-24-7

To Lee, the love of my life, who gave his unconditional love and support, and to my sister Sue, my best friend ever, who never stopped believing in me.

LETTERS TO THE CHIEF

JUDI LIFTON

INTRODUCTION

Chief White Feather was a real person in my life. I knew him because he came through Willmar, Minnesota (where I lived until I was thirteen) talking and singing about the American Indian and the Great Spirit. I knew nothing about his private life until much later when I was writing a memoir and my mother surprised me with an article she had found in the *Pietisten* saying that Chief White Feather was a descendent of Sitting Bull.

Before this book went to press, I decided I'd better collect more information, and here's what I found.

The chief was born in the early 1900s, died in the late 50s and was a grandson of the fourth wife of Sitting Bull. His father was Sioux and his mother was Chippewa. His family name was Teyet Ramar and his nickname was Chief White Feather Sitting Bull. He graduated from Shelton College.

As a Sioux Indian Chief, he appeared publicly and gave lectures on the American Indian. He was a pianist, organist and singer/opera singer, knew four languages and could sing in seven. Chief White Feather also sang for president Roosevelt and the King and Queen of England.

I was told that the *New York Times* called him "the most gifted American Indian in public life." After a family tragedy, he changed from secular to religious music.

Much of his existence remains a mystery, but it hardly matters. I just know that Chief White Feather's life affected mine and that he and my friend Es inspired me to write the Creed of the Tribe of Feathers and this book. While the letters are accurate in their description of my life in Willmar, they were "letters of the heart" and never mailed to the chief.

PROLOGUE

How was I ever going to get through this? My hometown had vanished, I'd been uprooted from my friends and plunked down in the middle of a big city. I sat alone in a house locked to keep out strangers, feeling suffocated with no place to go. Even my bicycle looked lonesome as it leaned sadly against the wall of the garage.

Before we had left our house in the small town of Parker Falls, an older relative named Es, who lived down the street, pleaded with me to stay in contact with our mutual friend Chief White Feather. "He's very sick and may be dying," she said. "The Chief just sits silently in a chair. Maybe a letter from you now and then would cheer him up."

Since moving to the city, I had sent a few letters to the Chief, but my slow handwriting couldn't keep up with my thoughts. Sensing my frustration with writing, Mother had given me her typewriter to try out but didn't understand. Using a pen was not the source of my discomfort... it was my loneliness.

With an aching heart, I embarked on another letter, this time clumsily pecking away on the typewriter. Tears spilled down my face in disbelief of all I had lost. I knew one thing, though—by the time I wrote down all my feelings, I would be a great typist.

Es was right, I needed to do this, and it made more sense to write letters to the Chief than to make entries to myself in a diary.

Chief White Feather and Es were extremely important to me as I was growing up in Parker Falls. Es's house was my hideaway, a special place where I could run for undivided attention and friendship. She was Mom's eccentric cousin who lived around the corner with her husband Jake, a professional photographer. I loved being around her. She was an oil painter and musician by day, a dreamer by night. I spent endless hours watching her paint as the sun poured through the windows. She hummed as she worked, always wearing the same apricot smock. We talked a bit as she mixed and dabbed her paints, but mostly I just sat with my elbows on the table eating cookies and drinking milk. As I savored my treats, I listened to the canary who sat on his perch in a brass cage and, with boisterous vigor, threw seeds onto the table. This always made me laugh and feel like there was no better place to be in the whole world. As Es painted, her canvases came to life and pulled me into another new world, just like the books I loved reading.

I'll never forget the day, I was four, when I rode my tricycle over to Es's house and walked in to find Chief White Feather. I was so surprised that I wasn't sure if he'd stepped out of one of her paintings. I had never met a real live American Indian before. Chief White Feather traveled the Midwest, stopping in various towns staying at Es and Jake's when he came through Parker Falls. The Chief was like an Indian Gypsy; he wore his hair in black braids and carried a headdress of white feathers in a canvas duffle bag. His mission was to tell stories/sing about his culture and the Great Spirit, who ruled the universe. Over the years, I listened to the stories that he told and to the discussions that he and Es had. Many of the discussions were about being committed to life and keeping strong internal beliefs. The Chief sometimes performed in an auditorium in town, and Es accompanied him on the piano with me watching from the front row.

The most memorable moment of my life was witnessing Chief White Feather and Es become blood brother and sister. When I was very young, I watched in wonder as they became spiritual siblings by piercing each other's ears and inserting identical sets of diamond posts. Afterward, they swore allegiance to one another and to the

Tribe of Feathers, promising to wear the earrings to their graves. To memorialize the event, Es set a camera on a tripod and told me to sit on the sofa while she focused the lens. The Chief put on his headdress and came to sit next to me.

Es set the timer, then came and sat on my other side. "One, two, three," she said.

United by the moment, we posed for the camera.

In my last handwritten letter to the Chief, I had asked, "Did you need me as a witness to know it was real? I still have the photo, and it's one of my most prized possessions. Are you sitting there looking at yours? I hope I've made you smile. You have a great smile."

As our friendship grew and I grew older, Chief White Feather urged me to understand all parts of myself and to learn how to live in harmony. He nurtured my inquisitive mind and somehow knew that I would explore life to its fullest. Wishing to acquaint me with the tools of resilience and courage, the Chief included me in his spiritual family and taught me the Creed of the Tribe of Feathers. The Creed is forever in my thoughts.

> To our own self be true and others will trust
> A belief in the Great Spirit is also a must
>
> We must explore all our faces to know who we are
> We must not judge our fellow man from near or afar
>
> Men and demons will tempt us to do as they say
> But only One spirit within, must we obey
>
> We must love ourselves to feel the music of life
> And forever stab Fear in the heart with a knife
>
> We must think like a bird in order to fly
> Actions and words are the seeds left when we die
>
> And we must never give up trying

ONE

MY FORMAL EDUCATION BEGINS

October 15
Dear Chief White Feather,

Did you suspect the last time we three were together that you would not be returning to Parker Falls? I remember you were very serious when you said, "Don't change your beliefs or yourself for anyone. Your soul is forever all you have."

I felt the sadness in the air. And the tears welled up in my eyes. You hugged me and said, "Don't ever be afraid, you have a reservoir of power within."

We sat in silence for a little while. Then I had to leave. I hugged you so hard my arms hurt. I remember the twinkle in your eyes and the love in your smile.

That was the last time I saw you.

Now, I'm sitting at the living room table in a new and strange city, thinking about how much my heart aches. I miss my old friends and my school. Today I walked alone the eight blocks to my new junior high school that has nine hundred students (three times bigger than my old school). I envy my little sister, who walks just three blocks to her school. I wish I were a kid again.

I remember how I could hardly wait to start school back in my hometown. I was so excited for the day to begin, I tiptoed into my parent's room and whispered in Mom's ear, "Is it time yet?"

"Go back to bed. It's too early," she replied. Finally, when I heard Dad get up, I got up too. I dressed and raced downstairs. Mom stood by the stove making oatmeal. "It's your big day, Judi. Have some hot cereal and toast so you won't get hungry before you get home."

She filled my bowl. I topped it with lots of brown sugar. I couldn't imagine what school would be like. I had asked endless questions of my parents, brother and sister who had attended the very same school. Now it was my turn.

Mom offered to walk with me. "Maybe you'd rather have your big sister," she said.

"No. I want you."

Side by side, hand in hand, we began the five-block journey. My sister Sheryl raced by, then turned around and yelled, "Hey Judi, meet me on the front steps. We'll go home together for lunch. And don't lollygag."

I already knew the way to Garfield School. We drove by it on the way to church. And I had ice skated on the skating rink with Dad a few times.

Mom pulled open the heavy wooden school doors, and we followed the polished granite floor to my classroom. A very tall woman wearing heavy dark-rimmed glasses stood in the doorway. Her beady eyes in the big frames reminded me of an owl. She had lots of little lines around her mouth like she drank everything from a straw. I gulped as she sternly looked down at me.

"Good morning, my name is Miss Pearson. What's yours?"

Taking a deep breath, I answered, "Judi. And this is my mother."

Miss Pearson's face remained somber as she pointed toward a chair. "Sit over there," she commanded.

I looked to Mom for help, but she released my hand and said,

"It's time for me to go."

I felt like a little boat set adrift. My stomach was queasy. *This is horrible*, I thought. My dreams about my first school day were shattered. As I sat down, I noticed the boy next to me was on the verge of tears. Turning to him I said, "Hi, my name's Judi. What's yours?"

"My name is Gene—Gene Furland. And I wanna go home."

"Well, we can't," I said, "so let's be friends, and it won't be so scary."

Gene wiped his nose on the back of his hand. "Okay," he answered quietly.

Just then, Miss Pearson cleared her throat. Our first day of class had officially begun. "I trust you are all sitting in the chairs I assigned you. Now I will take attendance."

We all sat anxious and fearful, hoping we were in the correct seats. Three or four classmates were told to switch. Gene and I looked at each other, relieved that we were still together.

Miss Pearson continued, "You must stay seated in your chairs. You can only get up for activities or if I allow you to go to the bathroom, otherwise you will be marked absent."

We all sat quietly, overwhelmed by the severity of our teacher.

She cleared her throat, adjusted her glasses and spoke again. "Every day we have a story, music time, a nap, show-and-tell and exercise. If the weather is nice, we will play outside. Otherwise, we will stay indoors. You must get my permission to go to the bathroom. You can only go two times. If you have an accident, you must wear my bathrobe until your clothes are dry. Any questions?"

The entire class sat shaking and silent, shocked at the coldness of our beady-eyed teacher and wondering, who would wet their pants first.

Our question was answered in the next hour. Would you believe it was my new friend, Gene Furland? Off went his pants, which were put on the radiator by an open window, and on went Miss Pearson's pink chenille robe. We all shrunk in horror! We glanced at our humiliated classmate who was wearing the huge robe and wished for the morning to be over so we could tell the world how mean Miss Pearson was.

My sister met me in front of the school. "Hurry up," she said. "I don't have much time to get home, eat lunch and race back here."

I tried to tell her about my day, but she just pulled me down the street, apparently disinterested in my story.

At lunch, I told Mom about Miss Pearson. She thought I was exaggerating. "You have to take the good with the bad. Maybe next year you'll get a better teacher," she said. Then she proceeded to tell me about her old teacher who used to hit the kid's hands with a ruler if they weren't holding the pencil right. Mom was trying to make me feel better, but it wasn't much help.

Wait until next time for a good teacher? I thought. *This is only the first day of the bad one.*

That night I dreamed about ugly and mean witches. I wrestled with those witches all night and woke up exhausted for my second day of school!

I was too young to realize that Miss Pearson had just introduced me to the word injustice, a word not in my vocabulary at five years of age. The only thing I knew was that no one in my world had ever been as coldhearted.

My classmates and I were unanimous in our dislike of Miss Pearson. Maybe she made us better friends.

I couldn't warm up to Miss Pearson. But as the days moved along, it felt like we were getting used to each other. That is until she told Mom, during one of the parent-teacher conferences, "Judi asks too many questions and is always eager to be first." As if that weren't enough, Miss Pearson added, "Why does she always wear the same horizontal striped T-shirt?"

Mother's answer to her was, "Judi is an inquisitive spirit. She enjoys school, so why does it matter if she has a favorite shirt?"

I was pleased that Mom stuck up for me. After all, it was only fair that if I had to excuse Miss Pearson's mannerisms, she had to excuse mine!

But I did love school in spite of my teacher. Storytime and music were my favorite parts. Any kind of stories were fine with me. Music hour was the best because twice a week, we were given combs wrapped in waxed paper. We placed our lips to the paper and hummed. It sounded like muted horns. Miss Pearson called it the kindergarten kazoo band. I was a pretty good hummer and very attentive during these sessions. Sometimes, but rarely, Miss Pearson even let me lead the band.

My friend Gene spent four out of five days in the cumbersome Pink Robe, his hands buried in the long sleeves, too embarrassed to participate in activities. Anyway, he would've stumbled on the train of the robe. Luckily, no other kids wet their pants at the same time as Gene or I'm sure Miss Pearson would've made somebody run around naked for lack of another robe.

One day before recess, so Gene could go out and play, I suggested to the teacher that Gene borrow the corduroys I had worn like leggings with my skirt. I felt so sorry for him and knew if he had more exercise and fun, he would forget about his problem. Miss Pearson scowled at me and said, "Go out and play, or I'll lock you in the closet."

One day in December, we were so restless that Miss Pearson told everyone to put their hats and coats on and go outdoors. She organized us for relays. Suddenly our fun was interrupted by a chilling scream. Everyone stopped in their tracks!

Gene, who had been running, had stumbled and fallen face first onto a pencil he was clutching in one hand. I guess he'd forgotten to put it away before recess and ended up with the pointy end going right through his bottom lip. We all stood in a circle gawking, fascinated by the pencil protruding from his lip. Before we could have a second look, Miss Pearson pulled Gene up by his hand and whisked him across the playground and into the school. We heard her yell at a janitor who was shaking his mop by the back door, "Watch those kids!"

We were all so shocked at this turn of events that none of us moved before Miss Pearson came back to the playground. "The nurse is taking him to the hospital," she said.

The next morning, we stood in a cluster, wondering if Gene would return. I breathed a sigh of relief as he got out of his car and tromped into school, immediately noticing that his chin had turned black and blue.

Gene solemnly walked a few steps toward us and pulled down his lip in greeting. We stared in awe at his lip sewn up with three stitches in black thread and bulky knots. I asked if I could touch his lip. Some classmates said "Ick" or "Ugly" and turned away, but the majority looked at Gene with great admiration.

That day went down in history.

Gene became our hero. And he forgot to wet his pants.

You know what? Even though we continued to sit together, things changed after that. The class admired Gene for the catastrophe he had bravely endured. Miss Pearson was relieved that she no longer needed to launder her pink robe. And she let Gene direct the band more often than anyone else.

Gene became a new person. He even grew a few inches. I noticed one day while he was directing that his pants were shorter. Or was he just standing tall?

Did I make you smile, Chief? Let me know. I think of you often and wish we were back in Parker Falls.

I wish it would be like old times and you would come and give a concert and stay at Es's house.

A big hug,
Judi

TWO

MOM'S PASSION

October 29
Dear Chief White Feather,

It's me again. Guess what? Mom was offered a position as a choral director here in the Twin Cities. She immediately accepted. I'm glad she has a chance to direct again. Music is her passion. I remember her parting words to the junior choir (which I sang in), "Someday you may leave Parker Falls. But remember, music stays with you forever because songs are carried in your heart."

It started me thinking about one summer afternoon with you and Es. A warm breeze was blowing through the open window, and the sun danced through the glass. You and I were sitting at the kitchen table. You were drinking coffee, and I had a cup too, except I was dunking cookies in mine. Es stood by her easel with her back to us. She would dab her brush in one color and then another, mixing the paints on the pallet before touching her brush to the canvas. Her figures were always so alive I expected them to wink or smile. Painting was her real passion, even though she played the piano and organ.

Anyway, on the day I'm talking about, I remember my eyes drifted from you to Es and the painting, and then to the sunlit grass outside the window. I wasn't really paying attention.

My thoughts were interrupted when Mom's name came up. I stopped to listen. Maybe it came up because Es was going to accompany Mom when she sang on the radio the next day. They were on WKLM a lot.

Es, much older than Mom, has played for lots of musicians, but she's told me many times that Mother was her favorite. In addition, Es had been a piano teacher for ages. She'd earned recognition from the music and art communities, and her opinion was often sought.

One such time was for the high school operetta. The singers had to be chosen, and Es was asked to be one of the judges.

"I can remember the occasion very well," Es told me. "Tryouts were in the large auditorium of the high school. The music teachers from the town, myself plus a guest Miss Sonja Eckstrom from St. Cloud, were the judges. Sonja had attended a conservatory in New York and become an opera singer. She had come back home to St. Cloud to teach after she retired. Miss Eckstrom agreed to direct the Parker Falls operetta and give lessons to the lead.

"Let's see now, the four of us were supposed to decide on the cast. We decided the female and male contestants would be auditioned one by one. Your mother, the last to audition, stepped up to the microphone. Despite being very petite, she exuded confidence. Turning to the pianist, Marguerite nodded for him to start playing. When she began to sing, we held our breath in delight. Her voice was clear and sure. All of us could feel the emotion and strength that came out of her small frame. Sonja turned to me and whispered, 'Marguerite sounds as if she learned to sing before she could talk.'"

"The vote was unanimous that your mother would be the lead in the operetta. We all knew we had a future star on our hands. Parker Falls would be put on the map. Your mother ran home to tell the good news and we applauded ourselves for discovering such a talent in our community."

At that point, Chief, I remember interrupting her. "What happened?" I asked. "Why didn't she become famous?" Then I heard the rest of the story—how Grandma Anna had forbidden my mother to take that part because she did not want HER daughter to be in show business and disgrace the family!

"Why didn't you talk to Grandma?" I asked.

"We all did," Es explained. "But Anna could not be persuaded, and your mother ended up singing in the choral group instead."

I had tears in my eyes as I stared out the window. "Poor Momma," I said. "But if she would have become famous, she couldn't have been my mother."

You and Es laughed when I said that. I laughed, too.

That's what I was thinking about last night, Chief. I was thinking that even though I'm sad that we moved from Parker Falls, I'm still glad Mother didn't become an opera star. And I'm glad I was born into my family.

Do you think she ever regrets being a mom? I know she had another dream, a new little house that she and Dad planned together. They built it when I was about eight. Everyone was excited about it. Finally, we moved in, and we were all so happy. In fact, I found a four-leaf clover, taped it in my album, and printed beneath it, "This is from our new and best house."

I guess Mom and Dad realized the house should have stayed a dream. The payments were too much for them, so back to our old house we went. We kids could've cried forever, but Mother cheered us up. She read to us, told us stories and reminded us that we had a good family. Maybe during those times, she was dreaming of singing in front of the masses, looking pretty in her opera costume and having roses thrown at her feet.

Mom has never admitted that she has any dreams. Maybe she's just keeping something special for herself, or maybe she didn't want us to think of her in any way but as a mother. But now that I'm older, I realize she really needed her dreams. Without them, she COULDN'T have given us such a love for music and COULDN'T have pushed us to think about our own ambitions.

I guess I should tell her how lucky I feel that she's my mom. After all, she could've had her name in Who's Who in America—"Marguerite Anderson of Parker Falls, Minnesota, (1914–present) soprano soloist with the Metropolitan Opera 1940–60, most famous for her voice in *La bohème*."

Today, if her accomplishments were listed in *Who's Who* it would read: "Marguerite of Parker Falls (1914–present), CREATED FOUR STARS IN LIEU OF ONE, FASHIONED FOUR VOICES, WHO HAVE NOT, YET, SUNG…

Do you remember this story, Chief?

I'm signing off, will write again soon.

Love,
Judi

THREE

THE PRINCESS

November 10
Hey Chief,

Thoughts of Grandma Anna keep coming to me. I figure she just couldn't stand up to the church and encourage Mom to star in the operetta. Grandma has never spoken out. She's timid and preoccupied with her own life. At least she was when we grandkids were around.

Grandpa Oscar took such good care of her. He called her "my princess." And I do believe she actually thinks of herself as royalty. Did you know that Grandpa came from Sweden when he was a teenager? By the time he married, Grandpa had his own painting and wallpaper business. Since the wealthy merchants in town were the ones who could afford his services, Grandpa swapped his work for their goods. He pampered Grandma. She always wore a set of pearls and, in the winter, a beautiful fur coat. They owned one of the first refrigerators in town.

Mom says that she and her sisters each had only one dress, which they washed out every night and was from the best store in town called Butter's Dress Shop. Mom's classmates thought they were rich, but she said, "You could almost call us poor. Dad swapped stuff for impractical things. He probably didn't have much choice since the grocer rarely got his house painted."

Anyway, Grandma and I have never been close. When the family has get-togethers, she chats with her daughters and doesn't have much to do with us grandkids. Mostly, I'm with my cousins. I used to do things with Grandpa Oscar before he died. Sometimes we fished together, and sometimes I just rode with him when he ran errands and ate candied orange slices out of the bag that sat between us. Of course, we talked and laughed too. That was four years ago. But Grandma Anna hasn't changed as long as I've known her. She's still preoccupied, only now it's with her memories and fantasies.

After Grandpa died, I became Grandma's errand girl. We lived about five blocks away, and I was elected to be "at her service." My older sister had a daily paper route that kept her busy. Since I was only busy on Thursday when I delivered a community flyer called the *Weekly Reminder*—pages of advertising stapled together—I guess everyone figured I had time to help out. My other cousins were either too young or too old, so that made me the chosen one.

Every time I came racing over to Grandma's house on my bicycle, in response to her call, I found her in one of two places—either by the side of the house weeding honeysuckles or sitting in a red velvet rocker in her dimly lit den, lost in thought and humming as she listened to the old 1940 console radio. When I went into that den, I felt I had run into a time-warp and wished the world would knock her into her honeysuckles or off her rocker so she'd wake up and be with me in my time. But she never did. Most times, I found Grandma wearing one of her flowered house dresses with a red woolen sweater attached at the neck with a pearl clip. She wore black leather shoes, the kind nuns wear with a fat, one-inch leather heel, black laces and screened toe.

When she noticed me, she'd look up and say, "Oh, it's you!" and give a meek smile. Chief, I admit I really didn't want to hang around her. I arrived when beckoned like "reckless Willy" charging up her gravel drive as fast as I could so I could do the errands and get out of there. But I was raised to be respectful, so I always stood there patiently waiting for her to give me instructions.

Usually, I received two pieces of paper. One piece had the items for Star Grocery and the other for Piggly Wiggly Grocery. If it were a special occasion, I also had to shop at Stein's Fruit Market. Then I had to ask Mr. Stein to let me taste whatever was on the list because "that's what Grandpa Oscar did." The lists had to be kept separate at all costs, and if one store was out, I didn't have the right to make any substitutions.

When setting out on my mission, I would put my feet on the pedals and take off like a shot hoping that I and the groceries made it back in one piece. My greatest fear was that toilet paper would be on the list, and I couldn't get everything else in my basket unless I drove one-handed holding a bag to my chest, and hoping my sweaty hands wouldn't moisten the brown paper bag, and that a sudden stop wouldn't send me and the groceries tumbling.

When I got back to Grandma's, I was usually required to have a cup of coffee and a rusk with her. Mom told me I had to stay if she asked me to. "It's a good way to get to know her," Mom explained.

There wasn't any cozy kitchen table in the house, just a formal dining room with a long, dark oak table covered with a lace tablecloth protected by a piece of clear plastic where Grandma and I drank our coffee. A matching buffet, china closet, and the surrounding oak wainscoting halfway up the wall made the room feel crowded. I usually sat facing a gloomy picture of a poor man with his head propped on his hands, praying over a loaf of bread. I always felt sorry for him, whoever he was, and very grateful for my cinnamon sugar rusk and sweetened coffee.

After we prayed and said, "Amen," Grandma would often put a record on the Victrola. Usually, it was her favorite singer, George Beverly Shea, singing the hymn *Is there Blood upon Your Hands?* She loved his rich baritone voice and would hum along with parts of the song as we sipped coffee. I found that song very depressing but would smile nevertheless, much preferring my favorite song *How Much is That Doggie in the Window*.

Sometimes, if she wasn't humming, we talked. Or she talked, and I listened. Most of her stories centered on her life on Swede Hill. I listened more attentively to the ones about when she was a young girl. When I was a little kid, I thought Swede Hill was "Sweet Hill" and figured that her mom and dad were full of good times and laughter if they lived where the "Sweet" people lived. I was disappointed to find out it was a hill on the far side of town where Swedish immigrants had settled.

After we finished our coffee and rusk, Grandma often gave me a nickel, and off I went. I kind of felt sad that we weren't closer.

Things changed for the better one day when I brought my four-year-old sister Susie along. I left her with Grandma while I ran my errands. When I returned, there she was sitting on the red velvet footstool by Grandma's feet, attentive as a puppy dog waiting for dinner. From that day on, Susie asked to visit Grandma with me. Excitedly, she'd run into Grandma's house, take her hand and make Grandma show her the long seal fur coat in the closet. She'd pet it and blissfully look up at Grandma. Then they'd walk over to the buffet together, open the top drawer and take out the satin box containing a strand of pearls.

I'd leave Susie sitting on the stool, knees bent and hugging her legs, eyes focused on Grandma. She looked adorable in her corduroy overalls, T-shirt and Grandma's pearls.

When I came back to take her home, she'd stand very proudly while Grandma took the necklace off her. Then Susie would kiss Grandma on the cheek and say in a very adult voice that must have been picked up from my brother, "I do believe, Grandma, that you are a Princess."

Grandma would look down and smile at her with great pleasure, the kind my presence never gave her.

If we rode off on my bicycle, Susie would sit on a special extension Dad had rigged over my back fender. Enchanted and inspired by our grandma, she'd hang onto my shoulders as her dark curls flew in the breeze and tell me tales of her visit.

I've got to stop for now, Chief. I think next time I'll tell you about Swede Hill.

Love,
Judi

FOUR

SWEDE HILL

December 1
Dear Chief White Feather,

You already know about Swede Hill from Es, don't you? As a child, she lived a few doors down from Grandma Anna, but they never chummed around together. Es was more outgoing and rambunctious. Her sister Minnie, though, was Grandma's best friend. Both were quiet, sweet and unadventurous. People called them the "perfect girls." I think they pretended they were of royal blood and modeled themselves after stories they had heard of great-grandpa's family.

I just found out my little sister wasn't too far wrong in calling Grandma a princess because great-grandpa did come from a respected, extremely rich family. Mom finally decided to tell me the real scoop about my grandparents. Maybe she didn't feel I was old enough before. Or maybe it was because, now that we've left Parker Falls, I can't run around and brag about my eccentric relatives. Mom knows I like to do that. She cringes every time I talk about Aunt Ida, the snake charmer. I'll write about Aunt Ida another time.

Here's what Mom said. "Great-grandpa Olaf had one of the largest dairy farms in southern Sweden. He had a number of dwellings for the farmhands and house staff and a mansion for his family. Olaf and Emma's three sons and two daughters had been raised with the luxuries of maids, cooks and coachmen. John, my grandpa, fell in love with one of the cooks, Johanna. Unfortunately, Johanna became pregnant. Olaf was furious and banished John to America. 'You are a disgrace to our family,' he told John. 'I'm sending you far away to the New Country. You will not get one krona of your inheritance.' But before John left for America, he eloped with Johanna. Since he had no financial support, he had to leave his wife behind, and she gave birth alone.

"Eager for adventure, John's brothers Ole and Muntz asked their father if they could go to America too. Olaf gave them tickets plus their inheritance. Ole came to Parker Falls and opened the only hotel in town, becoming very wealthy. Muntz attended a seminary in New York City and worked at the YMCA. One night while working at the front desk, he was shot to death during a robbery when he wouldn't hand over the money. In Parker Falls, John took a job on the railroad. It took him years to save enough money to bring Johanna to America. Sadly, she arrived alone—their baby had died.

"Grandpa built Johanna a little house on Swede Hill. It was a copy of the three-room house where she was raised. But Grandpa John treated it like it was a copy of his grand house and insisted that the dining room be kept formal for company. As a result, this front room was never used and became a family joke that it was saved for the King and Queen of Sweden. The kitchen was a large room with a pump, pantry for canned goods, a wood cooking stove and a porcelain table. The middle room was crowded with a bed, pull-out sofa, buffet, treadle sewing machine and a large oak table. If the minister came to visit, he was served in the middle room. Once, when he visited with his son, the child said, 'Why are we eating in the bedroom?'

"When Johanna and John's children were born, the house didn't get any bigger, but the sleeping arrangements changed. Grandpa and Emil slept in one bed, Grandma and the two girls—Anna and Victoria—in the other.

"There was an outhouse, a huge garden in the back yard, and a cellar to store vegetables and fruit for the winter. In the summer, it wasn't unusual to see Johanna shelling peas or doing some other task while sitting on a straight back chair on the front porch. She enjoyed watching the traffic pass their house, and that's where my mother first saw my father."

Sorry, Chief, I didn't mean to give you so many details. I think Mom gave us a good idea of what Swede Hill was like, and the new facts about my heritage sure cast some insight as to why Grandma thinks she's privileged.

I guess great-grandpa John never forgot his roots. Grandma Anna told me he wore a hanky under his collar whenever they went to church and pulled it out after the two-mile walk. Only then did he feel properly dressed and proud to be ushered to the front row. The service was in Swedish, which was fine with Johanna (who never learned English.) Anyone attempting to talk to her in English would get a very blank look before she turned away and waited to be spoken to in her native tongue.

Grandma also told me that on a clear night, her mother would walk outside and look up at the sky. The tears would run down her face as she said, "The same moon shines down on my family in Sweden. I wish I were the moon, so I could see my family." She would weep in sadness, pacing in circles and looking up at the moon, until she had no more tears.

At other times she was warmed by nostalgia and entertained her daughters with stories of her life on the farm in Sweden. When neighbors discovered what a good cook and baker Johanna was, they came knocking on the door for her recipes. But no one could match her wonderful cakes or her delicious stews.

Many Swedes immigrated to Parker Falls. The climate in Minnesota was familiar to them. Before long, the community on

Swede Hill expanded down the hill and into the valley. I've heard stories from both Grandma and Mom about numerous Oles, Oscars, Esthers and Johannas who lived in their neighborhood. It must've been a real challenge to keep them straight. I guess that's where all the Swedish jokes came from. Like, "Who did it? Was it my Oscar?" "No, it was Johanna's Oscar." "Which Johanna?"

I mean Es's mom's name was Johanna, and when her husband died, she married another man with the same last name of Petersen. Pretty funny, huh?

The best coincidence of all is that who should be leaving Sweden to search for his Aunt Johanna, who just happened to be Es's mom? Grandpa Oscar, of course. And who should be a teenager at this same time and looking for a suitor? Grandma Anna, of course.

So, Oscar moved in with his cousins and found a job at Peterson's Mortuary cleaning the stables and grooming the horses that pulled the hearse. As he walked down the road to work, he passed Anna's house. If she was on the porch, Oscar couldn't help but notice.

Can't you see Anna looking demurely at him, or furtively looking down at her shoes as she saw him passing? Her big eyes and coy smile must've thrown Oscar totally off balance. I bet she watched and waited for him to come up the hill and then went into the house, timing it so Oscar just "happened" to see her. Anna, in her shy and beguiling way, invited Oscar's courtship.

Her Swedish prince had arrived.

I guess I'll close for now. All those family details wore me out. Talk to you later.

Love,
Judi

FIVE

MOURNING UNCLE JOHN

December 20
Dear Chief White Feather,

Can't believe that I forgot to tell you something very important about Grandpa Oscar's new job. Yes, he groomed the horses for Peterson the mortician. But get this. The place was called Peterson's Furniture and Mortuary. There wasn't a separate funeral home like there is today. Instead, caskets were bought at the furniture store, and families took the body home for viewing. On occasion, people left the open casket in the furniture store for the public to view, such as the time when a little girl in Mom's neighborhood died. Since the family had five other children, they didn't feel it was appropriate to bring the casket home, so little Miriam lay in a small casket in the display area of the furniture store.

"She looked like a tiny angel in her white lace dress," my mother said.

I wonder if Grandpa Oscar drove the horses that pulled the hearse holding Miriam's little casket. And I wonder if anyone took a photograph of her? Mom says it's a common practice in Sweden. Maybe that is why Es and Jake became photographers.

The first thing Es did after her cousin arrived in Parker Falls was to bring Oscar down to the studio and take his picture. He looked pretty comical in a tight suit coat borrowed from Jake and a weather-beaten fedora brought from Sweden. His folks must've smiled and shed a few tears when they saw him. They understood why he had come to America. His father, a tailor, wanted Oscar to share in the family business, but since they lived in a small village, there wasn't enough income for two of them. The only jobs available were in the coal mines.

Es took a sepia photo of Oscar, glued it to a gray paper board and turned it into a postcard. Chief, do you have some of those cards? Have you noticed that most faces are somber? Oscar's wasn't. He was so happy to be in Parker Falls that a smile showed through the twinkle in his eyes and the slight upward movement of his lips. Of course, since his body was larger than Jake's, the suit coat looked way too small, and the hat was wrinkled. But the message of the photo rang loud and clear. "Thanks for giving me your blessing. I'm with family and have a good future here. I'll make you proud. I'll write and come home to see you."

Oscar never placed a foot on Swedish soil again. He purchased a ticket to visit his parents before his wedding. However, Anna begged him not to leave her side. She wept and carried on in fear that Oscar would never return. It was told she said, "I don't want to be like Momma, and at night look up at the sky weeping and wishing to be the moon so I can see the one I love in Sweden."

Oscar relented, cashed in his passage and never returned. But you know he never looked up at the moon and cried. Oscar loved and embraced his new country. I asked him once if he was lonesome. He smiled and said, "The Swedes in the 'old country' and in America speak different languages, but their laughter is the same. Sometimes, when I hear laughter around me, I close my eyes and think I'm in Sweden. But when I open my eyes, I'm happier to be here."

Es and Jake enjoyed taking pictures and continued to document Oscar's life for the folks in Sweden. They sent photos of Oscar and

Anna when they married and endless photos of their four children—my mom, her two sisters and her brother.

Oscar's career changed from grooming horses to hanging wallpaper and painting. Eventually, he saved enough money to move from a small house they were renting on Swede Hill into their own house on the other side of town. My mother, the oldest, was a teenager. Naturally, Es took a picture of their new house.

A few years later, Es and Jake had their camera along for Mom and Dad's wedding and also twelve months later to capture photos of baby Don followed by my sister Sheryl's birth and Uncle John's (Mom's brother) enlistment in the Navy. Es insisted that Uncle John come to her studio in uniform for a formal photo. The picture sits regally on the table in Grandma's living room. My favorite picture of John is in our family album. Mom took the photo with her Brownie box camera. John, wearing his uniform, is sitting on a chair in the bathroom. It always makes me laugh to see the linoleum floor and clawed foot of the tub.

I'm sorry that I never knew my uncle. Everyone says he was a very gentle and loving man. He died when I was dust under the bed. His boat hit a land mine. Mom says that the pain of John's death took the twinkle out of Grandpa's eyes. Sheryl was a baby, and Don was five years old then. It took years of smiles and hugs to rekindle the light in Grandpa's eyes.

John's death caused Grandma to be even less social. She closed the carved oak door that slid from the wall between the sunny living room and the den. Grandmother sat in her rocker insulated from the world in her dimly lit cocoon, withdrawing into her private thoughts and dreams. At times she read or listened to the radio. Grandma changed the formal living room that had always been a showcase—like the front room in her parent's house—into a shrine for John.

My brother and sister survived the quiet household. But when I grew into childhood, I made Grandma nervous. As a little tyke, my curiosity and eagerness to explore made her leery of having me around. If Mom stopped by to see Grandma, she assigned my older sister Sheryl to be my bodyguard. Her instructions were to "keep an eye on Judi." Sheryl took her job seriously. When we walked in the back door, her mission was to usher me upstairs, which was safe to explore. Sheryl would grab my arm and drag me through the kitchen and dining room. In the living room, she'd say, "Don't you dare touch a thing." I'd immediately put on my brakes and challenge her. "We've gotta see Uncle John." It haunted my young mind that no one spoke of his death except to say, "John met his Maker when his ship was blown to the heavens." I had visions of fireworks and its sparks falling into the water, and the big fish eating my uncle like goldfish eat wafers floating on the water and then swimming away to the far shores of the sea with a piece of my uncle.

So, we stopped to look at John's Purple Heart medal and his photo. It gave Sheryl and me the willies to see a photo of an uncle we didn't know looking out at us in a navy uniform. He seemed to be looking across the room at a lilac satin pillow with fringes that he mailed to Grandma from overseas. Sentiment oozed from the poem hand-painted on the silky surface with the letters of MOTHER. Another present from John was the parquet table. It sat in a stand, legs folded against the underside, showing a picture of trees and fluffy clouds designed into the wood by inlaid pieces. Sheryl watched me carefully as we walked by. I longed to feel the smooth surface and to touch it. But my sister pulled me around the corner and pushed me up the stairs.

First, we peeked into Grandma and Grandpa's room, just making sure that everything was the same and that Grandma's nightgown still hung on the back of the bedroom door. We smiled at one another, remembering Grandma lying on the fabric while Mom traced her body. Each time Mom sewed a gown, Grandma complained it wasn't wide enough. "I don't want it crawling up my legs," she'd say. "Let's measure and make it wider."

We quickly walked through John's bedroom and into my mom's and her sisters' (she had two sisters) old room. I looked at the frosted perfume jars while Sheryl sat by the vanity posing in front of the mirror, trying to keep her eyes on me while she studied herself. She loved to use the pearl-handled comb and brush to style her hair.

Soon we heard Mom's musical call from downstairs, "Sheryl, Judi, we're leaving." We came running down the stairs, asking Grandma on our way out if she would give me a perfume jar and Sheryl the hairbrush. Her answer was, "The dresser would look empty, maybe someday."

But "someday" hasn't come yet. Now I'm fourteen. The vanity and its decorations sit collecting dust, and my life in Parker Falls is over.

Memories are not enough. I want to be back in my town. How about you, Chief? Don't you feel the same way? It's been months, and no one has heard a peep from you. Es wrote and said you are breathing and blinking, "but otherwise, he is silent." Are you alive inside? Or are you lost forever? It's almost Christmas.

I am crying for you,
Judi

SIX

CHRISTMAS

December 21
Dear Chief White Feather,

I'm worried. It's almost Christmas, and I haven't heard a peep from you. We'll be driving to Parker Falls during the Holidays, so I'm going to visit Es and find out if she knows anything.

Remember the winter you came for a Christmas concert? It was the year I started school. You asked for donations for a little boy on the reservation who needed an operation.

The next morning, before you left, I came over to Es's. You and me and a kid from down the street made a snowman. I ran home and got some feathers I had saved from Dad's pheasant hunting. We arranged them as if it were a headdress and dubbed it our "Indian Snowman."

This was the same winter Dad splurged and bought us a toboggan for Christmas. Dad tried to keep it a secret until we got home from our traditional Christmas Eve dinner at Grandpa and Grandma Frank's house but found it impossible to hide an eight-foot toboggan from three snoopy kids. After it was discovered, it was torture waiting until Christmas Day to try it out. You and Es chuckled when I told you about our first ride at the golf course. You called it "The Christmas I was helped by an angel." Of course, that was some time ago. I hope you can remember.

Did you know Dad comes from a family of ten kids? Most of my aunts, uncles and cousins live within a hundred miles of my grandparent's house. Actually, it's a small farm. You could say Grandpa's a gentleman-farmer, except he isn't rich, and my grandma does the work. During most of Grandpa's working years, he lived in Chicago writing religious educational material while commuting by train to visit his family. He chose Parker Falls to raise his children because it was a small town on the railroad line, and at that time, the railroad gave free rides to clergy.

After thirty years, Grandpa left his position in Chicago and became a preacher at a country church. It was a special little church that had selected my grandpa to receive its financial support when he attended the university. To show his gratitude, Grandpa asked if he could be their minister when he retired from Chicago, and that was where our family gathering took place.

On Christmas Eve, my five aunts and female in-laws hovered around Grandma in the huge kitchen steamy from the boiling of potatoes and lutefisk—dried cod from Sweden that had been soaked in lye, washed, boiled into a gelatinous mass and eaten with thick white gravy. I must tell you, Chief, that to eat a portion of this delicacy is a rite of passage into adulthood. It's as serious a ritual as the requirement for a young Indian to forage alone in the wilderness for food and shelter in order to become a brave.

As children, we began training our palate at five years of age. It began with one forkful of lutefisk, which was instantly spit out. Each Christmas, this ritual was practiced until, at the age of thirteen, most of us were able to eat an adult portion. It's my theory that this is why many Scandinavians became Vikings—to avoid eating lutefisk.

At this Christmas, which is like most others, the men sat in the living room with the Christmas tree drinking coffee and swapping the latest tales. The children, tots to teens, separated into groups.

My brother, one of the oldest, was up in Grandpa's study reading. Grandpa was an author, educator and scholar—he's writing his second book now. His office has three walls of ceiling-to-floor bookcases. The books filled the shelves and spilled into piles on all available surfaces—wooden chairs, the floor, even his huge mahogany desk.

Meanwhile, a few of the teenage girls scattered into one of the four bedrooms to talk. The rest of us piled outside to beat on each other, make angels in the snow, have snow fights and play games. By the time we were called in, we were famished and ready to eat our mittens. After shedding our wet clothes in the hallway, we were given a heavily buttered piece of limpa (a rye bread with raisins and fruit) to quiet our stomachs. We knew that this was all we would get until we had our Christmas program and prayer. Resigned to this tradition, we inhaled our bread, licked our fingers and found chairs.

The living room was large. Earlier in the day, the men had brought wooden folding chairs over from the church so we could each have one of our own. There was a large tinseled evergreen tree in the room and an upright piano. One of my aunts was the accompanist for the program. My great aunts were given the easy chairs and sofa.

Grandpa Frank dressed in formal black tails. Because of his romantic ideals, on special occasions he wears tails with a gold watch chain in his pocket. Every year my aunts tell me how smart and handsome he looks. I think he looks like Abe Lincoln. When Grandpa stood in front of his chair in his stately suit and cleared his throat, the program officially began. We quieted and listened while he read the Christmas Story. Then he said a few sentences about the miracle of a virgin birth, and the Christmas program was off and running. Each kid said his piece or sang her song. There were thirty-four cousins in total, and usually fifteen to twenty showed up. Last on the program was carol singing followed by two Swedish hymns. Toddlers to teens attempted the words. Learning the pronunciation was another ritual, along with the lutefisk, to earning our passage into true Swedish-hood.

The finale of the program was Grandpa's Christmas prayer. All of us were instructed to get on our knees with the exception of pregnant aunts and great aunts Rachel and Martha. This was the prayer of all prayers. Grandpa left *no one* out of the blessing—all of the in-laws of his nine children, his grandchildren, and of course, all children were included. This was not merely a "Bless Judi." It was "Bless Judi, who is in kindergarten and learning important lessons in life. May she grow strong in Your will and sing forever Your praises. Please bless her neighborhood friend, Rachel, and her parents Edna and Irv. And bless Judi's Sunday School teachers, may they guide her to stay strong and resist temptations."

You get the idea?

We all wiggled and giggled and peeked until all the parents had pinched and pulled their children's hair more than once. In all the years we've attended, I don't remember anyone getting up to go to the bathroom, which is truly another miracle. I guess we have such respect for Grandpa that it never crossed our minds.

All bedlam broke loose when Grandpa finally said, "Amen." Card tables got quickly set up in the living room with chairs tucked around them. The kids each grabbed a chair and sat down. The adults sat by a long formal table in the dining room. The entire troupe eagerly awaited the platters of food. There was pork roast, mashed potatoes and gravy, scalloped corn, homemade breads, Swedish sausage, lefsa (rolled up potato pancake with butter and sugar), candied yams and meatballs. We finished the meal with blueberries over ice cream and plates of homemade cookies.

The adults collapsed the card tables, rearranged the chairs and refilled their coffee cups while we danced around waiting for the presents to be opened. All of us kids had two presents—one from exchange and one from Grandma and Grandpa (usually a set of pencils embossed with our name). The adults had exchanged names and would receive one present each. But Grandma and Grandpa received tons of presents. Grandpa opened them and announced who they were from while Grandma wrote the giver and the gift down in a leather notebook.

Finally, it was time to go home. Exhausted, with our stomachs full, we climbed into the car for our return to Parker Falls. I snuggled in the front seat between my parents and immediately started to think about the toboggan.

"Hey, Dad," I said. "We're going tobogganing tomorrow, aren't we?"

"After we come home from church and have our dinner," he replied.

Content, I leaned against him and fell asleep.

* * *

The year of the toboggan is only memorable for me. Sheryl and Don weren't that interested, and Susie wasn't born yet. Anyway, after dinner the next day, Dad and Don tied the toboggan onto the car, and off we went for our adventure.

It wasn't often our family had new things. Usually, it was homemade or hand-me-downs, so this was quite the occasion. The new toboggan was a masterpiece to behold. The end was curled like the end of a sleigh. The wood was fitted in alternating walnut and oak slats and varnished as shiny as glass.

When we arrived at the golf course parking lot, we could see a bunch of kids sledding. Dad and Don untied the toboggan from the car and placed it on the ground.

"Come on," Don yelled. "Let's go this way." He pointed to a hill in the distance. "There are too many kids over there. We'll have a collision and wreck the toboggan."

He and Sheryl took the rope and started to walk. "Hey, wait for me," I yelled as I attempted to follow, my short five-year-old legs sinking deep in the snow.

Dad stood by the car. "That hill is too steep for me. I'll stay and listen to the radio. Can you watch your little sister?" he asked my siblings.

Don turned around. "Oh, sure," he answered. "Sit on the toboggan, Judi. Let's go."

He and Sheryl started up the hill. It was a long slope, and when we arrived at the top, they started arguing about which way looked the best. Naturally, Sheryl chose one direction and Don the other.

"Listen," my brother said, "I'm older, and I get to choose."

"Let's flip a coin," Sheryl replied, yanking on Don's scarf to emphasize her point. And with the pull of the scarf, Don lost his balance and fell into the snow accidentally pushing the toboggan—with me still sitting on it—away from him.

I shot down the hill like a fish riding down an ice chute. It was only a few seconds before the snowy surface beneath me disappeared. The hill became a precipice, its overhanging face high above the land below. I flew over the edge like a raft launching off Niagara Falls.

And landed perfectly with a thud.

I sat there, shocked. My heart pounded in my ears. Then I heard my sister yelling at my brother on top of the precipice. "If my sister is dead, I'll never speak to you again."

It seemed ages before they got down to me. I was still sitting in the same spot.

Grinning, I looked up at them. "It was magic," I said.

Don hugged me. Sheryl hugged me. There was no more fighting, and we rode the toboggan peacefully. They made me swear that I wouldn't tell Dad.

And I never did.

Do you remember that story, Chief? I keep rambling, hoping you'll wake up. The best Christmas present in the whole wide world would be to see you smile.

Love,
Judi

P. S. After I see Es, I'll write again.

SEVEN

INDEPENDENCE

Dear Chief White Feather,

I was wishing with my whole heart that I would hear from you at Christmas. That would've been the best present ever, but no such luck.

We had planned on traveling to Parker Falls to visit, except it never happened. Winter storms moved in, dumping trainloads of snow from the sky. Since I never got to see Es, I begged Mom to let me call her up.

Es's advice: "Keep writing." Then she told me your nephew had called to say you'd had another stroke.

I wanted to come and see you, but your reservation is over three hundred miles away. The image of you sitting there unresponsive makes my heart ache. I hope you still believe in miracles—I know I do. Remember those last lines from the Creed of the Feathers?

> We must think like a bird in order to fly,
> The impact on others is our legacy when we die,
> And we must never give up trying.

So, I've made up my mind to just sit in front of my typewriter and talk to you through my stories about Parker Falls. And I won't bother you with questions. Maybe someday I'll be as great a storyteller as you.

If you wake up, please let me know. I'll find a way to come and give you a big hug, even if I have to take a Greyhound bus.

Back to my kindergarten days.

After I adjusted to the rules of Miss Pearson's class, the winter months passed and blossomed into spring. Sheryl continued to escort me home from my mornings at school. She walked far ahead, constantly yelling, "Hurry up." If her friend Christine was with us, Sheryl was easier on me. When it was just the two of us, it was pretty rough.

I followed Sheryl, trying to make my short legs keep up. To make matters worse, Mom bought my new school shoes a bit big, so I would grow into them. My socks crept down with every step and bunched into my arch. Naturally, I stopped frequently to pull them up. This drove my sister nuts, and she'd come running back, grab my arm and pull me down the sidewalk.

When we arrived at our front door, Sheryl would burst through hollering, "Do I have to walk this pokey kid home? I hardly have time to eat my lunch."

"She's your little sister, and she needs you," Mother would reply. "Now, sit down and eat your lunch."

Naturally, I would plead, "Let me walk by myself, Mom."

Sheryl's favorite response was, "It would probably take you three days to walk home!"

You can imagine my relief when in April, for my sixth birthday, Mother announced, "You know the way home, Judi. Your sister no longer needs to walk with you."

Sheryl was ecstatic. Me too. I felt so grown up to be on my own. The only trouble was that with no one to accompany me, I was totally distracted. By the time I'd watched a squirrel or tried to coax a cat over or kicked a few stones, I was exhausted and only halfway home. It was a wonderful coincidence that my Aunt Victoria and Uncle Oscar lived right at the corner where I was always ready to "drop in my tracks."

Victoria was my Grandma Anna's sister and married an Oscar just like my grandma did. Of course, I never got their names mixed up because I called Grandpa Oscar just plain old Grandpa and that left Uncle Oscar the only Oscar.

On my way home, I would walk up to their back door and knock. My Aunt would come to the door, and I'd look up and say, "Aunty, I'm very tired from working hard at school. And I walked all this way. Do you think I could have a little snack? Then I'll be on my way."

She'd smile and say, "Come in. I'll call your mother and see if it's okay."

While running through the kitchen and into the living room, I checked things over as Aunt Victoria called Mom. Uncle had built them a new house, and it was always bright and cheery with white walls and shiny varnished woodwork. There were lots of windows, and the sunlight poured in through the sheers. My favorite thing about it was the velvet rug that hung above the sofa. The background was blue with a deer bearing antlers and big eyes staring right out at me. The best part was that he was smiling. This brought me great comfort, and I always smiled back.

As I checked out the deer, Uncle appeared from nowhere. He touched my cheek and said, "How's my pretty little girl? You're not chewing gum, are you, because it will stretch your rosy cheeks?"

"No," I said, hoping that he didn't smell the gum I had spit out when I rounded his corner.

His teasing continued as we had lunch together. "Now, don't add any milk to your coffee. It's a bad habit and will make you fat."

"But I'm only six, Uncle. It tastes good with milk." Aunty smiled as she added a dollop of milk. Then looking over at Uncle, she exchanged a smile with him. I think they really loved each other.

One day Uncle Oscar challenged Aunt Victoria to an egg-blowing contest. They put pinholes in the ends of each egg and blew and blew until the egg came out. Uncle won! I got so excited when I saw the whole yolk sitting intact in the dish that I put my arm right on the empty eggshell, and it smashed to bits.

Uncle laughed and told the story of how he had won many egg-blowing contests when he was a kid. We didn't have such contests in Parker Falls.

Uncle was raised in a town about sixty miles away. Even though he was a Scandinavian and married my Aunt Victoria, folks continued to call him an "outsider." It never helped his reputation that according to local gossip, Uncle took a swig of whiskey now and then. No one ever saw him drink. He never went into any local bars. But the rumor was that Uncle "kept a bottle in his closet."

I guess gossip sometimes leaks out to kids in the hope we will stay away from "those people." In Uncle Oscar's case, I never saw any evidence to keep me away. Nobody was going to scare me off. I loved being around him and Aunty.

My sister constantly reminds me, "You always protect the 'odd' guy."

My brother's opinion, "You always have to be different."

My response, "I have to explore all angles, look at the whole picture and reach my own conclusions. Is that wrong?"

Anyway, back to Aunt Victoria and Uncle. Stopping at their house became a routine. My legs would come to a screeching halt at their back door. Then I'd plead, "After all, Aunty, six blocks is a long way for a little girl like me."

Usually, I arrived before Uncle Oscar came home for lunch. If I saw Uncle's big oil truck parked on the street, I knew I really had dawdled. My Aunt would greet me, "Did you get lost?"

I remember one day I begged Uncle for a ride home. "Not today," he said. "Your school clothes will get dirty."

Aunt Victoria came to his rescue. "Judi, I think this is a day for incense." She opened a drawer, found a small asbestos ring and handed me a little bottle with an eyedropper in it. "Now, put three drops on the ring."

I carefully did my assignment and helped Aunty set the ring on top of a bulb in her lamp. After turning the light on, we waited. The room filled with the fragrance of orange blossoms. It was heavenly—the sun and the smiling deer and the perfume. When I told Mom later, I could still smell the orange blossoms.

One day, after school, I was very lucky. It was raining. Mother didn't drive, so guess what? I rode home in Uncle Oscar's big truck. I sat on his old jacket so I wouldn't get my school clothes dirty.

I gasped in delight as I looked out at the street through the pouring rain. The windshield was huge, and the wipers were trying to sweep the rain away. But the water kept running down the glass. I felt like I was floating in a large plastic bubble with water streaming down its face. I looked out in awe from my dry space.

Uncle spoke up, "What's the matter, cat got your tongue?"

We drove up in front of the house. I scrambled onto the seat past the steering wheel and jumped into Uncle's arms. I didn't get any grease on my clothes. But I got some on my leg.

When Dad read me a story that night, I told him about my adventure. At show-and-tell the next day, I excitedly told everyone about the big truck my Uncle drove and my ride home. I pointed to the grease on my leg for evidence. My classmates were impressed.

Before we knew it, the school year was over, and we had to pass the requirements of graduation—printing our first and last names, and reciting our addresses and phone numbers. In addition, we had to tie our shoes. Miss Pearson said it was critical for our safety.

Everyone graduated that year. The pink bathrobe was retired to mothballs for the summer, and the school doors were closed. It was summer and time to play.

But it had been a big year for me. It was the first time that I had questioned the authority of an adult.

My world had changed.

Now I could walk alone to school. Plus, I could tie my own shoes. I felt older and smarter! I'll never forget Gene and how his life changed overnight. He moved that summer. I hear he's doing fine.

Love,
Judi

EIGHT

SUSIE ARRIVES

Dear Chief White Feather,

After the school year finished, Mom set down the summer rules. "I know you walked home from kindergarten and stopped at Aunt Victoria's, but now I want you to stay on this block. Her house is off limits unless you have my permission. Since Es is around the corner, you can visit her anytime, okay?"

I nodded, but I wasn't too pleased. I loved visiting Aunt Victoria. I also loved having coffee with her and Uncle Oscar. So, I came up with the notion that if I learned how to ride a bike, they would have to increase my range of travel. I asked Sheryl if I could borrow her bike.

"Only if you leave the seat alone," she said. "And remember, it's my bike, not yours."

I approached Dad knowing that he approved of anything mechanical.

Eager to help, he offered to teach me. He stabilized my sister Sheryl's twenty-one-inch bike as I stepped onto the pedals and sat on the seat. "Ready?" he asked as he pushed me off across the double lot toward our neighbor's house. I pedaled as fast as I could and stopped myself by running into the hedge.

Dad smiled, "Don't worry, you'll get the hang of it in no time."

He knew I was determined. It was easy for me to pedal, but stopping was the killer. I couldn't stand and back up the pedals to brake. It was too difficult.

Within a few days, I looked pretty beat up. Mother asked, "What happened to you? Did you bother Mrs. Swenson's cat?"

"No," I answered. "I can't stop the bike unless I run into the hedge."

"What are you talking about?" Mom replied.

I stared at her in amazement. How could she not know what I was up to? Recently, she hadn't been paying much attention to me. She had changed—always tired, her face puffy, her figure getting fat. What was wrong with her, anyway?

Rather than try to explain everything, I decided not to bother Mom. "Can I visit Es? I'll walk alongside Sheryl's bike and push it just to get used to it."

As I rounded the corner by Mr. Benson's, I saw him working in his garage. "Hello!" I hollered.

He looked up. "Where's that big smile I always see? What happened to your face, you chase a rabbit into the bushes?"

"No. This bike is too big for me. I have to run into our hedge to stop."

"I can help you with that," Mr. Benson replied. Taking out his wrench, he lowered the seat way down. "That should do it." He wheeled the bike onto the street next to the curb. "Let's make sure that when you sit on the seat, your feet touch the curb. It will be easier to stop and start. Now, let's see you ride."

Somehow, I got started and thanked him as I rode away.

Wobbling down the street, I suddenly realized that I didn't have the confidence to turn around, so I stopped and almost tumbled as I caught my foot on the curb. Hurriedly, I pushed the bike up a driveway and down the sidewalk toward our house.

"Hey, Mom," I yelled, running through the door, eager to brag about my accomplishment. I found her by the kitchen table looking pale and sick.

"I'm glad you're home, Judi," she said. "Run over to Aunt Victoria's and get me a heating pad, ok?"

I ran out of the house as fast as I could. Mr. Benson had gone inside, and I was glad because I couldn't stop to talk. Aunty was walking down the street to meet me. Picking me up, she gave me a big hug and said, "Slow down. Everything is all right. Your momma called and said she's going to the hospital to have a baby."

"Where will she get a baby?"

Aunty told me God planted a seed in Mom's stomach, and it grew into a baby.

"Then why doesn't Mommy go to church to have the baby?"

"Because God plants the seed, and the doctor takes the baby out. God doesn't have time for everything," she replied. "You'll understand this when you get bigger. Why don't we stop at Nelson's Grocery and get some licorice?"

She knew my weakness, and she also knew that this distraction would make me forget our discussion and get lost in the candy cases. Mr. Nelson's store had a wonderful selection. The candy was all behind glass. Somehow, he understood when I pointed and said, "I'll take one of those and one of these and one of those in the back." My favorites were red licorice twisters and a yard of red licorice, which was a thin piece of licorice rolled up to the size of a big quarter with a little jawbreaker in the center.

Between eating my licorice and laying in Aunty's hammock while she listened to me talk or told me stories, it didn't seem long before Uncle Oscar came home for supper. We had just finished eating when Dad knocked at the back door to announce that I had a new baby sister, Susie. He told us she had curly dark hair and was really cute. Also, he said, "Lena is coming from Dawson, and she will help around the house until Mother comes back."

The next morning, I walked over to Es's and stayed until lunch. Dad sent one of his workers to get Lena saying he would call when they arrived home. I remember that Es thought I looked like I'd been in a fight with a wild animal because of all the scratches on my face.

And she told me you'd be visiting soon, Chief. Do you remember if my face was still scratched up when you came to town? I bet it was, because I know it was a disastrous few weeks for me.

Shortly after Susie came home, I climbed up the face of the metal cabinet in the hallway to get some Q-tips. The metal cabinet rocked in its place, dumping the top shelf onto my body. Come to think of it, I must've looked a mess when you visited.

After Dad called, I ran back home to meet Lena. This was the first time I'd seen her. Her jaw was at an odd angle and her lips were scarred, which scared me.

"Where's Dad?" I asked.

Lucky for me, Dad was out in the back shed looking for something. I ran through our laundry room and out the back door. Finding him, I said, "Why does Lena look so weird? Her face is scary. Is she a witch?"

"No Judi," Dad answered. "She got kicked in the face by a goat when she was a little girl. Lena is nice, and I think you'll like her."

I really had my doubts, but I did what I was told and went back in for lunch.

Lena was really something, Chief. Not only did she look funny, but she was hard to understand because her folks were from the "old country," and she spoke very broken English. I just sat and watched her, considering my misfortune. How could my mother have left me with this strange lady?

That week may have been the longest week of my young life. Lena was too peculiar for me. Even her cooking was strange.

Everything she made was covered in a white cream sauce. It was fortunate that I was small because she served me little portions. After I choked down what she gave me, I went over to Es's or Aunt Victoria's. If it hadn't been for their cookies and glasses of milk, I would've lost my chubby figure during the week that Mother was gone.

I missed my mother desperately. With Sheryl babysitting and Don being a young teenager, there was no one to ask questions or keep me company. Lena sure didn't fill Mother's shoes.

I was too young to visit the nursery, but Don and Sheryl did and told me Susie was a little doll. One night, Don weakened and wrote a letter that I dictated.

"Dear Mommy," I said. "I hope you are feeling very fine. Today Lena canned. It gets kinda lonesome without you here. Sheryl is playing with another girl. Daddy said the baby has black hair and is cute. Love from your honey pie, Judi."

After Don wrote my letter, I still didn't feel much better. Mother was gone, and I felt deserted. Finally, Mom and Susie came home. I ran upstairs and hid under the bed, figuring that with all the commotion, I wouldn't be missed.

Mom came up to find me. Bending over to look under the bed, she said, "Let's take your rocker down, and you can hold baby Susie." We went downstairs. I sat in my rocker, and Mom put a little bundle in my lap. My new sister looked up at me with big blue eyes and curly dark hair.

Susie didn't even cry when I said, "Hello."

I smiled in happiness. Maybe we would be good friends. I felt a lot better now that Mother was home, and Lena was gone.

That night my baby sister slept in my old crib. Twin beds were put up for Sheryl and me. The room seemed a little crowded with three in one room, but Sheryl didn't complain about the change. She babysat for the neighbors and felt confident that a little sister wouldn't be too difficult to handle.

I wasn't convinced that a baby was easy or any fun. For one thing, it cut into my story time. Susie always needed attention, and my Golden Books were getting dusty.

One day I asked Mother if Susie could go stay with Lena until she grew up. Mom laughed, and my story telling schedule was resumed. Sometimes Don and Sheryl were coaxed into reading, but Dad read more often. He became my favorite reader because he'd try to trick me and change the stories to see if I was listening.

Having the baby around kept Sheryl extra busy, so she wasn't using her bike. I really got the hang of bicycling and was elated at my new achievement. My world was expanding, and I welcomed it with eagerness. By fall, I was allowed to ride over to Aunt Victoria's for coffee.

Dad never raised the seat on the bike. He was distracted by reading stories to me or dealing with emergencies like finding a plumber after Don rinsed Sue's diaper in the toilet and let go of it when he flushed the poop away. The diaper stuck in the drainpipe, and Dad had to call for help. To add a little more excitement to our lives, after he fixed the plumbing, Mom was upstairs rocking Susie to sleep. Sheryl and I were downstairs. She was playing the piano and I was singing away. Suddenly, the cracked plaster ceiling came crashing down onto our sofa. Of course, it had been that way my entire life. But it had expanded, and with time the plaster was just hanging from the ceiling. We had all forgotten about it until it fell on our heads.

Mom always said that Dad's strength was running his business, not house repair.

Sheryl and I cleaned up the mess. She grumbled the entire time. After Susie fell asleep, Mom came down and made us popcorn. As we sat around the kitchen table eating popcorn, I began to cry.

"I'm glad Mommy and Susie weren't on the sofa," I finally said. "My baby sister would look like Lena."

Sheryl and Mom started to laugh.

Well, Chief, it's late. I'd better turn out my light and go to bed. Remember, I'm writing stories now instead of letters. Maybe a miracle will happen, and you'll wake up and tell me what you've been thinking all this time.

I'm sending lots of love and reminding you that we're friends forever.

Love,
Judi

NINE

DRIVING LESSONS

Dear Chief White Feather,

With a new baby sister in our house, things were different. It seemed that Mom was always rocking or feeding Susie, but it was okay by me. I had a captive audience for my chatter. I could tell Susie liked my stories because mostly she smiled. When my little sister would start fussing, I'd race over to Es's house for cookies and milk, or Mom would send me over with choral music for Es to practice.

I might have forgotten to tell you that right after Susie was born, Mom became the choir director. She couldn't pass up the opportunity. The minister and his family had moved away, and his replacement didn't have any musical ability, so Mother was offered the position. Es remained the organist.

Each week, both of them had to be there early to rehearse with the choir. Since neither woman drove, Dad started picking up Es. He had made a barter arrangement with her husband, Jake, in which Dad would drive Es to rehearsal, and our family would get an additional discount when Jake took our family photos.

Es was always very casual about squeezing into the car with two adults and four children. She acted like commotion was an everyday thing. On one occasion, she questioned why Mom didn't drive. "You're younger than me and could easily learn," she said. "Why don't you get your license so Bob won't have to haul us around?"

Mother laughed and said, "Oh, he doesn't mind. Anyway, I'm not ready to buckle down and learn."

But one day that changed.

It was September and the Sunday of our "summer's-end picnic." There were a lot of get-togethers, but this one was extra special because all the aunts and uncles, great aunts and great uncles, plus grandma and grandpa showed up. And there were scads of cousins. It was a big deal. Mom was in a hurry to get to the park and help her sisters set up the tables. She told us to meet in the choir room right after the service. "Don, watch little Susie," she instructed. "Sheryl, straighten the choir robes. And Judi, collect any music left on the chairs and bring it to Es."

All of us moved quickly so we could be on our way. After finishing, we went outside to get into the car, but when we exited the church, we couldn't find Dad.

Mom asked Mr. Olson, who was standing nearby, "Have you seen Bob?"

"Yup, Red wanted to give him a ride in his new car. They just left."

Mother's jaw dropped.

Es turned to her. "I can call Jake."

Don interrupted with his idea. "Mom, you should drive home. Dad has shown me the ropes a million times. The keys are in the glove compartment. Anyway, it's time that you learn. Come on—I'll teach you."

We could tell Mother was miffed, so we all chimed in with encouragement. Even Es joined in by saying the streets were very quiet on Sundays, so there would be no harm in driving slowly down the street.

Mom puffed out her chest and said, "Why not? I believe I will drive home today."

Feeling the excitement, we all quickly got into a 1957 Oldsmobile before she changed her mind. Don and Mom sat in the front, and the rest of us crowded into the back. Es held Susie in her lap. Even though I was smiling, I was a little worried. I'd sat alongside Don when Dad explained how to drive a car, but Don had no real experience and needed a few more birthdays before he could even touch the wheel!

First, Mom tried to adjust the seat, but it didn't budge. She was a small person. Dad was large. "I can't sit back this far," she said. "My feet hardly touch the pedals."

"We need some muscle to move it," Don added. "When I count to three, all of you push from the back, while Mom and I pull from the front. One, two, three…"

The seat was a monster. On the third attempt, it groaned and moved forward. Mother was now in position to drive. Taking a deep breath, she turned the key. The car started and jumped. Then all was silent.

"Try again, Mom," Don instructed, "but push in the left pedal and move the shifter into the middle, and then the car will be ready. Now shift upwards."

After a few tries, we were off. Sheryl and I laughed hysterically as we lurched down the street.

Es whispered, "It's like being on a bucking horse."

We were raising so much commotion that Mother turned around and said, "Shush or you will have to walk home." At that moment, the wheel hit the curb, and the car conked out right in front of Pederson's Funeral Home. Mr. Pederson happened to be outside. Coming over, he said, "Are you having car trouble?"

Mother glared at him and replied, "No, I'm teaching myself to drive. Bob was busy, and we're in a hurry, so I'm driving home."

Mr. Pederson looked shocked but cleared his throat and said, "Then I advise that you keep your eyes on the road. He leaned over and looked at Sheryl and me in the back seat. "You children must remain quiet, so your mother doesn't get distracted. Now start the car and take your foot off the clutch nice and easy. And be careful." He waved as we we leapt away from the curb.

Mother drove slowly down the middle of the street, creeping along without further incident. As we approached our block, Es said, "Never mind about dropping me off. You might not get started again. I'll walk from your place."

As we drove up to our house, Mother decided to park on the wrong side of the street. "That way, I can see the curb and won't hit it again," she said.

Our neighbor, Mr. Watson, came running out of his house. He ran around to Mom's side of the car and crouched down to speak through the open window. "What happened? Is Bob in the hospital? Why are you driving?"

Mother looked him right in the eye and said, "It's time I got my driver's license, Irv. Bob was too busy to take us home. Enough is enough."

By the look on her face, Mr. Watson knew she meant business and quickly scurried back into his house.

We all piled out, hollering and clapping.

"Good job," Es said. "I knew you could do it."

Just then, Dad drove up with Red. "What happened? I couldn't find the car, and someone at church said that you drove it home."

The five of us turned to look at him.

Don spoke up, "I taught her just like you taught me, Dad. She did really well."

I guess we all looked so formidable—or pitiful—that Dad smiled and said, "All right, you win. Tomorrow I'll start giving

Mother lessons."

When we arrived at the picnic, the story was told and retold. Don was in his glory, bragging that HE had taught Mother to drive.

I watched Mom. Her face was glowing as she walked around chatting and laughing. Catching her attention, I waved and ran off to join my cousins at the playground. Dave was starting to push the merry-go-round.

I jumped on and grabbed the metal bar. Holding tight, I leaned my head back to feel the air.

"Hey," I said pulling myself upright to make an announcement. "When Mom gets her license, we can come here any time."

Love,
Judi

TEN

WINTER SPORTS INTRODUCE SPRING
AND A PUPPY

Dear Chief White Feather,

Sheryl didn't seem to miss her wheels. After the birth of our sister in September, my skills were needed around the house. Mom asked me to run many errands, and without Sheryl's bicycle, it would have been impossible.

The autumn came and brought lots of brown, crunchy leaves and cool temperatures. I spent more time in my little rocker holding baby Sue. I often stood by her crib, told her stories and sang to her. Pretty soon, she began to smile when I talked. It made me feel real important.

As the days grew darker and the clouds looked like big, gray cotton balls, we knew that snow was on its way. Sheryl and I were excited, but Dad grumbled, "Now I have to winterize the house." This meant that a small room on the north side had to be closed off and plastic put over the door. Dad also would need to wrap tarpaper around the foundation and pack bales of hay around it to keep the winds from blowing through our hundred-year-old house.

Sheryl complained about the appearance. "I'm embarrassed," she said. "Our house looks like it belongs to a bunch of hicks. No one else in town lives like this."

"I'll bet they're not as toasty either," Mother answered.

To be "toasty" we needed to dress warmly indoors and out. Mom and Grandma made us heavy quilts and flannel pajamas for the frigid nights. When we awoke in the morning, our noses usually felt cold from the frosty air that sneaked in through the cracks, so we'd quickly crawl out of bed into sweaters and pants. When we played outdoors, all of us had warm coats, boots and snow pants for the below-zero cold. You should have seen the lot of us.

Dad loved to take pictures and develop them in his darkroom. Outfitted in warm hats with fake-fur-lined ear-flaps tied under our chins, we were the most motley-looking group imaginable. Of course, our big mittens, zipped boots and much-too-big ski pants with flannel-lined corduroys underneath added to our quaint appearance. But the best part of the photos were the smiles on our faces.

We knew that winter had truly arrived when Dad called his friend Joe to clean our oil-burning stove, which sat like a huge, old-fashioned TV in the dining room. Since Dad didn't feel comfortable cleaning the burners himself, Joe came to the rescue. He was a Seventh-Day Adventist.

Dad explained to me that Joe was a good man even though he had a different faith and ancestry. I nodded in respect but was confused because how could he go to church on Saturday when the Sabbath was Sunday? Mystified, I stood by and watched as Joe cleaned the burners. He had black hair and tanned skin. No Swedes or Norwegians looked like that!

"Mr. Antonio, are you a Swede?" I asked.

"No, I'm Italian."

"What's an Italian?"

"Well," Joe said, "Italy is a country down south from Sweden where it's very warm, and the people get darker from all the sunshine. Italians invented two very good things—macaroni and spaghetti."

"Then I like Italians very much," I said, "because my favorite dish is macaroni and cheese." I walked away with the two men smiling.

The entire town welcomed the winter season. The men had ice fishing, and the kids had sledding and skating. All the schools had rinks and warming houses. By Thanksgiving, everything was ready.

One snowy afternoon during the winter Susie was born, Dad told me, "Today I'll teach you to skate."

Off we drove to Foot Lake, a small body of water across town that was bumpy and lumpy and somebody had swept with a broom to prove there was ice below. Since there was no warming house, there were few skaters around. This spot was the "training rink" for all children.

Dad tied double runners onto my boots, took my hands and walking backward, pulled me around on the ice. Patiently, he lifted me up whenever I fell. Then he'd say something like, "Now you try skating yourself. I'll walk by your side." During these training sessions, I clung to him, barely moving and as unsteady as a newborn lamb.

After a few Sundays, ice skating didn't seem so difficult.

"You've graduated," Dad said. "I think you can stand on your own two feet. I'll go with you to the rink to make sure."

I put on an old pair of Sheryl's shoe skates and two pairs of woolen socks. Dad tied my shoelaces, and after placing a wooden guard on each blade, he drove me to Garfield School. I tried to be excited, but inside I was worried that I might never be as good as my brother and sister.

Don was famous for skating backward and flirting with the girls, and Sheryl was a rink leader in "crack the whip." After organizing her friends in a long line, they would pivot from the person on the inside and swing in a fast circle like a lasso over a cowboy's head.

Whoever was on the outside edge was in serious trouble and would be moving so fast that most of the time, they'd holler and end up in the snowbank surrounding the rink. That is, everyone except my sister Sheryl.

As we walked from the parked car to the rink, Dad gave me a pep talk. "I know you can do it. All you have to do is just skate into the middle of the rink and practice. Everyone else will be chasing around the edge. Got it?"

Nodding, I wobbled toward the center, blades pointing outward and ankles pointing inward.

"I'll be in the warming house talking to Sam," Dad said. "You all right on your own?"

"Sure, Dad," I yelled as I crashed to the ground.

Sheryl saw me and skated over to pick me up. "I got her," she shouted. "Don't worry." She put her arm around me and escorted me to the center of the rink. "Don't look at your feet," she said. "Look straight ahead and skate a little faster. And act tough even if you fall."

I practiced skating until I was brave enough to skate between the kids to the warming house. I was still unsteady, but I managed to get up the two steps to the door. Inside, I saw Dad talking to Sam and went to sit next to them. It was a noisy and cheerful place. Within a couple of minutes, everyone had come in from the cold and was clomping with their blades on the wooden floor, eager to sit near the stove. Some fell onto the benches, laughing. Others were groaning. The energy of the skaters was contagious. I felt very grown up to be among them.

Suddenly, Dad realized I was sopping wet. "Come on, Judi," he said. "Let's go home and have Mother make some popcorn."

Dad put skate guards on my blades. Walking back to the car, I discovered my balance had improved. Maybe I was motivated by the image of buttery popcorn, hot chocolate and laughter around the kitchen table.

When the snow eventually turned to slush, I knew it was spring and time to celebrate my seventh birthday. It seemed like a great way for the season to change. On my big day, Susie was napping, and I was helping Mom make cookies when Dad came in. You remember how big he was, Chief? Almost six feet tall and two hundred and fifty pounds. He was almost never without his gray fedora and dark gray suit. Dad had a real presence about him.

"How's my little girl on her birthday?" he asked.

"Fine, and what did you get me?"

Laughing, Dad put one hand in the pocket of his suitcoat. His hands were big. I spent many hours as a little kid putting my hands against his just to see how big they were and if they had grown. Many times, we played "stack our hands," which meant one of my hands would go on one of Dad's and then his hand on my other one. The idea was to rotate hands as quickly as possible, pulling out the hand from the bottom and putting it on top. Sometimes, Dad tried to keep my hand in place, and other times, we would go so fast we'd get mixed up. Every time, though, we ended up laughing.

Anyway, Dad stood there smiling and repeatedly asking, "What do you think I have in my pocket?"

Every time I guessed, he repeated, "Guess again."

Finally, Dad withdrew his hand. In his palm was a tiny black puppy with a red ribbon tied around its neck.

I squealed in happiness, "Is it really for me?"

"Yes, it's your birthday present."

"I think I'll name him Rex," I said. And that day marked the beginning of our great friendship.

I quickly realized that Mother didn't share my excitement about the puppy. She immediately placed the ironing board—slammed it down, actually—across the kitchen doorway. She put papers in the corner and managed to train Rex in four days—I'm sure a world's record. I was happy that he was such a smart puppy because his life would have been in jeopardy if he'd been a slow learner.

After a few months, Rex was kept outside by his doghouse. By the end of the summer, he had grown to the size of a small beagle, except he was thinner and taller with short black ears. Rex's fur was soft with a little feathering on his legs and some white on his face. He was easygoing and smart enough to play fetch. But Rex's two greatest attributes were that he could run very fast, and he never left my side.

Wherever I went, Rex was right there. I could walk, run or bicycle—and there was Rex. When I went to Es's, he waited outside. If I went to a friend's or the library, he didn't mind just sitting and waiting.

His behavior was exemplary until the summer day I was biking uptown to the drug store to buy Mother some aspirin. I decided to take a detour to see if the mysterious Gravel Gertie was outside. I heard gossip about her because my parents and neighbors told me she drove a truck. I was dying to see what she looked like.

In Parker Falls, people were farmers, retailers or factory workers. "Unusual people" were few and far between. Except for you, Chief, and Es, the only unusual people I knew were those I read about in books.

My father said that when Gertie's husband died, her brother Slim, being an honorable man, gave Gertie a job driving a truck for his business. Slim let it be known that since "on-time delivery" was crucial to his cement business, who could be better at delivering stuff than his reliable sister?

Slim was very sociable and could often be seen having coffee at the local donut shop and chatting with the other customers. Gertie could only be seen driving around in her gravel truck. Otherwise, she was a hermit. Sheryl said she had seen Gertie once wearing a baseball cap. Pictures of her in a cap floated through my head, but I couldn't quite imagine what that really looked like.

The few times I rode past Gertie's house, I got a little scared and raced by.

On one particular day, Rex and I were traveling past it when Rex suddenly saw a squirrel and dashed right through Gertie's hedge. This put me in a tough spot because how could I leave my dog?

Getting off my bike, I used the kickstand to park it then peeked through the hedge. I could see Rex with paws up on a tree barking at the squirrel, which chattered back at him. No one was around, so I walked toward the house and called out, "Come on, Rex, let's go." Just then, a small woman with a red bandana tied over her hair came out of the house and yelled, "What's all the commotion out here, anyway?" Then she saw me.

Timidly, I replied, "It's me, Gravel Gertie. I'm trying to get my dog outta here, and I'm sorry for the bother."

Hearing my quavering voice, she smiled. "Aren't you Bob's girl? What are you doing so far from home?"

I cleared my throat, figuring I'd better tell the truth. "Yes, that's my dad. My name is Judi. I'm on an errand for Mom but rode out of my way to see if you happened to be outside. I wanted to see what you looked like. I figured that if you drove a gravel truck, you must be a lady who looks like a man. But you don't. You're tiny, and you look like a lady."

I felt like I was going to get a bawling out, but Gertie said, "Sit down on the steps, Judi, and let's talk a bit." I obediently sat down as she continued. "Why shouldn't I drive a truck? Your mother drives a car. Is that any different?"

I tried to think about it. I was in a jam and didn't know how to get out. Rex had trotted over to my side, so I took ahold of his collar and tried to be brave. "Well," I replied, "I rode in my uncle's big oil truck and really loved it. It was way up high and made me feel very important. I think it must be nice to drive a truck. I just don't know any lady who does that. I'm very pleased to meet you, and very happy you're small. Maybe when I get as old as you, your brother will hire me."

Gertie threw back her head and laughed. "Well, I guess that's possible. There are lots of things to choose from. Maybe you'll sell cars for your dad."

"I don't know much about cars, but when I get older, maybe I could learn. It was sure nice talking to you. I guess I better finish my errand or Mom will wonder what happened to me. Come on, Rex, let's go!"

At supper that evening, I asked my father if I could sell cars for him when I was older. He avoided answering me and reprimanded me for snooping at Gravel Gertie's.

I took the scolding and said that I wasn't going to make fun of her anymore. She was okay by me, and from now on, I would call her Mrs. Gertie.

Mom thought my idea was a good one.

Sheryl told me I was pretty dumb to let Rex trick me into stopping because he would have come home sooner or later.

Don said Dad would never let me sell cars. "You have to go to college," he explained smugly.

Later, when I talked to Es, she said, "Judi, you just celebrated your seventh birthday. I think you have plenty of time to figure it out."

ELEVEN

DREAMS OF ALASKA

Dear Chief White Feather,

Did I tell you, Chief, that Grandpa Oscar was a fisherman? He fished all summer long, and in the winter, too. I guess he just loved fishing.

One winter day, as my brother Don and I sat drinking cocoa and eating popcorn, he vividly described his ice fishing experience with Grandpa. As the oldest child and only son, Don was doomed to endure the sports of hunting and fishing even though he despised both! Sun and swimming were on his list of pleasures, but sitting in an icehouse on a cold day in December was the same level of punishment as having chocolate cake and ice cream taken away forever. Don gave me this lurid description—"We stared down a deep black hole at our lines fading into the water. Finally, after waiting and waiting, a fish took our bait. The worst part was whacking the fish over the head to kill it. Bright red blood splattered all over the ice. My feet were freezing, and the fish lay dead on the ground. Now, what fun is that?"

We both knew that our family was more of a docile, non-whacking kind of group. But I wasn't going to let that stand in my way. I loved adventure. Sensing Don's frustration, I came up with an idea. "Next time I want to go in your place," I said. "I'm old enough now. I'll be eight on my next birthday. Pulleease ask Grandpa."

My brother laughed. "I'll think about it."

The lack of interest in sports came from Dad's side of our family. Grandpa Nat's definition of a good sport is "anyone willing to participate in a lengthy discussion." Scholastic competition was encouraged and demanded. Sports were never mentioned unless you were talking about joining the debate team. When I became a softball pitcher in junior high, it changed history—a breakthrough into athletic sports.

I inherited my throwing arm from Mother. For years I had watched her take mice out of their Velveeta-baited traps, walk outside, wind up and pitch the little dead mouse across the empty lot next door. I swear, with her vigorous throw, she could toss it right into the hedge on the property line fifty feet away.

Anyway, I had some other reasons to go fishing. Number one— since I was old enough to remember, I had been tantalized by all the little huts (we called them ice houses) sitting on the six nearby lakes. And number two—I had been reading about Eskimos since my Aunt Gert and Uncle Ralph had invited me to visit them after they moved to Unalakleet, Alaska.

So, I telephoned Grandpa and asked him to take me fishing. "It could be my Christmas present," I suggested.

"We'll see," he said.

At night I dreamed of ice fishing and how the experience would give me something in common with the new friends I'd meet when visiting my aunt and uncle in Alaska. Deep down, though, I knew my dream would never come true. My family stayed close to home. But that didn't stop my imagination. Faces of my new Eskimo friends floated through my mind. Well, I couldn't really see their faces because of their fur parkas. I fantasized about walking to the trading post and buying a parka for myself and sitting in their igloos having hot chocolate (if they had hot chocolate, that is) and laughing like crazy. My heart beat with excitement.

After exhausting my dreams of Alaska, I reviewed Aunt Gert and Uncle Ralph's wedding. It had been a special occasion for me, the first time I'd been part of a wedding celebration. Mother sent me to Penney's Department Store with Sheryl to buy a dress. I dreaded the shopping trip because I never got to choose anything, and my older sister would whine, "You have no taste in clothes." On this shopping trip, I saw a pale yellow taffeta dress that looked very soft and beautiful. If I had to dress up, why not pretend I was Cinderella? My sister had run into a classmate and was so busy chatting that by some fluke, we arrived home with the yellow dress. Mom said it wasn't practical, but I pleaded with her. After all, I was going to be an official dream-cake-deliverer with my cousin Karin.

Aunt Toots gave us instructions at the wedding reception in the church basement. First, she handed us big Easter baskets with small pieces of fruitcake wrapped in tin foil and tied with ribbon. "Now give one to all of the guests," she told us. "Tell them to put the fruitcake under their pillow and whatever they dream about will come true."

My eyes opened wide at the opportunity.

Aunt Toots smiled. "Didn't you know this was an old Swedish tradition?"

"What if I put two cakes under my pillow?"

Toots laughed and sent us on our way. I noticed that everyone took a piece. Most of the men opened the tin foil and ate the cake. The women put them in their purses. Later, Aunt Gert gave Karin and me a gift of perfumed sachet and said, "Come and visit us in Alaska."

That night, I put my little piece of foil-wrapped fruitcake plus the sachet (for good luck) under my pillow and dreamed of traveling to Alaska. I had looked at a map in one of my library books and found Unalakleet on the banks of the North Bay Sound less than two hundred miles from the Arctic Circle. Their home seemed even more faraway and mysterious. To add to the intrigue, Dad told me they were setting up a new radio station to broadcast democracy and religion to Russia. I felt proud to have pioneers in my own family and wanted to keep track of them.

As I lay revisiting these events, I realized that IF Grandpa took me fishing that I would have something to tell them in a letter. They were probably lonesome and would enjoy getting news from someone who didn't live in an igloo.

Luck smiled on me, and Grandpa called. "Let's go, Little One," he said. "I'm going out right after supper, and I'll take you with me. Maybe you'll become the fisherman of the family."

It was a ten-minute drive from Parker Falls to Willow Lake. Car tracks led us from a gravel road toward the lake.

As we drove onto the ice, the evening sky performed magic. A big, red, faraway sun slipped over the edge, its molten weight sinking out of sight. Excitement surged in my veins as we slowly moved across the ice. Wide-eyed, I held my breath in delight. Here we were, my Grandpa and I, in his warm car on a lake with thick ice covering the water. It felt like we were following a glass road into the Land of Enchantment. No sounds existed there except for Grandpa's tires crunching the snow against the ice. I sat cozily by his side, feeling happy to experience this miracle in life.

Grandpa stopped the car, and I jumped out. Holding his hand, we walked toward his little fishing house. Inside, Grandpa turned on his flashlight and showed me the hole he'd cut deep into the ice. He took a hatchet and broke the new ice that had skimmed the top. Hanging a line into the dark water, he said, "Let's walk around and see who's here. I'll fasten the line to the wall, so some big fish doesn't run off with the bait."

Walking around, we visited fishermen idly drinking coffee in front of bonfires with tall, yellow flames reaching towards the sky. Glowing embers created wetness and frost. I was captivated as I looked at the glistening ice and the chatting men. It felt like they were suspended in some dark space. Nothing was visible but the fires and the faces. Without stopping my thoughts, I tugged on Grandpa's hand. "Did you bring me to Sweden?"

He chuckled and leaned over, "Yes, maybe I did," he said. "When I was little, I spent lots of time with Papa on the village lake just like this one."

We wandered around checking on all of Grandpa's friends. One old man was standing over his fishing hole with a bow and arrow, a fire blazing alongside him. Bait floated on top of the water as the man patiently waited, eager to pierce the fish by surprise. The arrow was attached to a string, which was attached to the man's arm so he wouldn't lose the arrow in the dark water.

The fish weren't biting that night—not for us or anyone else. Unfortunately, I didn't get to see any fish get whacked over the head, nor did I dare quiz Grandpa about the technique. Don had sworn me to secrecy, fearing that I would expose his true feelings.

While driving home, Grandpa and I talked—me mostly—as we shared the sugar-coated orange slices he kept in a bag on the front seat. I told him that ice fishing was the best present he'd ever given me.

Enclosed in the Christmas card from Aunt Gert and Uncle Ralph were some photos. Their house was on a snowy plain with no igloos in sight. Many of the Eskimos were bundled up in regular clothes, but a few wore parkas. Nobody looked like the pictures in my library book.

My letter to Aunt Gert and Uncle Ralph lay unfinished in the bottom of my dresser drawer and the images of stopping by the trading post with my Alaskan friends began to fade from my dreams. My mind became preoccupied with something else. Grandpa and Grandma had become the proud new owners of a cabin on North Eagle Lake located a few hours away. Mom said our family would go and help put up the dock, returning later for a vacation. This was exciting because the only time we had spent more than a day away from home was to attend church camp, and we didn't call that a vacation.

During those cold winter and spring months, Susie and I spent endless hours talking about all the fun we would have. And some days, in anticipation, we put our bathing suits on. We must've packed and unpacked our shared suitcase a hundred times.

TWELVE

NORTH EAGLE LAKE

Dear Chief White Feather,

On my bedroom wall hangs a picture I made after visiting Grandpa and Grandma at their lake cabin. I love the picture almost as much as I loved the trip to the lake. My crude drawing shows a man and a redheaded girl sitting in a boat with red crayon smiles on their faces. The man in a brown hat holds a fishing pole, and so does the little girl. A piece of yarn—the fishing line—is pasted onto the end of the pole at one end and a big cut-out fish on the other end. The fish is hidden beneath one of the turquoise waves cut from construction paper. If I pull on the yarn, the fish jumps right out of the water. A yellow sun is glued among blue clouds with cookie-cutter edges that float in the sky.

If I were to create a whole comic strip, it would illustrate my anticipation over our upcoming vacation, the ride with Mother to the cabin, Susie's fishing adventure, and my fishing trip with Grandpa. But since words are my paintbrush, I'll tell you the stories instead.

At North Eagle, we visited other friends from Parker Falls. The land was wooded, rustic, and the lake was the best for fishing.

Everyone said that the drive was worth it. But this year was extra special because Grandma and Grandpa had their own cabin, and we were taking a real vacation and going to stay with them. Dad couldn't come because he had to run his business. Don pleaded to stay home since he was such a big shot in high school and felt too old to be with us. Sheryl had just discovered boys and wished she didn't "have to go to the boondocks for a whole week."

But their requests were in vain.

Susie and I were so excited about the trip we ignored our brother's and sister's complaints.

It was the first year that Susie was no longer a baby and old enough to be my friend. Since she had no memory of previous visits to North Eagle, she begged me for information about it. As we lay in our beds before leaving for our vacation, I told her stories.

"One time," I said, "Sheryl took me to a haunted barn in the woods where a witch lived in the hayloft. We didn't see the witch, but we saw a dog that looked like a wolf. The dog howled and snarled, and we ran away as fast as we could."

It didn't take much to get Susie convinced that we would be going to a world of scary animals, witches, and a deep clear lake where we might see crocodile skeletons.

Finally, it was time to get our gear together and leave for North Eagle. Mom packed everyone's clothes in two suitcases. All the stuff was placed on the back porch for Dad to pack into the car. We brought extra bedding, a cot, new canvas lawn chairs for Grandma and Grandpa, and Mom's usual baked treats—bread, rice pudding, ham and scalloped potatoes.

"And where am I supposed to put all of this?" Dad asked. After getting no response, he continued. "Anybody know where there's some rope? You'll look like the Real McCoys, but it's the only solution."

The trunk was packed, the cot and lawn chairs were tied to the roof and we were ready to go. Don studied the map as Mom backed out of the driveway. Susie and I yelled and waved. "Bye, Dad. We'll miss you. We'll bring you lots of fish. See ya."

"Okay, everyone," Mom announced, "keep yourselves busy. I have to concentrate on driving across the country."

Sheryl was sitting in the back seat with Sue and me. "I can't believe how much you exaggerate! It's only three hours away."

Mom ignored her comment. "Just keep your eyes on your sisters. I'll take care of the driving."

Before long, we were playing the alphabet game—searching for each letter of the alphabet on the road signs. Mom interrupted. "In another half hour, there's Sundstrand's Dairy. Does anyone want an ice cream cone?"

We stopped to use the bathroom and buy our treats. Sheryl chose the new flavor, peppermint stick. After eating half the ice cream, she decided she didn't like it. "Come on, Judi, swap with me. This stuff upsets my stomach."

"Right," I answered. "You just want my cone because it's bigger."

Not appreciating how seriously the ice cream disagreed with my sister, we continued down the road until suddenly Sheryl yelled, "Stop! I have to throw up."

Mom slowed down as fast as she could. Sheryl's cheeks were ballooned out, and she was pinching her lips. As the car stopped, Sheryl puked all over the floor, some of it spilling onto the seat between us.

"Everybody hang on. Wind the windows all the way down," Mom pleaded. "There's a gas station up the road."

At the Sinclair station, Mom removed the dish towel she had wrapped around her scalloped potatoes and got a bucket of soapy water from the attendant. "Go sit on that bench over there and stay put. Sheryl, clean yourself up the best you can."

Opening all the doors, she washed everything off and then, as an additional precaution, sprinkled around some Evening in Paris perfume from the blue glass bottle she carried in her purse for special occasions. Then she called us back to the car.

"All aboard! Don, would you please switch seats with Sheryl?"

My brother immediately moved to my side of the car. "You sit on the other side," he said to me. "I'm not sitting in that wet spot. I'm the oldest."

"If your butt weren't so big, it wouldn't get wet," I shot back.

Mom intervened. "Judith, you know better than to talk like that. If you don't settle down, I'll turn around and drive home."

Everyone was silent until Sheryl said, "Hey, there's the sign for Camp Roma Bait Shop. That's where we turn."

Mother was lost in her thoughts and didn't hear the warning.

Sheryl boosted her volume. "Mother, you're missing our turn!"

Her daydreams suddenly shattered, Mom quickly jerked the steering wheel to the right and turned the corner as if she were a race car driver. Dad's knotted rope securing the overhead gear could not take the stress. The cot and lawn chairs shot off the roof like rockets on the Fourth of July, landing with a clunk in the ditch. I laughed so hard I thought I was going to wet my pants.

Mom stopped the car. She was trying to be stern, but she started laughing too. Then she turned to Don. "Can you please get our things out of the ditch?"

My brother cautiously walked through the long grass and retrieved our stuff. Relieved that nothing was broken, we placed the cot across our laps and propped the chairs out the window. The cabin was just a short distance away.

When we drove up to the cabin, Grandma came out, glanced at our harried-looking Mom and said, "What happened to you?"

Mom hugged her parents and said, "Ask the kids."

We all joined in, revealing the details of our adventures. Then Susie and I went off to explore.

The cabin sat on a wooded hill a hundred feet from the lake. A narrow, well-worn path wound down to the lake. Edges of rocks stuck out of the dirt. I warned my sister, as Mother had warned me, about all the catastrophes that could happen if we were not careful.

Susie and I raced back to the cabin, shouting, "Can we go swimming?"

Mother turned to Don, "Will you watch them?"

It was amazing that with all the time we spent at the lake, none of the adults could swim. "Us kids" were the first generation to flap our arms and try to be amphibious.

Grandpa was a fisherman, but his only body parts that ever touched the water were his feet when he pushed his boat away from the dock. Grandma was a "water gazer," which meant she looked down at the water when she sat in her lawn chair on top of the hill.

My parents were a bit more adventuresome. Mom put a suit on and hung her feet in the water at least twice each summer. Dad only went swimming late at night "after all the mosquitoes are sleeping," he'd explain.

Obviously, that left Don and Sheryl responsible for our safety.

We all walked down the path to the lake. North Eagle was so clear that I felt like I was standing in a big fishbowl. I watched the minnows swim around my legs and the crayfish scurry away from my feet. Susie played in the sand with a porcelain cup that Grandma had given her. As she dumped sand over her toes, she watched mesmerized as it ran over her feet, then looked up and smiled at me, happy with her great discovery. I walked onto the dock, laid down on my stomach and swished a stick in the water, trying to persuade a floating bobber and broken fish line to come my way.

Sheryl and Don started a water fight with such a ruckus that I stood up to watch. They were screaming, splashing and dunking each other. Suddenly, I turned to check on Susie and she wasn't there. I looked down and there was my little sister flat on her back beneath the clear water looking up at me with her big blue eyes. She was lying very still—the only movement was her brown curly hair floating in the water.

"Help," I yelled. "Susie's drowned."

Don came charging through the water, Sheryl close behind. Their splashing wrinkled the water, distorting the image of my sister, who was lying quietly below the surface.

Holding my breath in fear, I watched as Don picked her up out of the water. Grabbing Sue under her arms, he lifted her high into the air.

Sheryl whacked her on the back with a good thump.

Susie sneezed—a really big sneeze—like a puppy would if he put his nose in pepper.

I jumped up and down, yelling, "She's alive. She's alive."

Mother came running down the hill, "What happened?"

Don was sitting on the dock with his arms wrapped around Sue. "Everything's all right. She fell over in the water."

Susie looked up at Mom with a big grin on her face. "Guess what, Mommy? I caught a baby fish in my cup."

Mother lifted little Susie from Don's lap and hugged her tightly. "Come on. Let's go have some lemonade and cookies."

THIRTEEN

MY FISH

Sorry, Chief. I meant to get to the story about Grandpa and me fishing, but I got sidetracked telling about other adventures. The stories will fit together, I promise.

First, let me tell you about Grandma and Grandpa's cabin. It was one big square structure with a huge, overhanging roof. Big eaves shaded the place, and if we lifted up the glass windows and hooked them onto the inside rafters, the eaves kept the rains out and let cool air through.

The inside was plain with a wood divider between the kitchen and bedroom. The rest of the walls were just bedspreads hanging from stiffly strung wire. Grandma would pull the cloth back during the day or across at night for privacy. In the open area, there was a second double bed, two rockers, a day bed with pillows on it, and an oval wood table with two long backless benches painted in green enamel. That's where we ate our meals. I can't forget Grandma's mahogany Victrola that she brought along for the summer or the pump organ that Grandpa bought from someone down the road, "so Grandma can sing to God's creatures when I'm out fishing," he told us.

I guess musical talent runs in our family. Grandma took lessons from Es, and so did Mom. My sisters and I took years of piano lessons. Don was born with music in his blood—at least that's what Mother says. "Pretending the kitchen table was a keyboard, Don would play the songs he learned from kindergarten. Dan (Dad's brother) stayed with us while he was attending college. He was so impressed with little Donnie that he insisted we find a piano. Mrs. Rasmussen, a neighbor at the end of our block, heard about this and offered us hers.

"'It's a huge upright,' she said, 'but if you can move it, you can have it.'

"Dan and Dad bought lumber and casters to create a means of rolling the piano down the street and up our steps.

"Little Don immediately climbed up on the piano bench and played *Happy Birthday*. He didn't miss a single note."

Since that day, Don was called a genius. Of course, the rest of us did not witness his keyboarding debut, but Mom swears it is true.

Back to my story about North Eagle and Grandma's pump organ. Obviously, when Don saw the new organ, he couldn't resist entertaining us. He played our favorite songs in any key that we started singing in. Reading, playing and singing were the passions of my life, so I sang enthusiastically. Sheryl and I carried the melody while Mom and Susie harmonized. Grandma smiled as she quietly hummed along, and Grandpa tapped his fingers on the arm of the rocker, probably thinking, "Don might not be a fisherman, but he sure knows music."

Our song fest lasted until Don's legs got tired from pumping the organ. Then Mom announced it was time for bed, but first, we all had to "do our business."

Unfortunately, the business had to be done in the outhouse.

It was a sign of bravery for each of us to go out by ourselves (except for Susie). Walking into the darkness with a flashlight, I entered—leaving the door wide open—and threw some powdery lye down the hole in hopes of killing some of the stink. I held my breath as long as possible and tried to "go" as quickly as I could, but it was not easy. Sheryl told me she could run in, "go," and run back out while holding her breath the entire time. And, of course, I believed her.

Grandma and Grandpa got the bed closest to the kitchen, Mom and Sue, the other one. Don slept on a cot. Sheryl and I were put on the day bed, her feet by my face and vice versa with a common blanket over our stomachs and chest. The bed became a war zone. First, Sheryl poked her feet in my face, and then I grabbed the whole blanket, protesting that she could freeze to death. On and on this went until Mom threatened, "Judith, one more peep, and you'll be sleeping on a green bench by the table without a blanket."

One morning, I was awake and heard Grandpa closing the screen door. I ran out and asked where he was going. He whispered, "Fishing." I begged to come along. He said, "If you bring me a paper and pencil to write a note AND not wake the whole cabin up."

Miracles happen, and somehow, we got down to the lake and into the boat without waking anyone else. Grandpa shoved us away from the dock and rowed out before starting the motor. "Here's breakfast," he said, offering me a handful of his favorite sugar-coated orange candy slices. Smiling, we headed for his fishing spot.

I know that Grandpa sacrificed that trip for me. I asked so many questions and bounced around so much that he didn't catch any fish. But he showed me how to row quietly into the long weeds because "that's where the fish are." And he showed me how to put a worm on a hook, making me do it myself. Most importantly, he showed me how to wrap the drop line around my finger so I could "feel" the fish bite and tease them with a little tug. He advised me not to talk so much because "if fish hear voices, they swim away."

So, I tried to be a good fisherman and be quiet, sit still and not talk. Several times, when I whispered questions, Grandpa smiled at me because he knew I was trying.

Lucky for me, I caught a fish. I thought it was a whale! Grandpa helped me bring it over the side of the boat. It was big and ugly with whiskers and smooth skin. Grandpa said it was a scavenger fish that ate all the dead stuff at the bottom of the lake. "Grandma won't cook it," he said. "All the trash the fish ate makes its meat taste strong." But he told me we could take the fish home and show it to everyone.

Boy, did I feel like a hero. It didn't bother me that Sheryl and Don were unimpressed because little Susie was so happy for me she kept repeating in a sing-songy voice, "Judi caught a big fish, Judi caught a big fish."

I hugged her real hard.

When Grandpa threw the fish back into the lake, I yelled, "Good luck, you homely old fish. It was nice knowing you."

I grinned at Grandpa and said, "I'm gonna be a great fisherman someday."

FOURTEEN

THE CITY POOL

The next time we went to North Eagle, Dad came with us because things were quiet at the garage. You remember my dad Bob, don't you? He was the big guy that drove us to your meeting if Es's husband was busy. Like I told you before, Chief, he always wore a gray felt hat with a full brim and loved to talk to people.

Before we left for the cabin, Dad announced, "I'd like to stop in Alexandria on the way up and have coffee with Gus. You can visit with your friends. Get yourselves organized. We'll be leaving bright and early Saturday morning."

"I'll stay home," Don said. "Pete is a hood, and we have nothing in common. Last time I saw him, he was thinking of dropping out of school."

"You can be a good influence on him," Mother replied.

Sheryl choked on her cookie. "That's my brother, real goody-two-shoes."

"Enough!" Mom said sternly. "Why don't you and Judi do the dishes?"

It was unheard of for Dad to be away from his business. I couldn't remember him ever passing up a chance to sell an Oldsmobile. Of course, we knew that now he'd pester us on the drive by singing his rendition of "In My Merry Oldsmobile," plus any other tunes he could think of.

Saturday arrived, and we were on the road by nine o'clock as Dad tried to entertain us with his singing. I smiled at my good fortune.

I was really looking forward to seeing Grandma and Grandpa, but not as eager to visit Alexandria, where Mom and Dad had lived right after they were married. Dad loved to remember those "good old days" when he managed a new welding supply store owned by a friend from Parker Falls. Across the street from Dad's store, Gus had sold used cars.

Dad and Gus became coffee buddies. Janet (Gus's wife) and Mother became friends. Janet taught third grade, and Mom directed choir and taught Sunday school. Their friendship grew to include the four kids in each family, who just happened to be the same age. Kenny was my age, Marlene was Sheryl's, Pete was Don's, and Leanne was the same age as Susie. The only clashes that occurred were between the two boys.

Before long, we got out of the car in Alexandria. Dad and Gus immediately wanted to go to their favorite diner for coffee and asked if we wanted to take a swim in the new city pool. Relieved that Pete was working and not available, Don stayed with the two moms and read a book. The rest of us left with Gus and Dad.

It was the first time I swam in a pool. Instead of the usual sand and seaweed, I walked on the floor of a big cement box filled with water. The water smell and taste of chlorine seemed very strange.

Kenny swam with his friends. I watched Leanne and Susie while Sheryl and Marlene whispered to each other and watched a couple of guys at the end of the pool. A cluster of boys near me were discussing Nancy, who they sometimes called Slut. They described her as though they had seen her changing in the bathhouse.

My curiosity was up, so I walked over to Marlene and asked, "Is Nancy Slut here today? The guys over there are talking about her."

Marlene turned bright red, and so did Sheryl.

"Slut isn't her last name, dummy," Sheryl stammered. "It's a bad word, and you're not old enough to know what it means."

"I sure am," I replied. "I'm old enough to ride my bicycle anywhere I want, so I think you'd better tell me. Otherwise, I'll have to ask Mother."

"Okay," Sheryl said, "But if you ever tell Mom I explained it, I'll call you a liar."

After swearing secrecy upon my heart, Sheryl told all. "Now go watch Leanne and Susie, so they don't drown," she commanded.

I walked along the pool, feeling very grown up. I knew I had learned an important word even if it was one Mom would not approve of. When I returned, the two little girls were splashing each other. I continued watching them while eavesdropping, too, hoping to improve my vocabulary.

Sheryl interrupted my concentration, "Come on, Gus and Dad just drove up. Let's go."

We jumped into the car, still in our bathing suits. "Sit on your towels," Gus said in his gravelly voice. "It's only a few blocks to the house. I'm sure that Janet and Marguerite have food for us. Just stay out in the backyard until you dry off."

We all sat around the picnic table eating and laughing. I was glad we came and could never have guessed it would be the last time we would be together. Shortly thereafter, Dad lost respect for his old friend. "Gus took up womanizing and left his wife and family for a twenty-five-year-old waitress," he explained.

Mom still wrote Christmas cards to Janet and the children, but this visit ended our Alexandria adventures.

When we arrived at the cabin, Grandma and Grandpa were happy to see us. Grandpa grabbed Dad and said, "Bob, the walleye are biting. Why don't we go fishing after supper?"

Dad and Grandpa were pretty good friends. Did you know, Chief, that Dad helped Grandpa do painting and wallpapering to earn money for college? He even helped paint a church steeple. I guess Dad didn't know he was afraid of real high places until he lost his balance. He looked down while descending the ladder and came crashing to the ground like Humpty-Dumpty. They rushed him to the hospital. The first thing he said when he woke up was, "Where's Marguerite?"

My Aunt Marion often repeats this story at family get-togethers, and then adds, "That's when we knew Bob and my sister would marry."

Now here Sheryl and I were, umpteen years later, walking with our grandpa—Dad's friend—down the hill to take the boat and buy bait for their fishing trip. After Grandpa started up the motor, we puttered along the shoreline and tied the boat to Camp Roma's dock. Up the hill we went to buy minnows.

Grandpa put his arms around us, smiled, and made introductions. "Here's Sheryl, who is smart and has a paper route. This little one, Judi, caught a big bullhead a few weeks ago and thinks she's a fisherman."

Mr. Roma smiled and offered us popsicles as a greeting. He and Grandpa exchanged winks, and then we walked back to the pier to get our minnows.

Mr. Roma took the lid off the screened tank in the lake. I crouched down and looked in, "Hey, there are a million fish in there."

"Well," he responded, "Why don't you fill your Grandpa's bucket?"

I took the little net, which had a handle like a coat hanger, and scooped a bunch of minnows into a bucket with a bunch of small holes on the top. Grandpa tied it to the outside of the boat, so when we moved, the water flowed through the bucket and kept the fish alive.

He told Sheryl that she could drive us home.

Dad was waiting on the dock as we rode up. He held Susie's hand as he gave instructions. "Okay, Sheryl," he said. "Drive right to this post, and Oscar can throw me the rope. I'll tie up the boat. Let's eat and then we'll go fishing."

We sat down to creamed macaroni and a ring of bologna. But first, we had to close our eyes while Grandpa prayed in Swedish. Translated, he said, "Thank you Father for all we have. Help us be joyful on earth until you take us to our heavenly home."

Then the noise and eating began. Grandma frowned as she watched Grandpa cut his food into small pieces and mix them together. I thought he was being silly, so I asked, "Why do you mess your food around like that?"

Grandpa looked up and smiled. "Because it gets mixed up in my stomach, anyway."

We all laughed, even Grandma.

The men were still out fishing when we went to bed. Mom said we would take Grandma to church tomorrow because Grandpa was staying home to fish.

Guess where we ended up? The service was held in a bank. Not an empty bank, but a real bank with a vault on the left and the teller windows in front. Folding chairs were set up as imaginary pews, and someone brought an accordion to accompany the singing. Sheryl and I started giggling, and Mom told us to "shape up or we could go to the car." Then she gave me a painful pinch on the thigh, which killed my grin and made me look straight ahead. When the service finally ended, we dashed into the fresh air.

Outside the bank, two women sat by a card table with a sign taped to the front edge—"Ladies Circle taking donations for Fred's son." On the table were plates of homemade donuts. When Grandma came out and read the sign, she took a hanky out of her pocket with some coins tied up in it. She unbundled the money and gave it all to the lady. "I'm very sorry I don't have more," she said.

The ladies smiled and put some donuts in a brown bag.

I asked Grandma what happened to Fred's son. She said that the tractor rolled over on him, and he lost a leg. We were all quiet on the way home, our minds filled with thoughts of a young boy with one leg and our stomachs pestered by the aroma of fresh donuts.

At the cabin, Grandpa greeted us with his smile. "I'm glad you're back. Come on, Bob," he said. "Let's go fishing until dinner."

"First, I need a cup of coffee and a donut," my dad replied.

After they left, Mom gave us each a sandwich, a glass of milk and a donut. "That will have to carry you until the men come back from fishing," she said.

Grandpa and Dad made a remarkable catch. Enclosed is the snapshot of us standing alongside the fish. There must have been two dozen huge fish hanging by their gills and strung on a line between two trees. That's Don and Sheryl smiling as though they had caught them.

Dad and Grandpa scaled and cleaned the fish before putting them in a washtub filled with ice. Sheryl and I helped. We had scales all over our hands and clothes. So did little Susie.

"Okay, kids," Dad said. "You'd better take a dip or Grandma won't let you in the cabin."

The cool water and swimming had made us hungry, and the smell of fish frying brought us to our seats around the table. Grandpa mixed his fish with mashed potatoes and peas. Mom glared at me when I started to copy him.

After dinner, Dad packed the car. We left for home as the sun was setting. Susie sat in the front seat between Mom and Dad. A dishpan of fresh fish on ice was cooling Mom's legs. Dad was so tired from cleaning all those fish that he forgot to sing. Don, Sheryl and I were in the back seat. It was one of those rare times when we were so pooped that instead of picking on one another, we leaned against each other and fell asleep until the car was parked in our driveway in Parker Falls.

Mom shook us gently and said, "Wake up. We're home."

FIFTEEN

BEREAVEMENT SERVICES

The arrival of cool September breezes and falling leaves brought the summer to a halt. The cabin had to be closed up. Over the winter months, Susie and I spent many nights talking of last year's adventures, eagerly waiting for the next summer when we could go back to North Eagle.

The snow finally melted, and the crocuses and May flowers appeared.

We knew the summer had officially begun when school closed its doors on the Friday before Memorial Day. The following Monday, a big service at Parker Falls Cemetery was held for veterans. Grandpa and Grandma would never leave for Eagle Lake until after the ceremony. Their son, my Uncle John, had died in the war, so they were entitled to sit in the "seats of honor." Grandpa sat still as a granite monument, his face frozen in grief. Grandma sat by his side, her hands clenched on her lap, tears running silently down her cheeks.

The program started with a navy captain reading a list of all the vets who had died in World War II and the Korean War. This was followed by a speech by an army commander and a closing prayer by the mayor. The finale was the only bright moment for Grandma and Grandpa because they could hear their grandson, Don, play *Taps*, followed by a ten-gun salute.

For many past services, Jack Olaffson, a veteran of the Korean War, had played *Taps*. But during his last years, his trumpeting skills had deteriorated. It had become excruciating to hear him splat the sacred notes while people shook their heads in disbelief or snickered in discomfort. The committee had finally decided that the next trumpeter must be talented and not necessarily a veteran.

My brother was selected.

Don, who played the piano and trumpet, was a musical celebrity in Parker Falls. It helped his reputation that Uncle Reuben wrote a column in *The Tribune* called "Man About Town." Reuben kept the community posted on all activities, including those of his nephew. He bragged that Don at age 13 or so was the "youngest ever" to play *Taps* at the Memorial Day service.

Sheryl and I rarely attended the ceremony. We stayed on the cemetery grounds by the lake. Susie was not allowed to come along—Mother didn't find us trustworthy enough after the previous summer when we almost let our little sister drown.

We liked hanging around the lake because after *Taps* was played, a gunshot salute broke the silence, and a small plane flew overhead dropping red poppies into the water. The lake was actually a murky swamp, so the challenge we set for ourselves was to retrieve as many poppies as possible without falling in. On one occasion, we took off our shoes and socks and got bloodsuckers between our toes. When we asked Mom's help in pulling them off, she reprimanded us for our shenanigans. The next year, she made us sit with her for the entire service. From then on, we tried to avoid catastrophes.

Sheryl came up with a brilliant plan. She brought twine and attached it to a branch. By throwing out the branch and gathering the string, she could rake in a lot of poppies. Of course, when we handled the wet paper flowers, red dye ran all over. In Sheryl's excitement, she had forgotten that I was standing next to her and raked some poppies onto my shoes and white socks. "How am I going to explain all these red spots?" I asked.

My sister groaned. "You're an idiot. Why didn't you get out of my way? Here, take my socks."

After the service, Mom was distracted by walking her parents to their car and never noticed my baggie socks or that Sheryl was wearing loafers with bare feet. On the ride home, she was preoccupied by a conversation she was having with Dad about our visit to North Eagle. Actually, Dad was telling Mom she should take us girls, and he would fly up with Don the weekend of the Fourth of July.

I guess I never told you, Chief, that the same year Grandpa swapped his services for the cabin at North Eagle, Dad swapped a new Oldsmobile for a small plane (remember, he owned a car dealership). Dad had just earned his pilot's license and to keep it active needed to put in so many hours of flying. "I have permission from Myron to land at his farm," Dad told us.

Landing in a cornfield does sound strange, but my family has always been a little goofy. Our neighbors on one side called us mavericks, and the neighbors on the other called us pretentious, so there you have it. My mother's side of the family is composed of entrepreneurs and artists, and my father's side is a bunch of intellectuals, so I guess we're a hodgepodge of backgrounds.

Enclosed is a photo of Don, Sheryl and me standing in front of Dad's plane. Notice my frown? My eyes were tired from looking into the sun. Susie had lost interest and fell asleep in the car.

After they landed, Dad and Don stepped out of the plane like they were president and vice president of America, all smiles and glad-to-see-us. Dad took our picture, gave us a hug and promised that next time it was our turn for a ride. Then he jumped into his yellow bird and flew back to Parker Falls.

On the way back to the cabin, Mom treated us to ice cream at Camp Roma. We felt rejuvenated and ready for a swim, so we walked down the hill carrying inner tubes. Grandpa was in his boat just offshore. The water was cold and spring-fed. Splashing around in tubes seemed more tantalizing then swimming. Grandpa smiled as he turned off the motor and drifted toward the dock.

"Hey, Grandpa," I yelled, noticing the string of fish that hung by the boat, "You sure are a good fisherman."

"Why don't you help me clean them?" he replied. "We can have them for dinner."

The next morning, we packed up and headed back to Parker Falls. I was going to camp with my friend Tina, and Mom had to wash our clothes and get me ready. This was the first time I would be staying away from home for a whole week, and I was very excited. Susie was upset that she couldn't come with me.

"How about I make you something special in craft class and bring you back a caramel Sugar Daddy sucker?" I suggested.

In addition, Mom promised her that before they turned around and drove twenty-five miles back home, we could all take a swim.

My little sister finally smiled, content with the promises.

The morning before I left, we were joking and eating our breakfast when the phone rang. It was a call from Mrs. Roma from the bait shop at North Eagle. Grandma had walked down the road to ask for his help because Grandpa was very ill. They were all at the hospital.

That phone call changed our lives.

Mom couldn't find anyone else to drive us to camp. Tina and I stayed home. Feeling sorry for me, Mother bought a small blue suitcase with blue trim and presented it to me. "Here's a present, Judi. You can bring it to the lake the next time we go see Grandma and Grandpa." Then Mom jumped in the car and drove up to North Eagle.

Two days later, she came back with a pale and somber Grandma. Grandpa had died. Grandma seemed dazed and kept whispering, "He can't leave me... he can't leave me." She sounded like a record with a needle stuck in its groove.

Dad made the funeral arrangements. Mother and two of my aunts began making food for the reception. I sat on a chair next to a wall that Grandpa had painted and papered not so long ago.

I heard Mrs. Bengtson, Uncle Reuben's mom, consoling Grandma. Every time she heard Grandma's repetitive whisper—"He can't leave me"—Mrs. B. patiently said, "Well, Mrs. Anderson, he has left you, and he's with his Maker."

I overheard my aunts talking about Grandpa, who only a few days before had said, "Anna, I 'ett too much. I have indigestion, so I think I'll rest a bit."

But his pain had gotten worse. When he got to the hospital, they called it a stroke. A nurse sat by his side as poor Grandpa rested in a tent filled with oxygen, and my Grandma, shocked by his condition, left the room and stood in the hallway pleading, "Don't leave me."

After Grandpa had fallen asleep, the nurse left. During her absence, Grandpa woke up and got out of bed to go to the bathroom. As he started to walk across the floor, he took only a few steps and dropped dead.

"Massive heart attack," the doctor had said.

Grandpa took his last ride home, silent and cold, in the back of the hearse.

Susie and I couldn't go to the funeral or mortuary. Our parents decided we were too young. But Sheryl gave us a report. "The church was packed and overflowing. Everyone loved Grandpa. Mom and Aunt Marion walked Grandma to and from her seat, and Grandma acted like a zombie. She sat tearless and pale as a wax figure during the service. I couldn't believe Mother sang Grandpa's favorite Swedish hymns without crying.

"Then an old friend told the story of how Grandpa Oscar found his way from St. Paul to Parker Falls. When he got off the train, a conductor happened to know a postman who was bringing mail to the Parker Falls Post Office a hundred miles away, and he gave Oscar a ride right up to the door of his cousin's house on Swede Hill."

And me? I couldn't comprehend that Grandpa was gone. I filled my new blue suitcase with my favorite things—a book of jokes, a penknife, an old spool of fishing line Grandpa had given me, and a pen and pencil to leave a note just in case Grandpa stopped by to take me someplace.

I hauled that suitcase around for weeks believing he would come. Then one day I put the little suitcase under my bed and laid down on the floor and just cried and cried. I knew I would never hear his laugh again, never share his orange slices, never go fishing with him, and never ever see him again.

SIXTEEN

THE DOGCATCHER

I just realized that I haven't talked about my dog very much since I told you, Chief, about Rex chasing a squirrel at Gravel Gertie's—excuse me, I mean Mrs. Gertie. Anyway, Rex and I were a real team. He was so dependable I took him for granted like books on the nightstand or warm flannel pajamas. He was my friend and ran with me when I biked, walked by my side and waited patiently for me as long as it took. Rex wasn't allowed in the house, but he had his own place complete with a door flap and straw for cold winter nights. If sub-zero weather hit, Mother allowed him to sleep on the back porch with an old blanket. But Rex never complained and took what we gave him.

Dogs had not been part of my parents' childhood. Two of my grandparent's favorite slogans were "children should be seen, not heard" and "dogs are outside for protection, not petting."

So, I don't suppose any of the old folks were upset when one Wednesday morning they heard Max announce on WKLM or they read in the *Tribune*:

NEW LAW PASSED AT TOWN MEETING! ALL DOGS MUST
BE LEASHED IN PUBLIC PLACES AND CONFINED TO THE

OWNER'S PROPERTY. A DOG CATCHER HAS BEEN HIRED STARTING JUNE 1.

My stomach heaved, and my face turned pale. "It's not fair," I said. "Everybody likes Rex. Why would they ever pass that law?"

"Lots of people have dogs," Sheryl said. "But somebody must be pretty mad about dogs crapping on their lawns."

I just sobbed. How was I going to make it without Rex by my side? For the next few days, I tried riding my bicycle while holding Rex's leash, but it was hopeless. Either he almost got strangled by my wheel riding over his rope, or I almost got killed from being yanked off the bike.

On June 1st, Dad chained Rex to his doghouse. Poor Rex howled and howled. Both of us felt miserable. For the first time ever, Mother let me bring him in to play, but it wasn't the same. Rex had always been free and lived outside. He couldn't understand why things had changed. Neither could I! Mom felt so sorry for Rex that after we went to bed, she let him run around the neighborhood for a little exercise.

Every time I saw the dogcatcher, I stuck my tongue out at him. He looked so plump and proud driving his new truck that I got aggravated just thinking about him. Unfortunately, we went to the same church. I vowed never to smile at Mr. Nelson again!

One day after school, when Sheryl and I were both home, I sneaked Rex into the house to share my peanut butter and jelly sandwich. The doorbell rang, and Sheryl opened the door. I could hear her say, "Hello, Mr. Nelson. What do you want?"

My heart shuddered as I hung onto Rex.

"Well," Mr. Nelson replied, "I'm here for your dog. He's barking all day and running loose at night. I've had complaints."

"Excuse me," Sheryl said. "I'll be right back." She came running into the kitchen, grabbed Rex from me and threw him out the back door.

I ran crying to the front door. "Mr. Nelson, go away!" I said. "I love my dog. He's my friend, and I don't want you to take him."

Sheryl interrupted. "I'm sorry, but Rex isn't here. Somehow he got off his chain, and we're looking for him too." Just then, Rex appeared at the bottom step looking up at the dogcatcher's butt. And he started barking.

Sheryl yelled, "Run, Rex, run!"

Responding to Sheryl's shout, Rex wheeled and ran with the chubby dogcatcher puffing behind him. Rex was smart enough to slow down and wait for the wheezing man to gain a little, and then off he'd run again, always beyond Mr. Nelson's reach.

Finally, the dogcatcher got mad and yelled, "I'll come back for him tomorrow and he'd better be here."

As Mr. Nelson drove off, I threw my arms around Sheryl, "You saved Rex's life. Let's call Dad. He'll help us."

Sheryl looked at me and said, "Something's fishy, Judi. Last Sunday I saw Dad talking to Mr. Nelson after church. He might've asked him to come here because Rex is so upset and barking all the time."

"Dad would never do that," I snapped. "I know he wouldn't. Let me call and ask him to help us."

I called, and when Dad answered, I told him what had happened. "Can you call and tell him never to come back?"

There was silence on the other end of the phone. Dad cleared his throat and quietly said, "I talked to him, Judi. Rex is so unhappy that I asked Mr. Nelson if he knew a good home for him. He said a friend of his has a sheep farm and would be happy to take Rex."

"But Rex is my friend!" I started crying. "I can train him not to bark, Dad. Why would you do something so mean?"

I handed the phone to Sheryl. I told her, "You talk to him. I never want to speak to him again."

Dad came home that night and tried to explain that he should have talked to me about it but couldn't. I was so hurt the tears would not stop. "Why would you ever do that, Dad?"

That night I lay awake thinking about the sheep farm where

Rex was supposed to live. In my life, I had seen only a few sheep in the surrounding area, and the more I thought about it, the more suspicious this so-called plan seemed to be. My heart ached so much that I couldn't bear to ask Dad about it.

The next morning, I raced downstairs to see if Rex was in the backyard. Maybe this whole episode was just part of a bad dream. It was Saturday. Rex and I could spend the whole day together. But when I ran out to the doghouse, Rex was gone. Mom was making breakfast and said that Mr. Nelson had picked up Rex.

I ran out of the house and jumped onto my bike and rode as fast as I could to burn off some of the pain. Finally, I parked my bike in front of the library and sat at a table and read an entire book—*Mrs. Pickerell Goes to the Arctic*. The title character used her umbrella and flew to the Arctic, just like I wanted to do that very moment!

After I finished the book, I still didn't want to go home, so I went to Es's. I walked in and just sat in my spot looking out the kitchen window into the sunny yard. Es continued painting as she talked to me. "Your mother called and wondered if you were here. She told me what happened. I'm sorry, Judi. I really am."

I started crying again. "I'm so sad. I'll never forgive Dad."

"Yes, you will," Es said. "Remember, he was little like you once. Now that he's a dad, you expect him to be perfect. But he's not any more perfect now than he was when he was small like you. I know your dad should have talked to you, but he didn't. He can't change that now. Sometimes you just can't change things back to the way they were. He disappointed you, but you must forgive him."

I didn't respond—just sat and looked out the window. Then I turned to her canary and said, "You're lucky. You seem happy singing away in a cage. Rex liked freedom and couldn't be happy like you." The sun kept shining even though I was sad about Rex.

As weeks passed, I continued riding my bicycle and spent more time with Es and my other friends. I still missed having Rex by my side. One day, I asked Mother if I could use some money from my piggy bank to buy a bird. Maybe that would help me feel better. After all, I could talk to it, and no bird catcher would take it.

"Ok," Mother answered, "but you're old enough to be totally responsible for its care."

I went to Woolworth's and bought a blue parakeet. I named it Peachy and bought a nice cage, a bell for her to peck at, and a swinging perch to jump onto when she felt like being silly. The clerk told me that with patience and time I could teach her to talk and sit on my finger. But she wasn't as independent as a dog, nor did she bark to remind me that I should take care of her. So, I forgot to feed her or change the paper when I should have, and the little blue bird got sick and died.

I buried Peachy in a shoebox and cried because it was my fault she had died. But I cried mostly because I couldn't change things and bring her back to beg for another chance. Then I realized I wasn't perfect either.

That's when I forgave my father.

SEVENTEEN

SERIOUS DECISIONS

One evening Dad announced at dinner, "Judi, I found you a job."

"You must be kidding!" Sheryl said. "Why would anyone hire an eight-year-old?"

"Because the wages are three bucks a month," Dad answered.

"What's my job?" I asked.

"A REMINDER route," Dad replied. "Uncle Rueben brought Jack Paulson to our coffee club this morning. He's decided to print a weekly flyer called THE REMINDER that advertises everything from groceries to auctions."

I was excited. "When do I start? I hope I don't have many houses. Remember, Dad, I work at the library Wednesday and Saturday."

Sheryl turned to me, "I don't call that work. You check to see if Miss Swenson has received any new books for you to read."

My REMINDER route made me feel very grown-up, Chief. I was proud to see "Judi" on the shelf that contained flyers for me to distribute. After placing the papers in my bike basket, I rode over to Fifth Street. I had one office building at the beginning of the street, but the other flyers had to be individually delivered. It took forever for the basket to be empty. I was exhausted and rewarded myself with a chocolate soda at Thrifty Drug.

Feeling rejuvenated, I decided I'd keep my route and save my wages for *Humpty Dumpty Magazine*. After two months of hard work, I finally had enough money. Mom wrote a check for my subscription, but afterward, I only had only fifty cents left. I spent it at the Parker Falls sidewalk sale. I couldn't resist buying a pair of blue and gold earrings and a tube of lipstick. The next week I wore both when I delivered the REMINDERS.

One customer did not like my new look. Maybe it was the combination of green pants, oxfords, T-shirt and costume jewelry. I'm not sure. Anyway, Mom received a call from some busybody who told her, "Did you know your little girl is running around in earrings and lipstick?"

Mom confronted me later that day.

"What's wrong with me dressing up?" I asked. "I'm just playing."

"You're too young to be wearing lipstick, Judi."

It was absolutely impossible to win an argument with my mother. She confiscated my lipstick, and I returned to my unadorned self. But I think my employment convinced Mom I was growing up.

One afternoon she told me to go down to Paterson's store and pick out some new shoes for the fall. Since the owner, Roy, was from our church, that's where we bought our shoes. I was very excited about making my first serious purchase without the supervision of any family member.

Mr. Paterson was busy when I entered the store, but he said, "Judi, look at your feet in my new machine." He told me to stand on a platform that had an attached box with a cut-out place to put my feet. I pressed my face into a viewing cup, pushed a button and looked down. My shoes looked like green shadows around my feet, which showed as dark green footprints. I kept switching the machine on and off, thinking this was quite a wonderful thing until Mr. Paterson finished with his customer and interrupted my play.

"Well, what's your opinion?" he asked. "Should your shoes be the same size as your last pair?"

I pulled my feet out of the box, looking at my scuffed shoes, wiggled my toes and answered, "These shoes feel good to me."

Before giving his opinion, Mr. Paterson placed my foot on a long silver board and slid a lever back and forth. "Guess what? You are one-half size bigger."

Next, he went to the back room and brought out my choices of shoes in my size. Boy, did I hate tie shoes. However, it was Dad's rule that we had to buy oxfords. "They keep your arches strong," he explained. "Any slip-ons must be purchased with your own money."

Brown and black oxfords were the norm, but this time Mr. Paterson opened a box and showed me a maroon shoe with white stitching on the toe. "These are the latest," he said.

"Did Diane or Muriel buy a pair?" I liked the new color but didn't want to have a pair like my friends at church.

"Nope, they bought something different."

Choosing the maroon shoes, I left the store, placed the package in my bike basket and rode home to show Mom.

She admired them. "Seems to me, you did some pretty good shopping."

When Sheryl came home, she said, "Those are boy's shoes! Look at the color and heel."

"No, they're not," I said. "They're a new style."

"Right," Sheryl said in a condescending tone.

That Sunday, because the children's choir was singing, Mom let me wear my new shoes to church. We singers walked onto the platform where I stood in the front row because I was small and because Mother, the choir director, made it a point to keep an eye on me.

Walking off the platform, I smiled at the audience and then looked down to watch my step. I gasped. Mike, who was right ahead of me, was wearing the same shoes as me. I was horrified!

"Why would Mr. Paterson sell me boy's shoes?" I asked Mother as we were putting away music.

"He probably forgot."

At the dinner table, the family discussed it. Naturally, Mom and Dad, being the diplomats they were, voted not to confront Mr. Paterson.

Sheryl stuck up for me. "That was rotten," she said.

Later, she took me aside. "I have an idea. Margaret fixed a pair of shoes that she didn't like. Let me take them to her house this afternoon and see if there's anything we can do."

She and Margaret scrubbed the leather with steel wool and then applied a dye. The color was a strange blue, but I didn't care. They weren't the same color as Mike's.

I felt indebted to my sister until she started pestering me to return the favor. "When school starts," she said, "I'll have so many activities that I could use your help with my paper route. You'd make more money than that crazy REMINDER route AND start saving for college. It takes more than reading books to become a librarian. You need some training."

"But I'm not even nine years old," I replied. "I don't have to make money yet."

"You need a change," Sheryl answered. "You're the only kid I know who goes to the library and gets four books and reads them all in one day."

"I also play with Rachel and Tina."

"Are you going to help me or not?" Sheryl asked.

"How can I? I ride your bicycle, and we'd need two bikes to do this."

I wasn't that interested in mimicking my siblings in everything. First, Don had the paper route, then he gave it to Sheryl. Now she wanted me to help her. All three of us were taking piano lessons. I could see where this was going. What kind of future would I have if I had to act like them?

Every time I turned around, people asked me if I was as smart as Don and Sheryl. I felt like a cookie stamped out of their cutter. Nobody saw me as Judi, and their blindness to my distinctiveness bothered me. It was no use discussing my thoughts with the family. The die was cast.

Feeling overwhelmed, I talked to Es. Consoling me, she said, "I know one thing for sure. You're smart enough to figure out how to be yourself."

Sheryl, though, was relentless and talked to Dad. "Judi needs wheels to help me with the paper route. How do you expect her to save any money if she doesn't make any?"

Always interested in business propositions, Dad was quickly persuaded. "Let's go shopping tomorrow after supper," he said. "We'll go to Spicer and visit John."

Excited about getting my own bicycle, I rationalized that maybe the paper route wouldn't be so bad after all. This would be the very first time I'd get anything new. Since Sheryl took such good care of her things, I inherited all her hand-me-downs. Okay, I know I just bought a new pair of shoes. But a new bike, just for me? I couldn't believe it.

When we arrived at the Corner Hardware, Dad's buddy John, the owner, was eager to help. I loved shopping at his store. It smelled of metal and paint, and I liked seeing the shiny hardwood floor. I took Dad's hand as we walked toward the bicycles. The boards creaked a welcome.

"Well, Bob," John said, "We have two bikes for your little girl. One is this blue and silver Schwinn, and the other is the red and white Continental."

My eyes just about popped out of my head. The Continental had skinny tires and a white seat. It looked so wonderful I knew immediately it was the one.

"Dad, I want the red and white one, okay?"

Turning to John, Dad said, "Where do they make Continental bicycles. I've never heard of them?"

John said they were imported from England. He'd been selling them for five years with no problems.

"Well, Judi, you'll have to get the Schwinn," Dad said. "I only believe in buying products made in the United States."

"I don't want the blue one—I want the red one. You promised I could pick it out."

"But I didn't know there would be foreign bikes," Dad replied. "Besides, those skinny tires will get caught in the grid of the drains."

I was speechless, almost, until I finally looked up at Dad and spoke. "I guess I don't want a bike. I'll walk until I grow into Don's bike."

John stood there, looking ill at ease. Finally, he cleared his throat and said, "There's a farmer down the road that does our bike repair. Why not take a ride and check out what he has? And take a bag of peanuts with you, Judi," he said, walking over to a brightly lit glass box containing warm redskin peanuts. He stepped up and put a scoop into a small wax bag and handed it to me. "Munch on these, and think about it. I'll be here until nine tonight if you need me."

"Thanks."

Dad received directions, and we drove to the farm. I chewed the redskins and said nothing during the journey.

Dad tried to start a conversation. "Why don't we turn around and get the Schwinn. It's a nice bike."

"I want to see what the farmer has."

It was dusk by the time we found the place. We followed a long gravel drive up to a weather-beaten barn where we could see through open doors an old man working on bicycles. He looked up as we got out of the car. He wore a striped engineer's hat and very thick fishbowl glasses. "What can I do for you?" he asked, squinting.

"John from Corner Hardware told us to stop by. He thought you might have something for us. Judi needs a sturdy bike for her paper route."

"I want a red bike—red and white, if you have it, with skinny tires." I tried to sound very firm.

The man took off his engineer's hat, ran his hand through his hair and replied, "I have something with skinny fenders but not skinny tires." He took us around the side of the barn where a dark red bike was leaning against the wall. A long neck rose above the front tire, and small handlebars branched to either side. The fenders were pointed instead of rounded and were smaller in width. It even had white stripes on the fenders. Because the fenders were pointed, the tires looked thinner.

"Is it made in the United States?" Dad asked.

The old man laughed and answered, "That's my bicycle from the twenties," he said. "The fenders and seat I took off from other bikes. I just painted it and leaned it here to dry."

I took the bike for a ride under floodlight of the barn. "It's good," I told Dad. "Can I have it?"

Dad still wanted me to get the Schwinn, but I said, "Nope. I've made my decision." Dad paid, and as he was putting the bike in the trunk of the car, the repairman asked me why I wanted his old bike over a new one.

"Because it's not the same as everyone else's," I said.

"You'll get yourself in a lot of trouble thinking like that," the man replied, then added, "but the world needs people like you. Now take care of my bike. I had lots of good times on it, and I hope you have the same." He stood there as we started to drive off.

I rolled down the window and yelled back, "I'll take care of it, don't worry." I waved until the man and his barn disappeared into the darkness.

When we arrived home, Dad wheeled the bike onto the back porch to show our family. Don hooted in laughter at the stripes on the red fenders. Now visible in the light, the lines were wavy and sometimes smudged, reflecting the poor eyesight of the painter.

After hearing the story, neither Sheryl nor Mother could understand why I thought the Schwinn wasn't good enough.

I might've lost face except Susie, standing next to me, came to my rescue. Tugging on my hand and looking up at me with adoration, she said, "Can I have a ride on your new bike tomorrow?"

EIGHTEEN

SHERYL TAKES CHARGE

Sheryl talked me into quitting my REMINDER route. I was grateful that she helped me get a bicycle, but it didn't change the fact that helping her with her paper route was going to be difficult. I already dreaded my new job, and I hadn't even started yet. What was I thinking of? My sister was very organized and fast at everything. Maybe that was why she called me "slowpoke." She loved competition, but I didn't. That made her a tough act to follow.

Already she had a "Carrier of the Year" plaque and a collapsible knife with her name on it. Her picture was in the paper receiving the award from the *Tribune* president. How could I live up to that, especially when I wasn't interested in the job?

Still, I was proud to have a famous sister and even brought the newspaper clipping to school to show my friends. I bragged about Sheryl, saying things like, "I bet my sister's the only paperboy who's a girl."

Anyway, here I was on my first day on the job.

"Okay," Sheryl said as we were finishing lunch, "Let's get our bikes. We have to pick up Tommy on the way."

Tommy was a man with a handicap who lived on the north side of our block. He rode a three-wheel bike and talked and laughed a lot. Sheryl told me that he was dropped on his head as a kid, but Mom said he was born that way. Tommy seemed old because he was heavy and almost bald, with just a little ridge of hair. I guess he went to school with my Dad and quit after the sixth grade.

"Tommy isn't stupid," Mom added. "He's just slow thinking and different."

The three of us must have been a sight as we rode down Second Street. My sister and Tommy talked while I sneaked peeks at him (or so I thought).

Sheryl pulled me aside before we were uptown. "Don't stare at him, Judi. Just because his tongue stays outside of his mouth and sometimes he has to stop and wipe his chin with a hanky, don't stare. Treat him as normal."

"But how can I do that? He's so peculiar."

My sister just glared at me. "Well, grow up!"

It took weeks of practice before I could "almost" look straight ahead when he was around. His speech was kind of warbly, but he kept us entertained during the ride down the street. I liked his jokes and laughed along with him. Sometimes I wondered if he knew more than he let on.

The fun stopped when we arrived at the *Tribune* building. It was time to get to work. My sister got off her bike and said, "Park this in the rack and meet me in line."

Tommy was in no hurry, and neither was I. His job was to deliver a few papers to the merchants on Main Street; mine was to help my sister. By the time I got inside, Sheryl was shouting at me from the front of the room, "Hurry up! Where have you been?"

I helped her count the papers into groups of ten until we had eight piles. Meanwhile, the impatient boys behind us started to yell, "Get a move on!"

"Shut up!" Sheryl hollered back and then irritated everyone even more by having me counter-stack the piles while she rolled papers and put them in her sack. I hoped we could get away before someone started a fight. I thought Sheryl might be trying to teach me a lesson in courage. If so, I didn't appreciate it.

I'd much rather she teach me how to have a big and powerful voice. Sometimes I'd sit on the swing in our pine tree and practice yelling, "Shut up!" But I could never copy my big sister—she was the best.

After getting all our newspapers, we each put a stack in our bike baskets. My assignment was to be Sheryl's shadow and stop when she stopped. While she ran up to deliver the *Tribune*, I was supposed to roll my papers and put them in the sack on my shoulder. That way, Sheryl could grab a few and keep delivering.

By the time I got off my bike and starting rolling papers, Sheryl was yelling at me to get the lead out of my pants. "You are the slowest person in the entire universe!" In exasperation, she came up with another plan. "Why don't you stop a few blocks ahead of me and start rolling papers until I catch up. Get it?"

"No, I don't get it. Why don't you just deliver to your houses and let me have my own papers?"

"Because you'd still be on the first block, and I'd be yelling at you from way down the street."

"So what? Just let me deliver a few. I'd be faster if you weren't bugging me."

"That'll be the day," Sheryl replied.

We argued constantly, but she was in charge, and I was her helper. She showed no mercy.

I guess we adjusted to one another because we made it through the fall months. As the temperatures chilled, the bicycles were put in the garage; our legs became our transportation.

I staggered down the street wearing two newspaper bags, one for the flat papers and one for the rolled. It was freezing and considering my short stature and thick layers of clothing—plus the shoulder bags crossing my chest—I looked like a chubby elf. My newspaper job seemed impossible, and I felt like *The Little Engine That Could* trying to make it up a hill that was too steep for its small size.

During the route one day during Christmas vacation, I was slowly rolling papers and trudging along, thinking my sister must've put a million miles on running back to retrieve papers from me. She was skinny that winter—maybe it wasn't a coincidence. Suddenly, an old lady yells at me from out her door, "Come here, Sheryl's little sister."

I shuffled up the walk toward her to a big surprise.

The woman opened her door and said, "Come on in. Do you like chocolate?"

I nodded, eyes peering out from my earmuffed cap.

Then the lady added, "My nephew gave me this candy, but he should have known better because these white things get stuck under my false teeth. Here you go," she said, handing me a box. "Merry Christmas."

I thanked her and walked back to the street happily eating my candy.

Sheryl, oblivious to my whereabouts, was collecting money and Christmas gifts from her customers. She ran up to me in a very cheerful mood.

I felt pleased with my good fortune and showed her my empty box. "Look, I got a present, too, chocolate stars dipped in white sprinkles."

The paper route took forever that day. When we were finished, my bags were overflowing with gifts for my sister. I complained that my shoulders ached.

"Here," Sheryl said, handing me the large box of Dots she was eating. "Maybe this will help."

Feeling the Christmas spirit, she shared her candy and proceeded to teach me one of her favorite songs, *Bringing in the Cheese*. This was the teenage rendition of *Bringing in the Sheaves*, a hymn from church—maybe you remember it, Chief? It went, "Bringing in the sheaves, bringing in the sheaves, we shall come rejoicing, bringing in the sheaves…"

We sang and laughed together as we walked down the middle of the street. The snowbanks sparkled in the night air, and for those few, rare moments, we were best friends.

By some miracle, we made it through the winter months. With the snow melting, we could use our bicycles again. And then came my birthday. Sheryl mellowed, and for my gift, she gave me twenty *Tribune* customers of my very own, though she still collected all the money. In July, she sold her paper route to John Easterling, a new boy in the neighborhood, and joined her friends to pick fruit and detassel corn. Sheryl was convinced she'd make a lot more money. I didn't miss being her helper or the meager income. I made a few bucks babysitting and helped at Brownie-day camp.

A few summers later, at Camp Koronis, one of my assignments was to compose a poem about a family member, write it on a piece of wood, and then decorate and shellac the masterpiece. For some reason, I decided to write a poem about Sheryl.

When I was chubby and little and small
My big sister guarded me, and she was tall.

She wanted me to walk fast and listen to her jokes
So kept prodding and yelling, "Hurry up you slowpoke."

We argued and fought and called each other names
But somehow, she never, ever, got the blame.

And now that I'm bigger and think about those times
I know I'd never choose any sister but mine.

NINETEEN

SWIMMING LESSONS

Did you ever visit Green Lake? It's a huge lake that takes forever to drive around and is always wavy and very cold. On the east side, a large public beach invited families to picnic, swim and enjoy the amusement rides there. Even though we liked our cabin on little Eagle Lake, where it was calm and shallow, we'd sometimes take a Sunday ride to Green Lake to buy popcorn, ride the Ferris wheel, or just park the car and walk around to visit with people we knew.

One Sunday, as we were standing in line to buy popcorn, Dad said, "I almost forgot. You and Sheryl will get free swimming lessons at Green Lake this summer. Now that I'm chairman of the Red Cross, this is one of my benefits. Actually, I get lessons for four children."

"But Susie is too little," I said.

"And Don has already passed Senior Lifesavers," Sheryl added.

"I know that," Dad replied. "But I get four passes anyway, and I've chosen who will go with you."

"Can't we each take a friend?"

"No, I've asked Lester's kids. He's the man I just hired at the garage."

"We don't even know them," Sheryl complained.

Dad told us that Lester was new in town and working as a mechanic at Dad's Oldsmobile dealership. Before he moved to Parker Falls, he had farmed with his two brothers thirty miles away in Raymond. Since there wasn't enough work for three men there, Lester found a job and left the farm. "He's living over at the Jacobsen place," he continued. "It would be nice if his two girls got to meet some kids before school started. They're exactly your age. You can introduce them to your friends."

"Hey, isn't the Jacobsen place where two train cars sit in the woods on the other side of Rural Avenue?" asked Sheryl.

"What train cars?" I asked. "I've never seen them."

Dad interrupted. "Those cars were moved in before I was born. They put the cars at the end of the road. I've never taken you there because it would be bad manners to turn around in someone's front yard."

Then Dad told the story of how John Jacobsen and his young wife had emigrated from Sweden. "He was employed at the railroad fixing steam engines. Years and years he worked there. I guess John bought some land and was saving to build a house. Unfortunately, one of the engines blew, and John was badly burned. He ended up losing an arm. The railroad felt responsible and moved two cars onto his land for them to live in. They employed him until he retired. The Jacobsens raised their family there. Their old Pullman house has been bought, sold or rented for the last twenty years."

I immediately wanted to go and see their place. *The Boxcar Children* was one of my favorite books. I felt quite knowledgeable about their lifestyle and dreamed of living like them with my dog in the woods, sleeping in a boxcar on a pine needle bed, eating berries from the bushes and drinking water from the stream.

In the book, the three children told each other stories at night, so they'd forget to be scared when owls hooted or crickets were noisy. Such an adventuresome life appealed to me.

Dad made it clear that he wouldn't drive us over to "gawk" at Lester's Pullman house. "Just wait awhile. Maybe his girls will ask you over."

The following day, Dad called Sheryl from work. "You and Judi get on your bikes and come down. Lester just stopped by with his daughters."

Twenty minutes later, we walked into the garage to meet the girls. After introductions, I talked to Kate, who was my age, while Alice chatted with Sheryl. The sisters looked alike—blond with lots of freckles. Kate was bigger than me, but that was okay—most girls my age were bigger. I immediately liked her and could tell we'd get along.

Sheryl figured out a plan for us to get to our swimming lessons. Sheryl and Alice were going to take Junior Lifesaving. Kate would be in Beginners with me. "Let's meet by Garfield School," Sheryl said. "That way, we can ride down to the courthouse together. The bus leaves at ten o'clock." Sheryl's plan was easier for the two of us because we lived only a few blocks away. Alice and Kate would have to bike about two miles. But they didn't seem to mind since they were used to distances when they lived on the farm.

As we rode our bikes to the courthouse on Monday, I asked Kate, "Can I come over to your house and play?"

"Mom and Dad are still fixing things up," Kate said. "My birthday is July tenth. Why don't you come to my party?"

"I'll ask my Mom, but I'm sure I can."

Our friendship was off to a great start. We loved the bus ride out to Spicer. Kate and I sat with the younger kids in the back of the bus, and our sisters sat in front. Being a natural leader, Sheryl led the songs we sang.

My favorite song was "One hundred bottles of catsup on the wall, one hundred bottles of catsup. If one of those bottles should happen to fall, ninety-nine bottles of catsup on the wall." By the end of the song, everyone was wound up and rowdy, and the bus driver had to yell, "Keep it down."

After we piled off the bus came my least favorite part—
changing clothes in the public bathhouse. Let me describe it for you,
Chief. The bathhouse was a cinder block structure in three sections.
On the right side was the boy's dressing room, in the center was the
storage room and candy store, and on the left was the girl's dressing
room. All entrances were on the front by the lake.

The worst thing about this structure, especially for us shy girls,
was that the walls had no roof. The sky was the ceiling. This meant
that when the rains came, the water would dump on our heads, but
more importantly, it meant that if a strong-armed boy was in one
of our swimming classes, he just might hurl his friend's underwear
over the walls and into our dressing quarters. When this happened,
we'd all scream in protest. We also lived in fear that some boy could
shinny up the wall and peek at our naked bodies. It was rumored that
this had happened a couple of times, so dressing under our towels
became critical.

We put our street clothes into a wire basket that we delivered
to the concession stand. In return, we were given numbered safety
pins that we fastened to our swimsuits and redeemed for our clothes
after swimming lessons.

On the day a boy's underpants came flying over the wall,
I was laughing and walking with Kate down to the water. I guess
I'd forgotten to close my safety pin, so when I came to back to the
concession stand to get my wire basket, the number had fallen off,
and I had to wait until everyone else had got theirs. What a disaster! If
my sister hadn't been such a big wheel, I would've had to walk back
to Parker Falls. But Sheryl held up the bus until I boarded. My face
was already sunburned, but when I climbed on and everyone cheered,
I turned even redder. It seemed forever before I got to the back of the
bus and sat down. Kate was laughing with the rest of the kids but had
saved me a seat and sympathetically handed me one of her candy bars.

Neither Sheryl nor I really enjoyed the swimming lessons,
especially in such cold water. I was used to the warm water at our lake

where I could float around on an inner tube and wave at the boats. The casual attitude we adopted there, unfortunately, was reflected at my swimming lessons. When we were instructed to do the "dead man's float," or "dog paddle," I was always moving my head to look at Kate or to see if my sister was out at the big raft. I would swallow water, cough, and have to stand up. My teacher would scold me, saying stuff like, "Pay attention, Judi, or you'll never learn how to swim."

When I got my card that said I had graduated from Beginners, I smiled in relief, but I knew that if my father's signature had not been at the bottom, I wouldn't have passed. Fortunately, Dad was so busy he never asked much about the lessons.

My sister Sheryl was a serious student and persevered even though she just about drowned while taking her deep dive test. To pass, Sheryl had to retrieve a cinder block from the bottom of the lake and then rescue her big fat teacher. Sheryl complained every week about her various assignments but was one of the few in her class who graduated. Kate's sister, Alice, didn't get her certificate. I guess she wasn't as tough as my sister.

The swimming lessons with Alice and Kate cemented our friendships. When Kate had her birthday party, Sheryl was invited too. I guess the two of us were the representatives of her new community. When Mom delivered us to the party, I gasped in delight. Sometimes, when I was daydreaming, I invented a secret hiding place that I decorated with my favorite treasures. But Kate's place surpassed my imagination.

The brown Pullman cars sat among trees at the end of a drive with a cornfield on the right. They had rounded tops and black tar paper around the bottom. As the light filtered through the branches and fell on the small glass windows, the Pullmans turned iridescent and looked like big fat dragonflies that had lost their wings.

Wow, I thought, *this is even better than the Boxcar Children.*

"Now both of you watch your manners," Mom instructed as she stopped the car.

Kate came running out to greet me. "Come on, I'll show you my house."

In the first car, a kitchen with a white breakfast nook adjoined a living area with wallpaper that had little roses on it. Kate's dad had decorated the ceilings in the same wallpaper. I laughed and said, "It feels like we're in a magic garden."

"We are," Kate said. "Mom's favorite book is *Alice in Wonderland*. That's how my sister got her name and why she chose the wallpaper."

We walked through her parent's room into Alice's bedroom.

"Someday, we'll get new wallpaper in here too," Kate said.

"But I like it. It's great!" I looked enviously at the bunks on one wall and dressers on the other. The wallpaper had big creamy ferns on a maroon background. With the rounded ceiling and windows, the place felt like a treehouse.

"What should we play?" Kate asked

"Let's pretend we're pioneers," I suggested.

Just then, Kate's mother walked in. "It's your birthday party, Kate. Come on outside and play some games. Your relatives came from Raymond, especially for you."

"But we're having fun here," Kate answered, pouting.

"Judi can come back tomorrow. Today you must share your time with everyone."

We played "pin the tail on the donkey" and "drop the clothespin in the bottle," then Kate's mom divided us into teams for a "tug of war." The best thing, though, was the birthday cake. Kate's aunt was a fancy baker, and she had made a cake that was sculpted and decorated to look like one of the Pullman cars. In pink, under the windows, she had written, "Happy Birthday, Kate."

We clapped our hands and sang *Happy Birthday*. When Kate blew out her candles, I closed my eyes and made a wish too—that we would remain friends forever and have as many adventures as the Boxcar Children.

TWENTY

MY ACTING DEBUT

Chief, have you heard of the Von Trapp family? I bet you remember them. They were a family from Austria who gave concerts around the world. Mom played their records and told us, "Listen and learn." The Von Trapps inspired her to launch us on our musical careers at very young ages—piano in kindergarten, instruments in grade school, and singing in school and church choirs. Sheryl plays the violin and several reed instruments, and Don plays the violin, several brass instruments, organ and piano.

I guess everyone assumed I would follow suit. One day, at Sheryl's violin lesson, Mrs. Chandler told her there would be free group lessons at my school. "It would be a wonderful introduction for Judi," she said.

Sheryl did her best to persuade me. "You could use my violin and be in the orchestra."

"Forget it," I replied. "I'm already taking trombone and piano."

"If you learned the violin," Sheryl said, "we could play duets together."

That wasn't a good selling point for me. After all our arguments on our paper route, I knew that playing a duet would be impossible.

Of course, Don added his bit, "If you learn a string instrument, there's more opportunity to play in a musical group in college. With a brass instrument, the only choice is band."

"I'm still in grade school," I reminded him. "You're the one going to college, not me."

"Try it for one year," Mom pleaded. "It won't hurt you."

So, I borrowed Sheryl's violin and started classes. But it was just too many instruments for me to learn. The violin remained in its case, and I hardly ever practiced, rationalizing that because the lessons were free, it was okay to slack off.

When it was time for the group recital, I was nervous and waxed the bow so much I couldn't get a squeak out of my violin. My teacher kept urging me to play louder. Suddenly it hit me that if I made any mistakes, it would be terribly embarrassing, so I smiled and pantomimed the entire number.

Sheryl was disappointed when I quit the violin. Don didn't comment. He was excited about a new opportunity playing the piano at the radio station for "The Gospel Hour." Since Mom was admired for her singing and was directing a large church choir, she was often asked to schedule music for the radio. Sometimes she asked us to sing on the program. I sang along with Mom—who had a beautiful soprano voice—while Sheryl sang alto, and Don sang tenor as well as accompanying us on the baby grand piano.

At church, people would pat me on the head and say things like, "My, you have a talented family. Just think—a little girl like you singing on the radio."

"It's not hard," I would say. "We just stand around the piano and sing like we do at home."

It was fun to be in the studio. Max Lynch, the announcer, sat on the other side of a large window and talked into his microphone. Everyone in Parker Falls loved him. His voice was deep and clear. Max tried to be witty and always introduced us by saying, "This is WKLM, your favorite radio station, giving you gospel songs from a wonderful local family. I went to school with Marguerite, and she was a songbird even then. Now here she is with three of her children singing…" And then he would name the hymn. "There's another little tyke in the family, and I'll bet she'll be on the air soon. Right, Marguerite?"

Every time he'd repeat that line, Mom would give Max an icy smile, and Don would mutter under his breath, "What an idiot. Can't he think of something new to say?"

We enjoyed singing on the radio. I think that's why Mom came up with the brainy idea of making Dad a record for Father's Day. Chief, do you remember Jack and Nettie? Nettie is a niece of Es's. Anyway, they had a recording studio in their home. Jack was a technician at WKLM, and Nettie was a pianist. They moved to Nebraska because Nettie got a good job as a professional pianist on a radio program there.

We still have that record we made. Don played his trumpet, Sheryl her violin, and we sang a few songs. Then I recited a poem, "Four and twenty blackbirds baked in a pie…" I took such deep breaths that I'm sure anyone listening could feel the waves of stage fright traveling through my body.

I'm no different now. I still don't like any kind of solo performance. I guess my idea of performing is when I was a safety patrol in sixth grade and walked the kids home at noon and after school. "Line up," I'd yell, and then hold my flag parallel to the ground and escort everyone home. It was fun because I'd turn around and walk backward and we would talk and laugh. The kids liked my interest in them.

I wish my teachers felt that way. They never seem too happy that I ask lots of questions. They want me to buckle down and become a star pupil and performer like my siblings and parents. Even in grade school, my choral teacher felt I should be in the spotlight.

One afternoon, during a music session, Miss Schill announced, "Attention, students. This Christmas, we will perform the Nutcracker

Suite." Then she added that I would be the star of the show. "You, Judi, will sit and dream by the fireside. You six girls (naming them) will be the plum fairies…" and on and on she went until everyone had a bit part.

The horrible thing about my role was that I was supposed to wake up from a kiss on my hand by a greasy-haired, fat-kid prince by the name of Billy. My classmates were in hysterics at my misfortune. I tried to talk everyone into swapping parts with me. When I found a volunteer, Miss Schill wouldn't hear of it.

My career was launched, whether I wanted it or not. Miss Schill ordered me to wear a white blouse and have Mother sew pantaloons for my costume. We were told our performance would be the Monday morning before Christmas. Everyone was welcome to attend. My dad had to work, but Mom said she'd be there. Susie was in the first grade and would be coming with her class.

The morning of my musical debut, as Sue and I were leaving the house, Mom handed me a large brown grocery bag, "Don't forget your pantaloons," she said, smiling.

I peered into the bag and noticed she had made them out of aqua crepe paper with an elastic waistband.

"How come they're made out of paper?" I asked.

"You're only wearing them once, so why waste good material?" she explained in Mom logic.

Off Susie and I went, braving the cold in our flannel-lined corduroys and flannel shirts.

"I don't want to be a star," I complained. "Why can't I just be in the choir with Tina and Carol? Maybe I'll get sick."

"But we never get sick," Susie answered. "Besides, Mom wouldn't believe you."

Arriving at school, I dressed in my aqua pantaloons and went to the gymnasium to get ready for the program. Miss Schill was shouting instructions and then spotted me. "Why are you wearing a flannel shirt and crepe paper pants? Where is the skirt with the white blouse, like I told you? The pantaloons are worn UNDERNEATH. Run to the office, and call your mother. Tell her to bring your skirt and blouse right away."

I ran as fast as I could to the principal's office. I called, but Mother was not home. Returning to the gym, I related the news.

Miss Schill was very angry but said we'd have to make do.

As the program was about to begin, she gathered us around and said, "Attention! Everyone quiet and take your places. The auditorium is full, and we must begin."

The curtain opened, the music started and I walked onto the stage in my aqua pantaloons and flannel shirt to sit in front of the Christmas tree. I was supposed to close my eyes and dream about fairies and drummers, and then they would appear.

As I was sitting there, I could see Susie in the front row on her little chair smiling at me. I smiled back and then crossed my legs and put my elbows on my knees to dream. Suddenly, I heard a rip as my crepe paper crotch disappeared, and my bright yellow underpants appeared in all their glory to the audience. Gasping, I quickly placed my left hand over the seamless pantaloons, rested my head on my right fist and closed my eyes, pretending to dream, hoping no one had seen my underpants. Peeking out of one eye, I saw Susie laughing along with the boy next to her. I squeezed my eyes closed and wished with all my heart that there would be a tornado.

But a tornado never came. It seemed like a century before I opened my eyes to my greasy-haired prince. I stood up, embarrassed, but relieved that my performance was finally finished. We all lined up for the curtain call, and as I bent at the waist, I looked down at my sister. She looked up at me with a big grin.

Mom drove us home for lunch and said I did just "fine."

I didn't believe her.

Susie tried to make me feel better and said, "Maybe nobody

noticed your yellow underpants."

I didn't believe her either.

Luckily, it was only a few days until Christmas vacation. My classmates teased me relentlessly, but I was so happy the disaster was over that I laughed with them. My friend, Tina, thought I had worn the flannel shirt just to get even with Miss Schill.

I never admitted to a thing.

TWENTY-ONE

MOTHER AND DAUGHTER ARE CONTESTANTS

Are you getting tired of my stories and letters, Chief? I'm so lonesome for Parker Falls. I keep missing Es, especially conversations we had while I watched her paint. If we weren't chatting, Es was humming, or maybe all was quiet, and suddenly, she would tell me something important. "You know, Judi," Es usually began and then told me what was on her mind, such as this little exchange: "Someday you'll need to find yourself a creative niche, a place that is your very own to explore and stretch your imagination."

"But I already have that," I answered. "I love my books."

"Well, that may be enough. But it's possible there's something else out there you could love and also share with others. For instance, I paint, and others can see my work. I play the organ, and others can hear it. Your Mother sings on the radio, and the world listens. Do you get what I'm saying, Judi? It's good for other people to see the passion in us—it gives them hope."

"It's kinda hard for me to understand, but I'll think about it," I replied.

For some reason, I remember that conversation as I'm typing this letter and suddenly realizing that writing has become my passion. Of course, I still believe that reading is a passion, too, even though I can't share it with others.

You, Chief, and Es too, have tried to get me to examine my thoughts and actions. I remember one time when I had come over to Es's house boasting that I had made twenty-five cents in a matter of minutes.

"How did you do that?" you asked.

"I sat on a bench at the tennis court watching two boys play tennis. One of them cussed when he missed the ball. Embarrassed, he turned to me and said, 'Hey kid, I'll give you a nickel every time I swear.' Crossing my fingers, I hoped he would swear a lot. And that's how I got my twenty-five cents."

You tried to explain how I took advantage of someone else's weakness and how I needed to decide if that was a good thing or not.

"Well, I go over to Rachel's and watch TV," I said. "Would that be taking advantage?"

You smiled and said it wasn't quite the same thing, but if I gave it some thought, I could probably figure out what you meant.

Eventually, I did understand what you were trying to tell me. Thinking about it now, though, I don't feel like talking so seriously. I feel like telling you about my friend, Rachel, who lived next door. I visited her a lot, especially when I wanted to watch television.

Ninety-nine percent of the families in Parker Falls are Scandinavian. They are divided into two groups, liberal or conservative, depending on which church they attend. Our church was conservative. From the pulpit, the minister preached, "Contact with worldly behavior cannot be endorsed." Much to our disappointment, it was further emphasized that "worldly behavior" included movies and television.

Everyone nodded and went home to watch their television. Unfortunately, we were not part of "that" group. Instead, we watched "other people's TVs." At first, I found this very confusing until Dad explained it to me. "Most of the congregation are poor farmers," he said. "Few have enough money to purchase luxuries, let alone have anything left over to give to the church. Besides, TV is impractical. We only get one channel."

Luckily for Rachel and me, our favorite program, *Axel and His Dog*, was on that channel. Axel was a peculiar-looking character in dark-rimmed glasses and a broom mustache that was attached to them. He spoke with a foreign accent and wore a striped T-shirt and bib overalls. Propped on his head, looking totally ridiculous, was an engineer's hat.

The only parts of Axel's dog that ever showed on screen were the paws, which were really someone else's hands covered in fake fur mittens resting on a log at the edge of Alex's view. That same invisible person made a "ruff" or "growl" that was very strange. The absurdity of it all made us laugh! The best part of this show was the "Little Rascals" movies, which were followed by Axel reading his choice of the original jokes sent in by the audience.

An original joke was just that—you had to make it up yourself. If you were lucky enough to have it read on the air, you received a membership card to Axel's Club. So, I sent in a joke. It read, "What has fifty-two feet but cannot walk?" (Answer: a hairbrush).

Rachel and I listened forever, hoping it would be read on the air. One day we heard Axel say, "From You-dee uff Parker Fallzz, Minneszota, in the US of A, vee half ay verie goodt yoke."

After he read the joke, the dog paws hit the stump, and the fictitious animal said, "Roof, roof."

Neither of us laughed when we heard it.

I turned to Rachel. "My joke isn't even funny."

"I think we were so excited to hear your name, we just forgot to laugh."

The next day at school, I felt like a celebrity. Kids came up to me saying they heard my joke on television. But I noticed that no one said it was funny.

When I explained all this to the family at supper, Sheryl said, "Good, I'm glad it was a flop. It would be a disgrace for any of us to be a famous television star, anyway."

"I'm not a star!" I said. "Just a joke teller—and mind your own business, anyway. Maybe I'll join the circus and be a clown. Then nobody will know who I am."

Later, when I went upstairs to read, Susie was right on my heels, "Can I come with you to the circus?" she asked sweetly.

"Yes," I answered.

Swearing each other to secrecy, we spent many hours planning our future as tightrope walkers, clowns and horseback riders.

By a strange coincidence, shortly after my name was announced on television, Mom was randomly chosen to participate in a contest on our local radio station. I was next door at Rachel's when Mr. Walkson yelled from downstairs, "Judi, run home real quick and tell your mother to say 'record.' It's the word for cash on WKLM, and it's worth fifty bucks."

I tore out of the house as fast as I could and raced down the front steps and across our double lot. As I ran into our house, I shouted, "Record, record—Mom, the word is record."

Then I noticed Mom was putting down the receiver. "Didn't you hear me? I was shouting as loud as I could. Mr. Walkson was listening and sent me over with the word."

"No, I'm sorry I didn't hear you. I guess it wasn't meant to be."

Mr. Walkson felt bad like he was responsible because he was kinda dozing when Max the announcer said, "All right, I'm closing my eyes and flipping through the phone book, and let's see now, I'll put my pencil on this name. Well, what do you know, it's Bob the Oldsmobile dealer's number. I hope his wife is home because I just saw him at the Chamber of Commerce meeting a short while ago. Remember the word—it's 'record.' Let's see if Marguerite is home and listening to WKLM. I'm dialing…"

Poor Mom, and poor Mr. Walkson, too, because he always had the word on a piece of paper by the radio just in case they chose him.

"To think I missed this opportunity for Marguerite," he told Dad. "I had a tough day at the railroad and was very tired. If they hadn't mentioned you, Bob, I would've missed it entirely."

Dad told Mr. Walkson he did his best. But when we were eating supper, Dad wasn't as forgiving. "Fifty dollars—we could have used that."

"You realize," Mom said. "I did not lose any of OUR money. It was never ours, to begin with. WKLM adds ten dollars every day to the pot until someone wins. The last four people didn't know the word either. Obviously, we ALL had better things to do than listen to the radio. Now quit complaining and eat your mashed potatoes."

On the rare occasions when Mom spoke like that, everyone remained very quiet. We quickly ate our mashed potatoes and excused ourselves.

Through the weekend, our neighbors and church friends gossiped about those fifty lost dollars. Finally, the following Monday, the station resumed the contest. I think Mother was relieved when a few days later, Mrs. Swenson won a hundred dollars. The conversation about Mother's loss stopped when everyone gossiped enviously about the winner.

When Mr. Walkson and Dad trimmed the privet hedge that separated our properties, neither of them brought up the contest. The Walksons had been our neighbors forever. The women borrowed cooking supplies from each other and talked back and forth while they worked in their huge vegetable gardens. Dad and Mr. Walkson trimmed the hedge a couple of times each summer. It was a big hedge, about a hundred and fifty feet long and four feet high. The men agreed upon a mutual time they could work on it. Then, as one stood on each side of the hedge, they clipped in rhythm, chatting about local events. Usually, they asked Rachel and me to pick up any trimmings from the ground. We gathered the branches and piled them at the back of our lot for a future bonfire. My little sister also helped since she knew there would be a reward when we finished. Meanwhile, the fathers talked and clipped as we raced around, teasing one another.

Later, we three jumped into the backseat, and one of the dads took us to the A&W Drive-In for root beer. We knew our fathers would each order two small mugs, and each of us kids would get one mug. Joking and laughing, we questioned why they would deliver seven root beers to five people. Dad said it was "more for the buck," and that everyone in town did the same thing.

One time, Rachel, Susie and I ducked down to confuse the carhop and make our fathers look foolish. But when the tray was hooked onto the window, we quickly popped up to claim our frosted mug. And then, like kittens over frothy milk, we greedily took a sip of the rich foam. After a few tastes, we lifted our heads, looked at one other and smiled in pure delight.

TWENTY-TWO

A DILEMMA WITH DELBERT

Rachel Walkson remained a good friend. She wasn't interested in riding her bike or playing in the park, but there were lots of other things to do. Usually, we hung around at her house. It was quieter there. Rachel only had one sister, Barb, who was five years older, and a lime green parakeet by the name of Delbert—and her parents, of course.

One day, as I rode by her house, Rachel came running out. "Come on, I have to show you something."

Guess what it was, Chief? Delbert the parakeet had learned how to sit on Rachel's lip and eat lettuce out of her mouth.

"Great," I responded. It didn't seem very sanitary to have a bird that had just walked on his droppings to be standing on her lip, but I didn't say anything. After all, Delbert was my friend too. He sat on Rachel's shoulder when we watched TV and sometimes jumped onto mine. Whenever we made a tent over the dining room table, he ran around, on top of the table, squawking and chattering. Delbert sometimes said his name, but that was his total vocabulary.

In the summer, when we sat on the front steps, Rachel let Delbert out of his cage. He flew to the inside ledge of the window to watch and scold us, obviously wanting to come outside. Rachel hung on the railing of the front steps, leaned close to the window and said to him, "Delbert, you can't come outside. There are cats in the neighborhood."

It didn't help matters that we gave the cats milk. If Mrs. Walkson saw a full bowl by the front steps, she reprimanded us. "Please stop feeding them. They'll tell all their friends, and we'll attract the entire feline community. If they start using the soil around our bushes for a litter box, your father will have a fit."

We nodded in agreement but ignored her advice. It was too much fun to watch the cats gather around the dish and lap up the milk.

One afternoon, I went into the house to get a Popsicle. I didn't close the front door quickly enough and a big, white fluffy cat ran in. "Help!" I yelled. "A cat just snuck in."

"Watch Delbert," Rachel screamed as she burst through the doorway. "I'll get him into his cage." Delbert, concerned for his own safety, jumped onto Rachel's shoulder. The second she opened the cage door, he flew in. I ran around, trying to grab the cat. Rachel followed behind me, clutching the cage to her chest with Delbert fluttering around inside, scolding the world.

Exhausted, we finally gave up. "Let's just guard my bird," Rachel said as we sat down on the floor in front of the sofa, the cage safely between us. "We've got to figure out a plan."

Minutes later, Rachel tiptoed up the stairs while I watched Delbert.

"I got the cat," Rachel yelled. "He was sleeping on my Mom's slippers."

Running up to join her, I ran into the room, "Look," I said, pointing to a big mess of diarrhea in the middle of the bed. Just then, the cat meowed, and Rachel almost dropped him. Regaining her hold, she ran downstairs and tossed him out the front door.

"What are we going to do?" I asked.

Rachel already had a plan. "I've seen Mother wash her bedspread, so I'll just say that we're helping her out."

It didn't sound very convincing to me. If I told MY mother that I was washing her bedspread for the fun of it, she would think I'd lost my marbles. However, Rachel was more of a homebody, so I hoped that Mrs. Walkson would reward the activity with praise.

Flushing the evidence down the toilet, we carried the heavy chenille bedspread to the basement. Rachel filled the ringer washing machine with water and put in Mrs. White's Bluing and lots of Tide. We scrubbed the spot on the bedspread, then stuffed it in the machine, gasping as sudsy water poured over the top onto the floor.

We let the bedspread wash, and after we stopped the machine, it was so thick we could not feed it through the wringer. It took both of us to pull it out and place it into the nearby laundry sink, where we tried to rinse it.

"This thing weighs a ton," Rachel said as we draped the dripping mess over the clothesline, getting ourselves drenched in the process.

I took a mop and pushed some of the water toward the drain. Rachel took a rag and cleaned up the washing machine. My body was trembling in anticipation of Mrs. Walkson's arrival. When I heard her come in the back door, I almost had a heart attack.

"Hello," she said. "Where are you?"

"Down in the basement washing your bedspread," Rachel answered. "I need to do it for a badge in homemaking for Girl Scouts."

I held my breath. It was a pretty smart reason to come up with. It even sounded feasible. I awaited her mother's reply.

"Sounds like you let a cat in, and it went to the bathroom on our bed," Mrs. Walkson said.

Rachel didn't respond. We listened as her mother's footsteps moved through the house and up the stairs.

"See you later," I said, running out the back door, down the drive and around the hedge. I didn't stop until I was sitting in the swing in my yard where I could see the Walkson house. It seemed like forever before Rachel came out and sat on her front steps. Running over, I asked, "What happened?"

"Mom said she noticed a big white cat by the front door when she came home. And if I dared to give away any more milk, she'd leave a cat on my bed until he pooped."

We laughed until our sides ached.

Mrs. Walkson must have forgiven us because a few days later, she let us make a Chef Boyardee Pizza for supper. Rachel and I thought it was great that we were allowed to make it ourselves. After adding canned mushrooms and hamburger, we sat down and devoured it as we watched television.

Mr. Walkson interrupted our show, "Remember, in fifteen minutes, it's Lawrence Welk."

Rachel rolled her eyes and said, "Don't worry, Dad, we'll be done."

After finishing our program, we went upstairs to Rachel's room. From under her pillow she produced a razor. "Look what I found while snooping in Barb's dresser today," she said. "I even found some blades with it. Why don't we practice shaving our legs? I've watched my sister shave a million times. Come on, let's try it."

In the bathroom, she took the soap off the sink, wet and lathered her legs and gave a demonstration. "How about it? Want me to do yours?"

"My hair doesn't really show, but go ahead and practice." Off went my peach fuzz. Presto, I had hairless legs. Rachel touched the bleeding spots with her dad's styptic pencil. I felt my legs between the nicks. "Wow, they feel smooth. Why don't you practice on my arms too? Maybe some of my freckles will come off."

"I've never heard of anyone shaving their arms, but why not?" Rachel lathered up my arms and shaved my hair away.

"I can't believe it. I think my freckles are even darker. Maybe where you scraped the skin and put that stuff on, they won't come back."

Rachel laughed. "I've got to wash the razor." After cleaning off the evidence, she returned the shaver to Barb's dresser drawer.

"I'd better be getting home," I said.

When I entered our living room, Susie was sitting on the floor doing a puzzle. She smiled and asked, "Will you help me?"

We both examined the pieces and tried to fit them into various spaces. Dad, who was reading the paper, suddenly closed it and looked at me. "Why are all those bites on your arms and legs?" he asked. "The mosquitoes aren't out yet." I sat there speechlessly as he continued. "My goodness, you have no hair on your arms OR legs. What have you been up to?"

Mother came rushing in from the kitchen.

I explained to them that Rachel and I had been practicing shaving. "We shaved my arms to see if it changed my freckles."

Both parents tried to be very serious as they gave me advice, Dad first. "Freckles are hereditary. Your arms will look like mine when you get older."

I hoped he was wrong. His arms were one big freckle.

Mother added, "No one in THIS house is allowed to shave until they are sixteen."

"Okay, Mom," I replied, eager to end the conversation. To Sue, I added, "Let's go upstairs."

After picking up the puzzle, we left the room.

Susie grabbed my arm, "When you get your shaver, will you practice on me?"

TWENTY-THREE

THE LITTLE HOUSE THAT WAS

Our house was one of the oldest in Parker Falls, part of a large farm that was sold and divided into many lots. I loved its sloping floors and big front porch. The location was perfect—eight blocks from uptown and eight blocks in the other direction from the new Washington Grade School. Grassy fields had always existed between our home and the school, but that was changing. New houses were popping up as quickly as Minnesota gophers.

Dad felt that Parker Falls was growing because the chicken hatchery had put up another building and hired more people. Dad usually knew the inside scoop since he owned "Bob's Oldsmobile" and drank coffee with the other businessmen in town.

Mom, however, felt the growth was coming because Swanson's Cookie Factory had relocated from St. Cloud to Parker Falls. Mom's knowledge was firsthand, coming from Trudy, a member of Mother's church choir, who had just married the cookie factory's manager. Oh, I almost forgot, Trudy was also a cousin of ours and Es's. Did you meet her, Chief? Anyway, Trudy, age 28, had worked at People's Bank since high school. Everyone assumed that she was going to be an old maid, but she had outsmarted us all. Not only did she marry, but she and her husband were building a new house on our street.

I frequently rode my bike over to check on the construction. I'd snoop around and then chat for a few minutes. I liked Trudy. She was boisterous and funny. The fact that her hair stuck out like a frazzled copper pan cleaner made me like her even more.

Trudy's bungalow was being built across from a tiny house that was a notorious neighborhood eyesore. The drab weather-beaten structure was centered on a lot with no trees, grass or driveway. A strange old man had lived there forever, parking his old junker right on the barren front lawn. On warm days, he sat on a metal chair in front of his house. I'd see him there looking into space, and I wondered if he was praying for a miracle to take him away from his dilapidated homestead.

Then, he died.

Weeks passed before I noticed any activity at the little house. A rusty car that looked just like the old man's junker squatted on the street in front. *Maybe the new owner was the old man's twin*, I thought.

Trudy solved the puzzle. "You know the geezer that used to live there?" she began. "After he died, my bank tracked down his only living relative in Coppertown, over by the boundary waters. Seems his sister, who died a few years ago, had married an Indian. They had a daughter by the name of Pearl. We notified Pearl that she had inherited her uncle's house and car. Yesterday, she arrived by Greyhound Bus with her little three-year-old daughter Star. There doesn't seem to be any husband. I hope she doesn't start any trouble."

"Why should she?" I asked. "Pearl has little Star to take care of. And besides, there's never any trouble in Parker Falls."

Trudy smiled and then remembered something else. "Guess what? There's also a boy your age who is moving into the green bungalow down the street. His name is Ricky Snickerson. My bank gave his father the loan for the house. The family owns the implement store on the outskirts of town. I think they have money. Maybe you can hook up with him someday."

I laughed. "I think since I'm only eleven, I won't get married for a while. See you later." I raced down the street on my bike, hoping to see Ricky. Every day, in fact, I pedaled over to see if he was there. Finally, one afternoon, when Susie and I were riding around, there was a kid out in the yard playing with his dog. We climbed off our bicycles and walked over. He was rather goofy looking with straw-colored hair and buck teeth. He was really skinny. I instantly doubted that I'd ever marry him.

"Hey," I said. "Is your name Ricky? I heard you were moving in."

He looked at me. "Yeah, that's my name. What's yours?"

After we'd introduced ourselves, I told him that our house was on the same street across from the park, "the one with the swing on the front porch. We'll be in the same sixth-grade class at Washington." Actually, there was only one sixth-grade class there.

He didn't respond.

The three of us stood around and played with Ricky's dog, Extra.

On our way home, Susie and I rode slowly by Pearl's house. We'd seen her only once and wanted to see her again. Pearl was tall and beautiful with long coal-black hair in a ponytail. Contrary to most of the town residents, she was thin, wore slacks a lot and had nice tan skin. I was so impressed by her looks that I told Susie I'd like to look like her when I grew up.

Susie giggled and said, "You're nutty. You're short with red hair and freckles."

"Wait a minute," I replied. "I might grow tall. And I can always dye my hair."

Pearl and Star was the topic of our discussions for the next few weeks. When school started, we forgot about them.

On the first day of school, Miss Dutch, my teacher, assigned me the desk across the aisle from Ricky. She divided the class into four sections. Somehow, Ricky and I ended up in the same math and social studies groups. He was as silly as he looked, always mumbling under his breath and rolling his eyes.

Unfortunately, I couldn't help but laugh at him. Out loud.

Within one week, Ricky and I ended up in the principal's office two times. My brother called me a delinquent. Even though I explained to Mom and Dad that "I didn't mean to laugh," they said it was inexcusable. The third time, when Ricky and I used squirt guns loaded with Kool-Aid and sprayed a mean kid at recess, the principal called my mother.

She confronted me the minute I got home. "What's getting into you, Judith?"

"There's a bully who always picks on Inky," I explained, naming a tiny kid with thick glasses. "Somebody's got to shape him up." (I used an expression my parents frequently spoke.)

Overhearing us, Sheryl, shook her head in disbelief. "You must be retarded," she said, using a word we had been warned not to call anyone. "If you wouldn't have used grape Kool-Aid on his white T-shirt, there wouldn't have been any evidence. Why didn't you use toilet water or perfume?"

"I guess I should've asked you first," I replied.

As fall passed into winter, Ricky and I became so disruptive that we were moved to seats away from each other. Unfortunately, it was during the time of student evaluations. Mom and Dad were very upset when they received my report card, and the "improvement needed" checkbox was marked next to my conduct. "You'd better not end up like Terry," they warned. (He was a teenager four houses away who stole a car and got sent to reform school.)

Nobody, though—not even my parents—could stop me from being Ricky's friend, especially since Ricky had traded his pocketknife for my pea shooter. I was smitten. I carried the pocketknife with me everywhere and bought only Snickers Bars with every nickel I had.

Susie constantly teased me. "Judi loves Ricky Snickerson, so Judi eats Snickers candy bars, eee eye eee eye oh…"

"Okay," I said. "If you don't quit pestering me, I won't ever let you talk to Ricky again."

That cured her. She thought Ricky was funny and enjoyed his stories on the way to school. Most mornings, if Ricky saw us walking by his house, he came running out the door with his jacket hanging from one arm and a peanut butter sandwich in his other hand, shouting, "Hey, wait for me!"

Sometimes, his cousin, Danny, walked home with us. When he did, Susie laughed even more than she did at Ricky's stories. Danny was really crazy. He was in the sixth grade with Ricky and me too. Danny was a big guy with very greasy hair who had flunked first and second grades. I had been a classmate of his in third grade. He was the only kid we knew with false teeth. He'd smile this impish grin, drop his teeth onto his tongue, and stick out his tongue. We'd howl and say, "Yuk."

Both Danny and I loved to tell the story about our third-grade teacher, Miss Johanson. One afternoon, she refused to give Danny a pass to the bathroom. He really had to go, so he stood up and took "it" out and peed in a puddle on the floor. Miss Johanson, who was very old and short-tempered, picked up the yardstick from her desk and whacked him on the head so hard the ruler broke in two. The pieces flew to the floor. Everyone in our third-grade class went into gales of laughter. Whenever either of us retold that story, we still laughed.

Susie thought the story was so funny, she repeated it one evening at our supper table. My brother promptly assured me that I had now graduated to a delinquent with a capital "D."

"I'll probably marry Ricky someday," I replied. "Then you can meet his cousin."

Sheryl turned to me, "You are so out to lunch. It's not legal to marry anyone that's not from our church."

"Mom, is that true?" I asked.

She nodded.

I felt sick to my stomach. There was only one kid at church my age, and I knew there was no way I would ever marry him!

That night in bed, when Susie and I lay talking, I said, "Maybe I'll be like Pearl after all. Even though I might not grow tall with beautiful black hair, I can find a cute kid and a house and forget about a husband. I don't think I'll work at a bar, though."

We both knew that Trudy was very upset with the job Pearl had chosen and that Pearl's daughter wasn't getting any religious instruction. "And to think that all seventeen of the churches have invited Star to Sunday School," Trudy said, repeating the gossip from the bank.

"Why would Pearl send her little girl to any of those Sunday Schools?" I asked my cousin. "Nobody ever has anything nice to say about her."

In spite of all the town chatter, though, Pearl made some good friends. I know because on Father's Day Sunday, when the town spent the morning in church, some folks appeared at Pearl's house with paint brush in hand, and they quickly painted the drab weather-beaten house shocking pink.

Before the churches let out, Pearl and her helpers had finished and disappeared. It wasn't long before the telephone lines were smoking. Susie and I spent the rest of the day sitting on our front porch swing, watching the entire town drive down our street.

I always wished that Pearl had been my friend. I could have sat on her front step and waved at all the traffic. It would've felt like I was sitting on the most important float in a parade.

After a few days, the neighborhood calmed down, and people stopped driving by—except for me. Pearl had become my heroine. Every day I rode my bicycle down the street just to smile at her pink house.

But the little house sat unprotected in the middle of a treeless yard, and as the summer moved along, its garish color, along with the town gossip, began to fade until the house was pale pink and all talk of it vanished from conversation.

TWENTY-FOUR

THE DEMISE OF THE LIVESTOCK

A few of my friends were adventurers, daring and fearless. It was their company I enjoyed the most. One friend, Tina, lived in a new house on our block. There also was Dianna, a farm girl who went to my church. I'm sure you know who she is, Chief—she sat in the front row with me every time you had a concert in Parker Falls.

Naturally, my parents preferred the company of Dianna since she was from the same religious and ethnic background. I often took advantage of their approval and visited Dianna's farm whenever I could.

After church, Dianna and I would get into their Chevy and drive past the Parker Falls municipal airport where the roads changed from asphalt to dirt. After another five miles, we'd park the car and walk up to their house. Dianna's father raised beef cattle, milk cows, pigs, chickens, plus enough corn and grain to feed the animals. Her two brothers helped with the fieldwork and cleaned out the barn. Mrs. Gustafson took care of the cooking, baking and hen house.

Dianna's family responsibilities were gathering eggs and milking. She'd wash the underside of the cow before her father hooked up the pneumatic milking machine. I watched this many times. What fascinated me most were the cow's udders. They hung, a big inflated sack of skin containing milk, with finger-like extensions below. It seemed unbelievable that the cow just stood there chewing hay and cud all day and then created something as delicious as milk.

Dianna didn't say much one day as I followed her around raving about the cow's magical ability. She began her chore by adding a special soap to warm water and then walking over to a cow and starting to scrub with a wire brush. "Don't just stand there talking. Help me," she said. "Hold onto one of these teats so I can scrub easier."

Obeying her, I gingerly grabbed a teat. It felt rough and funny, and I was very embarrassed. But the cow didn't mind. She just stood there swishing her tail and chewing away, ignoring our presence.

After we finished, Mr. Gustafson came over and squeezed the teats until the milk started. The first milk was considered unclean, so he collected that milk into a big aluminum basin. Mr. Gustafson asked me to help him, but I could never squeeze hard enough to get much milk. "You're just a freckled weakling," he somberly stated. But I knew he was teasing because his eyes twinkled, and fans of smile-wrinkles spread to his ears.

The cows looked comical with suction cups hanging from their udders. A sloshing sound resonated through the air as the milk pumped from the swollen sacks into shiny stainless containers that sat on the floor. When the udder was deflated, the cow's big watery eyes looked relieved, as though the creature realized that her duty had again been performed.

As we waited, Dianna and I placed the aluminum basin containing milk next to the bales of hay in the corner of the barn. We climbed up onto the hay and waited. "It's magic," I whispered as the cats and kittens appeared. Big and little, old and young, the cats stretched their necks to lap the warm liquid. With heads down, their butts and tails circled the basin. All were busy filling their tummies. After finishing, they lifted their milk-covered faces and meticulously washed themselves.

We laughed at how serious they seemed to be.

"Come on. It's time for us to eat," Dianna said.

Before walking into the house, we left our shoes in the barn-smelling mudroom. Mrs. Gustafson greeted us, "Wash your hands and help me finish setting the table. I see the men walking across the drive."

We set the table and waited until everyone was seated. Huge, steaming bowls of corn, pot roast, potatoes and gravy occupied the center of the table. A large pitcher of fresh warm milk stood above the food. Between two dinner plates rested a basket of bread.

The family quieted down, bowed their heads, and prayed in unison, "We are grateful to You for the riches of our harvest. Amen."

Dianna's brothers immediately started talking as they passed the food, scooping large portions onto their plates. I watched in amazement as everything edible disappeared as quickly as a Popsicle on a hot day. After washing the food down with milk, the family members sat back in their chairs, ready for conversation.

The Gustafsons were a jolly group. As they ate dessert, they told stories, some of them repeated for my benefit because it gave them a chance to laugh along with me. My favorite story was told by Dianna's mother.

"After Richard and I married," she said, "it was a big adjustment for me to live on a farm. In addition to feeding my new husband and his two brothers, I helped with many outside chores. Of course, I already knew how to cook. But I suddenly realized that Mother had never taught me how to make bread. It was a task she loved doing in the early hours of the morning, and we often woke up to the wonderful smell of bread baking in the oven.

"Now here I was, a new bride, and I wanted to impress my husband, so I decided to try my hand at bread making. My first attempt met with little success, and the bread was very dense. Richard ate it but said nothing. The next time, I mixed the flour, water, and yeast, but it didn't rise at all. So I added extra yeast and let it sit longer, but the dough just sat there and never rose a bit. Embarrassed to tell my husband that I had failed, I threw the dough to the pigs.

"The next morning, when I went out to feed the pigs, Auggie, my favorite sow, was dead. I ran and got Richard from the barn. He called the vet to come over and check for disease. After an autopsy, we found she had eaten all the bread dough. The warmth of her stomach had caused the dough to rise and burst through the wall of the intestine. Greedy Auggie gave us enough pork for the entire winter!"

One brother asked, "Did Betty Crocker send the mailman to pick up her cookbook?"

Mrs. Gustafson jokingly replied, "Well, I guess you boys wouldn't want to risk another piece of peach pie then, would you?"

After we finished the dishes, Dianna and her father took me home. "Do you want to come back next Saturday and help me pluck the chickens?" Dianna asked. "It's a crummy job, but if we worked together, it could be fun. Why don't you stay overnight, and we'll bring you to church with us in the morning?"

I impatiently waited out the week, eager to be an accomplice in de-feathering the chickens. When Saturday arrived, Mom drove me to the farm. I jumped out of the car and yelled, "Thanks, I'll see ya tomorrow," then ran over to the henhouse to help out. I stood in shock as I saw one brother holding the chicken parallel to the ground over a tree trunk as the other brother chopped off its head. The headless chicken was set down on its feet and ran around until it crashed to the ground. My jaw dropped in alarm.

Once I had seen a dead pheasant after my father had gone hunting. It was frightening to see the congealed blood in the bullet hole because I felt compassion for the fluffy, feathered bird. I had also seen death in a very brutal way months before when I was riding my bike in the neighborhood and saw two men lifting a stretcher into an ambulance. I could see the head of a woman, her scalp and hair burned. Mr. Olson told me the water heater in her house had exploded. Bicycling home as fast as I could, I threw my arms around my mother and wept. "Never, never die," I begged.

Of course, I was older now, and it was only chickens that were dying, but I was still uncomfortable with blood and death. As I witnessed the massacre, I didn't cry—I just stood there with my mouth open. Mr. Gustafson walked over and tried to explain things in a teasing manner. "Since their brains are cut off, they still have some thoughts left, so they run around." When he noticed that I didn't smile, he tried again. "I'm sorry. It's a way of harvesting food for us to eat."

Nodding, I continued to watch as six more chickens were decapitated. After they fell to the ground, they were suspended by their feet, dunked in scalding water and plucked. The headless chickens, now looking like bags of pimply pink skin, were thrown into a washtub to be gutted, washed and frozen.

Noticing I was speechless and pale, Dianna tried to console me. "Come on, put some of these feathers in a bag so we can finish, then I'll show you the new kittens."

I nodded and slowly moved into action. Dianna handed me the gunny sack, and I held it open as she scooped the feathers into it. It seemed forever before we left the scene of the slaughter.

Dianna and I walked over to the barn to check on the new babies. They looked like tiny, hairless pink mice with their eyes squeezed shut and their ears small and flat to their heads.

"Are you sure these are kittens, not blind mice?"

"If they were mice, would they be sleeping next to a cat?" she joked, climbing up the ladder into the hayloft with me close behind. Bales of hay were piled very high, almost to the ceiling. Dianna jumped from one to another like a kangaroo. I jumped like a kid with a gimpy leg and fell into the spaces between the bales. The hay scratched my skin, but I persevered.

Dianna squatted to pee. It seemed a better idea than running back to the house. For some reason, my attempts at squatting were never successful. Either I got my clothes wet, or if I sat on a bale of hay, the straw stuck to my rear end. Once I even found a squished bug stuck to my butt. Dianna laughed, "You're a city slicker, not a farm girl."

That night, when we were getting ready for bed, I was still thinking about the chickens. I told Dianna how it bothered me to see so much blood and death. Dianna understood and said she still missed a baby calf that she had raised on a bottle after its mother had died in birth. "But," she added, "I knew one day it had to go to the slaughterhouse. I cried and cried, but now I'm older and know that everything that lives must die sometime."

Our conversation ended, and my friend fell asleep. The stars sparkled outside the window, and the moon seemed to watch me toss and turn. I couldn't help that my mind was whirling and that every time I moved, the mattress made a scrunching sound.

Dianna always bragged about her comfortable bed. "I inherited my grandpa's old mattress. It's made of horsehair. Can you believe it?"

After witnessing the massacre of the chickens, I wasn't sure what I believed. I was wide awake and haunted by one thought: *Exactly what did someone have to do to get enough horsehair to fill a double mattress?*

TWENTY-FIVE

BUM'S ALLEY

When Dianna came to stay at our house, my little sister followed us around like a puppy. We didn't mind, though. Susie was cute, good-humored, and she laughed at our jokes. Plus, she was eager to participate in any of our adventures.

Sometimes Dianna and I invented magic tricks. The introductions to these acts of wizardry were my responsibility. I think you'll enjoy the story of one of our tricks, Chief.

Before performing this one, I told Susie, "Okay, we're going to let you in on a secret, and you must tell nobody, I mean *nobody*. Dianna brought along her magical carpet, and she will float on it out of the bathroom window into the sky. So we are going into the bathroom now and closing the door. We'll chant a bewitching rhyme to make Dianna disappear. You can sit right outside in the hallway and listen."

Susie's big blue eyes opened wide, and her curly hair bobbed as she spoke, "Show me where to sit."

I pointed to a spot next to the wall. My little sister obediently sat down. Dianna walked into the bathroom carrying a rolled-up rug under her arm. I followed and closed the door behind us. We started chanting, "Casper's cousin Malachi help Dianna fly into the sky."

As we repeated the magical words, I took the rug and shoved it way under the claw-foot tub. Dianna climbed up on the edge of the tub and hoisted herself out of the window onto the roof of the laundry room. Running down the roof, she leapt onto the small round-roofed tool shed below. Sitting on her fanny, she slid down the side to the ground.

At the same time, I opened the door to show Susie that Dianna and the carpet had disappeared. "Wow, it worked!" I said excitedly. "Dianna floated away. See?"

My sister wouldn't believe me and started checking in the corners and behind the door. When Dianna appeared outside the door, Susie turned as pale as a cotton ball.

"It's magic," Susie said. "Can I do it?"

"Maybe someday," Dianna told her. "Right now, let's keep it our secret, okay?"

A few weeks later, when Dianna was visiting, my little sister was right on our heels. Susie wanted to learn the magic carpet trick, but Dianna came up with another idea. "Why don't we bicycle over to Bum's Alley?"

"Yeah, let's go to Bum's Alley," my little sister echoed.

Parker Falls had been a railroad station since Grandpa was a kid. A dead-end street by the train yard had become a place where hobos sat around a fire, cooking and talking while waiting for a train. The town's people had named the street Bum's Alley. A few large trees sheltered the area making it less visible. Gossip was that the men sometimes curled up and slept on the ground. The bums never bothered anyone. I believe the town elders felt proud, even liberal, to allow these men to hang out. Parents purposely took their children for a drive, hoping as they peered out the windows at the bums sitting in layered clothes by the fire, that the youngsters would be forewarned and intuitively know, "Here is the fate of the irresponsible."

Dianna had never seen Bum's Alley and was dying to compare reality with the images in her head—scruffy characters who sat on logs or discarded tires swapping stories as they warmed their hands over an open fire.

"Come on," said Dianna. "Let's take the bikes and go. My brothers have seen it, but my dad won't take me there. I'll be a teenager in a few years, and then I'll be too old to go."

"What do you mean?" asked Sue.

"Because by then I'll have a boyfriend, and we'll be going to parties and stuff and won't have time. Besides, spying on people is kid's stuff."

My sister didn't respond because I interrupted, saying, "Well, we can't take our bikes across the tracks until we're in junior high. If we snuck, someone would probably see us and tell Mom and Dad—then we'd be in real trouble. Maybe we can talk Sheryl into going. That would make it legal. She *loves* to be a leader. Should I ask her?"

I did, and Sheryl liked the idea and immediately organized the activity. "Judi, you take your own bicycle," she ordered. "Dianna, you use mine, and I'll borrow Don's. Sue, you can sit behind me on the bike rack."

Bum's Alley was over two miles away. Sheryl gave instructions as we rode down the street. "Pedal slowly until we get there," she said. "You never know. The bums might chase us, and we need to be ready to beat it. Now, this is how we'll do it—we'll ride single file. That way, they can't get us all at once. I'll go first, Dianna second, and Judi, you bring up the rear."

"You make it sound dangerous," Diana said. "Did some kid get in trouble?"

Sheryl gave her a cold stare. "Clifford, who sits next to me in biology, said that a bum threw a rock at him when he and his brother rode by."

"Maybe Cliff made it up," I said. "I think you're just trying to scare us. Don't believe her, Dianna."

"Clifford is *not* a liar," Sheryl asserted.

After riding a few blocks in silence, we crossed the railroad tracks. Sheryl stopped and commanded us to line up. "The dirt road is just a few blocks farther. We need to practice our formation."

My big sister took a right onto Bum's Alley. Susie sat on the bike rack behind her, clinging to Sheryl's waist with both hands. As we rode single file, all of us were sneaking glances to check if anyone was hiding out there. I held my breath in anticipation.

Sure enough, there were three men sitting on logs talking. As we were turning around at the end of the alley, Sheryl announced, "Now ride by real fast so they can't come out and catch us."

Leading the three bikes, she raced down the road with Susie hanging onto her for dear life. Dianna charged after her.

Before taking off, I turned for a last look at the bums. They don't look so mean, I thought to myself.

At that moment, my tire hit some broken glass and popped.

I heard laughter.

Trembling, I got off my bicycle. To calm my weak-kneed self, I whispered, "Be brave, Judi." With heart pounding and hands sweating, I started to push my wobbling bike down the road. I tightened my grip on the handlebars and kept moving, eyes straight ahead.

Sheryl and Dianna were standing at the end of the road, motioning me to move faster.

When I was in hearing distance, Sheryl yelled. "Didn't you see that glass? What an idiot. Now you have to walk your bike all the way home."

"Do you think I would run over the glass if I saw it?"

"I can't believe you didn't watch where you were going! Let's get moving, or you'll never make it home. I'll walk with you until we get over the tracks, then you're on your own."

Sheryl pulled Susie by one hand and pushed the bike with the other. She started up again with her lecture, reminding me that I would never get anywhere in life if I didn't pay attention. After we crossed the tracks, she plunked Sue on the back of her bike and took off, shouting, "Don't break a leg or do something else stupid!"

Groaning in response, I turned to Dianna. We burst out laughing.

We had to walk slowly because of my flat tire, but we didn't mind. It was fun to review our adventure. "They didn't look so scary to me," I said. "Just think, they can see the whole world for free. Wouldn't it be fun to sit in a boxcar and look out through the open doors? Maybe we should try it sometime."

"Our folks would have a heart attack," Dianna said, smiling.

"I'm talking about when we're older. But we could start practicing this afternoon by going to the park and jumping onto the merry-go-round."

"Doesn't sound so great to me," replied Dianna.

When we finally approached home, my little sister ran down the block to greet us. "There's warm chocolate chip cookies and milk inside," she said. "Come on."

That night, after Mom turned out the lights and I was trying to go to sleep, Susie whispered from her bed across the room. "Judi, are you awake?"

"What?" I muttered groggily.

"If you decide to be a bum, can I come too?"

"Sure," I said, and then fell asleep, exhausted.

TWENTY-SIX

MY BEST FRIEND

Tina, my other adventurous friend, looked very different from Dianna—different from any of my Scandinavian pals, for that matter. She was part Greek, part Danish and part Egyptian. At least, that's what her dad said. Tina was my best friend in the whole world, so there's a lot to tell, Chief. I guess I should start at the very beginning.

Tina's family moved to our town because of a "position available" ad my Uncle Reuben placed in the *Optometrist Monthly* magazine. Reuben was part owner of our local newspaper, *The Daily Tribune*, and wrote a column called "Man About Town." In his column, he commented on community activities and responded to questions posed by the folks in Parker Falls.

I guess people kept asking, "Isn't our town large enough to support an optometrist? Traveling fifty miles to St. Cloud is a real inconvenience."

So, Uncle Reuben, man of action that he was, sent a classified advertisement to the appropriate magazine and printed in his column the ad he had written: "Wanted—optometrist for small rural town in Minnesota with honest hard-working Swedes and Norwegians. Community will pay for moving van and first month's rent in Torgeson's office building. Town has 17 churches and 5 good swimming lakes. Please respond to P O. Box 92, Parker Falls, Minn."

Local residents kept pestering my uncle for news of an applicant. My dad needed to replace his lenses, and so did our neighbor, Mr. Watson. Both wanted to give their business to the new doctor.

"Hang on," Uncle Reuben answered. "We haven't found anyone yet, but we will."

Finally, a prospective doctor responded this way: "I would like the opportunity to open an office in your town but will not graduate for three months. Could you wait until then?"

The community felt he might be too young for the position, so Reuben telephoned the applicant to get more information and summarized the call in his column. "Here's the scoop," he wrote. "Gary Duke worked in his father's dry-cleaning business until his younger brother was old enough to take over. At the age of 27, Gary started college and will graduate at the age of 30 from the Minot School of Optometry. Even though he was born and raised in North Dakota, his wife Jeri and their two children would be happy to relocate to Minnesota." He ended his column with, "Call me at the *Tribune* or send a postcard with your vote."

Most of the residents voted "yes." My father decided he could wait another few months for his lenses, especially since he'd learned that the Dukes had purchased a house two doors away and would be our neighbors.

It was an exciting day for me when I was playing in the yard and saw a moving van pull into the Duke's drive. Rushing into the house, I found Mom. "Hey, there's a huge truck and a big red and beige car by the eye doctor's house. Do you suppose his kids are here?"

"I imagine so. Why don't you run over and…" I was out the back door before she finished her sentence.

After running across the neighbor's back lawn and around to the side entrance of their house, I saw a man come out of the breezeway door. I figured he must be the new eye doctor because he didn't wear coveralls like the men unloading the truck. Also, he looked kinda special with his thick, shiny black hair, which stood tall and wavy above his forehead. His hair reminded me of my Grandpa with his thick, white hair, except Mr. Duke had a very tan face and a very big nose. He smiled when he saw me, a small and stocky girl with freckled, chubby cheeks, charging toward him.

"Excuse m-me," I stammered, overwhelmed by his unusual appearance. "Do you have a daughter my age?"

"You know," he answered, "it just might be that I do. Let's go find her."

We found his two girls in the kitchen with their mom. Mrs. Duke was very slim and pretty with an olive complexion like her husband. Just then, a big black poodle ran up. "This is our dog, Chula," the eye doctor said. "And these are my girls, Tina and Lizzy." The girls both stood there, staring at me.

"How old are you?" I asked Tina.

"Seven. I'll be in second grade. Lizzy just turned three. How old are you?"

"I'm seven too. My little sister is a year older than Lizzy. And I've got a big brother and sister and a dog, Rex. Can you play today?"

We smiled at one another, and I could already tell we would be best friends. The rest of the summer, we were inseparable. Mrs. Duke called us the unidentical twins. Tina and I had the same spirit of curiosity and ever-moving mouths, but our appearances were not alike at all. I was fair with blue eyes and a Buster Brown hair cut. Tina had dark skin, black curly hair, brown eyes, and brown glasses that she wore because her father was the eye doctor. Anyway, that's what I thought until Tina let me try them on. "Hey, this is like looking through the bottom of a jelly glass."

Tina giggled, "You look awful in my glasses. Let's go uptown and pick some out for you."

We loved going to Mr. Duke's new office. It was too far for us to bicycle, so whenever Tina's mom went, we rode with her in their

New Yorker. My father was in the car business, but I'd never seen a car like theirs.

Tina told me that Uncle George had given his old car to her dad for a graduation present because he was so proud of having a doctor in the family. My dad said that their New Yorker was still worth a lot of money even though it was three years old. I believed him because it *felt* expensive. The seats were beige leather and so deep that if I slid as far back into the seat as I could, my legs stuck straight out. Right then, I knew exactly how it must feel to be "Queen for a Day."

At the eye doctor's office, Mrs. Duke made phone calls, sent out bills, cleaned the office, and begged Tina and me to "stay out of the way."

It wasn't difficult to occupy ourselves. We tried on glasses until we knew the inventory inside out. We sat in the newly decorated "California-style" waiting room where there was a wallpaper mural of an ocean and palm trees casting shadows on the sand. We sat on the padded rattan chairs across from the palm trees, usually wearing our favorite cat-eye glasses, chatting and pretending we lived on the beach. No matter how often we came, we found plenty to do.

Sometimes, Mr. Duke needed our help, or so he said, "Now girls, which one of you is going to check the sand bath?"

Racing into his office, we got up on a stool and looked at a thermometer resting in a big bowl of sand to see if the temperature was up to the red mark. "It's ready," Tina announced. Then we watched Mr. Duke put frames into the hot sand and snap prescription lenses into them. Both of us believed he was very smart. Wearing stylish frames, we felt grown up and therefore entitled to this opinion.

Most people in town liked the new optometrist. The family's olive skin continued to be a point of discussion until Mr. Duke explained they came from a town where the Greeks and Danes intermarried. The community was relieved to find some Scandinavian blood in the family! Really, they weren't that dark—it was just that everyone else in Parker Falls was so pale. Their acceptance into the community was cinched when Mr. and Mrs. Duke joined the Methodist church, and the congregation found out that Gary's older brother was the pastor of the First Methodist Church of Minot.

My parents would have preferred that they join our church, but since they were "regular churchgoers," my friendship with Tina was allowed to continue. My folks even permitted me to sleep over at Tina's one summer night.

This was the first time in my life that I slept over at a friend's house, and I was very excited. Since Tina shared a room with her sister Lizzy, we wanted to be by ourselves, so we begged to sleep in the enclosed breezeway between the garage and the house. After pushing the two love seats together, we piled them with blankets and pillows until it felt very cozy.

Mr. Duke came out to say good night. "I bet you a double scoop ice cream cone that you'll get scared and come in."

"Don't try and spook us," Tina replied.

We lay there talking and laughing as the daylight faded into grays and then blackness. A streetlight stood in the distance, dim and blinking as though it were falling asleep, encouraged us to do the same.

Suddenly, a wind came up. The glass in the patio windows rattled, then and rattled some more. Our eyelids flew open.

"Maybe a window will fall out, and a stranger will sneak in and find us," said Tina. We were petrified with fear and began discussing what to do.

"We can't sleep inside," I said. "Then we won't get our ice cream cones. Besides, everyone would call us 'fraidy cats.' Let's be brave, okay?"

"I'll try. But with all this noise, someone might come in and kidnap us. We'd never hear them."

"How about if I put my finger in one of your snarly curls? Then I'll pull your hair, and you can sneak out and get help while I hang onto the love seat so they can't kidnap me?"

"Good idea. I knew we'd think of something."

So, I hooked a finger in one of Tina's curls. It wasn't easy holding my arm out across the space between the seats, but I did it.

We kept checking back and forth.

"Are you sleeping?"

"Are you scared?"

Finally, there was silence.

As sunlight finally poked through the windows, I woke up with Chula licking my face. Her warm, stinky dog breath invaded my nostrils—the only invasion of our breezeway adventure.

Quickly, I sat up and said, "Hey, Tina—wake up. Your dad's gonna take us for ice cream."

TWENTY-SEVEN

THE DUKE FAMILY

That summer, I spent more time at Tina's house. If Mr. Duke happened to be around, it was extra fun because he played jokes on everyone.

One afternoon, as we were all sitting around the table after lunch, Mr. Duke turned to me and said, "Did you know I was a magician? Let me show you one of my favorite tricks. Before your very eyes, I will pump food from your stomach and out of your ear. Then you'll have room for some of Jeri's wonderful dessert."

"You can't do that," I replied.

"Yes, he can," Tina said, nodding. "Really."

Hesitating, I extended my arm. Mr. Duke moved it up and down, placing his other hand by my ear to catch the food.

"Well, what do you know, now you'll have enough room for that cake." As he showed me a handful of gooey food, my eyes just about fell out of my head. Then he added, "Oh dear, I'm stuck between Lizzy and Jeri on this bench, can't get to the garbage can." He raised his arm and ate the nasty stuff in his hand.

"Yuck!" I said as the family burst into laughter. Then I realized what Mr. Duke had done and started giggling.

"You spit *your* food into your own hand!" I explained.

Tina's dad was notorious for silly ideas like that. One Saturday evening in August, he announced, "Today is Candy Day. This morning, when you were sleeping, I hid your favorite treats around the house. Now it's time to see if you can find the hiding places."

I helped Tina and her little sister, Lizzy, search for the hidden candy. Immediately, we looked behind the piano.

"Hey, here's a bone for Chula," I said, picking it up. Hearing her name, the big black poodle came running over. Growling, she clamped onto my arm, piercing my freckled skin with her teeth.

"Ouch. What a mean dog," I hollered. Without thinking, I grabbed her ear and bit down with all my might.

Chula ran off yelping. Mrs. Duke came tearing from the laundry room. "What's going on?"

As she washed my arm, Tina explained what happened. Within a few minutes, she had put iodine on my wounds, and I was given two pink bubble gum cigars for being tough. Then Mrs. Duke appraised the situation and delivered her assessment. "You seem fine to me. Let's look for the other candy."

We found a big bag of M&M's for Lizzy, a bag of Fireballs for Tina, plus Tootsie Pops, Neccos and root beer barrels. But Mrs. Duke couldn't find her surprise. After coaching from her husband, Jeri Duke looked in the bedroom. As she was opening a dresser drawer, she let out a gasp. In a drawer with her lingerie were chocolate-covered cherries, which unfortunately had melted all over her underwear because of the August temperatures.

Mr. Duke laughed. "I forgot about the heat."

As they hugged and kissed, we three girls cheered. Then all of us sat in the breakfast nook and had root beer floats and laughed about the cherries and me biting Chula.

Mr. Duke's joviality showed itself in other ways too. In the fall, he started to practice tap dancing for a fundraiser the Jaycees were having in December. Mrs. Duke was his pianist. Tina, Lizzy and I enjoyed being the audience. With a cane as a prop and Jeri at the piano, he began a rehearsal for us.

I sat on the floor cross-legged with my elbows resting on my knees and my head on my hands. As Mr. Duke twirled his cane and danced, I watched his feet clack and tap, up and down and side to side, backward and forward like two little acrobatic elves.

When the performance was over, Mr. Duke bowed, then bowed again as if he were in Carnegie Hall. We shouted and clapped until Jeri stood up from the piano and took a bow with her husband.

As the holidays approached, excitement grew. Grandma Duke was coming for the holidays to see her son dance in the Jaycees program. I had never heard of that organization until Tina moved to town. Questioning my father, I found out why nobody in our family was a member. The group was too liberal. Dad liked the Gideon's because they gave Bibles to all the sixth graders for Christmas.

"But the Jaycees are raising money for a new park. Isn't that good too?" I asked but got no answer.

The day Tina's grandma arrived, my mouth fell open in shock. This was the first gray-haired grandma I had ever seen with a youthful figure and stylish clothes. Her hair was short and wavy, and she wore a suit with a tight-fitted waist and nylons without seams.

My grandmas had saggy breasts, cotton housedresses for weekdays and silky ones for Sundays, and wore shoes like nuns in a convent. Granted, one of my grandmas had her hair done and wore pearls on Sundays, but Grandma Duke was in a league of her own.

I asked my mother, "How come Tina's grandma is so pretty? Is it because she's not Swedish?"

Mother acted like she didn't hear me. Later I overheard her talking to my Aunt Alice on the phone saying something about "hormone shots" and "only three children."

During our vacation from school, I spent a lot of time at the Dukes. In fact, I spent so much time there that one day Mrs. Duke said, "You girls are getting on my nerves. Why don't you play a game?"

"What game?" Tina asked.

"All right, I'll give each of you four wet wash rags. Go into the hallway with only a crack of light coming from the living room. Throw the washrags at each other until I tell you to stop. The rules—each stay at your own end. No chasing, hitting, wrestling, or biting."

It sounded great to us. We ran to the bathroom and came back with our rags sopping wet.

"Oh, no you don't! You'll ruin the walls," Mrs. Duke said. Tina and I groaned as she wrung out the water.

Placing one of us at each end of the short hallway, she closed all the doors. "Now, start!" she yelled from the other side of the door.

Throwing the washrags back and forth, we pelted one another, howling and screaming at the top of our lungs. Once I ran to the other end to retrieve my washrag, but Mrs. Duke must have been listening because she yelled, "Judi, sit back down and obey my instructions."

When we'd finished playing, we looked like two Holy Terrors. Tina's mother laughed. "I trust you aren't so wound up now? How about sitting in the breakfast nook, and Grandma will play a game of Candyland with you."

We had just set up the board when the telephone rang. "It's your mother," Mrs. Duke told me. "She said to come right home and get ready for church. Your family is singing at the service tonight."

"Oh my gosh, I forgot!" I replied. Putting on my coat, I asked, "Can we play Candyland tomorrow?"

Grandma Duke nodded.

As I was headed out the door, I turned to ask, "Do you want to come to our church tonight? We'll be singing Christmas carols. Mom's directing a songfest. There's only a ten-minute sermon, and our family is singing a few numbers. It should be fun!"

"Maybe next time," Mrs. Duke replied.

When I arrived home, my family stood around the piano to practice our hymns. (I doubt you ever heard us, Chief.) Don sang tenor, as usual, Dad added a grand bass voice, Sheryl alto, and I sang soprano with Mother. Susie sang along too. Little Susie was only three, but her voice added to the ensemble. Of course, with her curly hair and blue eyes, she looked like a singing cherub.

During the Christmas sing, we all sat in the front row and waited for Mother to motion us to come up. Our first number, "Joy to the World," was a great success, and I could see my parents' chests puff out—even though we were taught that pride was immoral.

Later in the evening, we sang, "Angels We Have Heard on High." Our musical family sang the first verse perfectly. On the second verse, my older siblings and our parents used the hymnbook. Unfortunately, nobody knew the song by heart. Dad lost his place—got nervous, I guess—and then he started laughing silently. His entire body shook, and he had a grin on his face. Sheryl, standing next to him, realized that something was wrong and looked up at Dad. Then she stopped singing. I was standing on a stool in front of the lectern, still singing as loudly as I could because I had memorized the song. When Sheryl looked over, though, I got distracted. Then realizing our dilemma, I put my hand over my mouth and tried to keep from laughing.

Susie was standing on the other side of Don holding his hand while singing out to the audience. She was totally unaware of what was going on. So, she, Mom and Don finished the last two verses by themselves while the rest of us stood there red-faced and grinning. Then we all sheepishly walked back to our seats.

When we were all in the car riding home, Dad said, "I think it's a blessing somebody finished the song."

Sitting in the back seat, I could tell from looking at Mom that she was still very miffed. Susie, sitting between them, was totally oblivious to the tension and started chatting away. "You know what, Mommy? Uncle Oscar said I looked like an angel. Can we sing again?"

"Sure," Mother replied, "as soon as the cows come home."

My little sister's curly head bobbed as she giggled and said, "Oh, Mommy, you're so silly. We don't have any cows."

TWENTY-EIGHT

THE BUTTERFLY

At Tina's house, we watched *Truth or Consequences*, which always made us laugh. This time, someone sat on a chair wearing a clown mask. A blindfolded contestant was supposed to feel the masked face and tell the audience if it was his uncle or his brother.

While we watched the show, we were also trying out some new glasses Mr. Duke had just brought home to his family. The glasses had lenses that stuck out like pyramids. Little mirrors were glued to the inside of the surfaces so we could look at the television screen while lying on our backs. As the man on the show was feeling the mask, we were switching the glasses back and forth while we talked and laughed.

"These glasses are like being in the funhouse at the county fair," Tina said.

"Where did your dad get these? It's magic to look up and watch TV when the screen's way over there. We've got to show them to my little sister. Come on."

Losing interest in the fate of the contestant, we took the glasses to my house. All of us lay down on the floor and took turns looking at the various objects in the room. Susie was as excited as we were.

Mother, hearing the commotion, came into the living room. "I have some chocolate chip cookies right out of the oven. Interested?"

Into the kitchen we went. The breakfast nook was my favorite spot in the house. The red Formica table made the room feel happy. We were discussing the mystery of the glasses when Mom came over and dropped a packet on the table. "Why don't you cut apart your school photos for me? I need to send one to Aunt Rachel."

Tina burst into giggles as she held up my picture. "Look at your bangs! They're crooked."

"It's how my hair turned out. I cut my own bangs and set my hair in rollers." Wads of curls hovered over each ear, reflecting the small metal rollers I had used. I must admit, I did look pretty goofy.

The night before, when my older sister had seen the photos, she reprimanded Mother. "Why did you let Judi go to school like that? It looks like she hung a couple of rat's nests over her ears."

Tina and Susie kept giggling about my hair as we ate our cookies, but I kept on with my story. "Notice the beads I'm wearing in the photo? Those are Sheryl's poop-it beads."

"What do you mean, 'poop-it' beads?" Tina asked, trying to hold back her laughter.

"One Christmas when I was little, we were counting our gifts before we went upstairs to bed. Sheryl couldn't find the necklace Aunty Victoria gave her and looked all over. All of a sudden she started yelling, 'I know what happened! I saw Judi eating something off the floor. She must've eaten my beads.' Mom got caught up in the frenzy and gave me a big spoon of castor oil, even though I kept repeating, 'I didn't eat them.'"

Later, when I was in the bathroom, I heard Don shout, "I just found the beads on the desk."

My story was interrupted by a phone call from Mrs. Duke asking Tina to come home.

"I have to go home and practice the piano," she explained. "See you tomorrow." My friend ran out the door.

Mrs. Bloom, Tina's teacher, lived on our street. I desperately wanted to take lessons from her. She gave out easy music to play, which made the recitals nothing but a tea party. I begged and pleaded, "I've already taken lessons from Mrs. Udahl for three years. Can't I try Mrs. Bloom?" But no, I had to continue taking lessons from Mrs. Udahl, the only person in town who studied at a conservatory. Mom's favorite thing in the world was music, and she wanted us to learn from the best. Es could have taught me too, Chief, like she did Mom, but that wasn't an option.

So, every Saturday, off to Mrs. Udahl I went, the Schubert Classical Piano book in my bicycle basket and a dollar fifty in my coin purse for her fee. Brother Don was already a musical wizard, and Sheryl was not far behind. At the age of five, I started learning to play piano.

Mother advised, "Listen to what you are told, and we'll start practicing together. I'm sure you'll do just fine."

Of course, I already knew my teacher. Once each year, she held her student recitals at the Lutheran Church. Mother and I had gone to hear my brother and sister perform there. Mrs. Udahl was a sweet, soft-spoken lady who was married to a famous lawyer twenty years older who spent most of his time in Washington at the House of Representatives.

My piano teacher was the only person in town who made me feel like a tomboy, probably because she always dressed so nice. She wore a silky dress with a lace collar and a crisp white linen hanky tucked at her wrist. Every week, when I noticed her princess-like hands and satin-polished nails, I tucked my striped T-shirt into my pants and quickly sat down only to realize that once again, I had forgotten to clean my nails. For that one moment, I wished I was frilly and neat because then I would look up at her and grin. She smiled at me anyway and said, "Let's begin with the scales." Placing my hands on the keys, all other thoughts were quickly forgotten.

I never minded my lessons. The music room had two pianos facing a wall with windows at my back and left. I enjoyed that I could look out and see the weather. I had one piano, and Mrs. Udahl had another. She listened to me play, ready to demonstrate if I did not correct my errors after her softly uttered reprimands. Sometimes my lesson would be delayed if Mr. Udahl were on television. Then we left our pianos and moved into the living room to watch the program. When he was on TV, her husband always sat kingly and composed as if he were a Shakespearian actor and spoke of matters beyond my grasp. I found the glow on my teacher's face more interesting than the program.

Mrs. Udahl was not a talkative person and spoke to me in hushed phrases and through the stickers she placed on my music. If I received bird stickers, I knew she was not pleased. If I got flowers, then she was encouraged. When Mrs. Udahl was serious and wanted me to "buckle down," she gave me blue (the lowest) and red stars. Silver and gold (highest) were for a good lesson. Rarely did I get a silver star.

Evenings, Mother urged me to practice. "Remember you have to practice two hours before your next lesson. I will not throw my money into the wastebasket. You may as well sit down right now and spend a half hour."

In the summer, it was very difficult to be disciplined, and on occasion, I ended up practicing two hours the day before my lesson. At least once a week, Mom sat by my side to check fingering, posture and progress. Or she set the metronome, adding, "You're not playing for a funeral." The kitchen was close by, and Mother's comments like "watch your notes" or "pay attention" frequently floated through the air. Following her instructions, I became a decent pianist. Singing was more fun, but piano was all right, except for the recitals.

Every year I had to endure a public performance, and each time it was traumatic. My hands would be sweaty, and my piece much too difficult. Because I'd rather be outside playing or inside reading, I was never prepared like I should've been. "Mastery is a by-product of good practice," Mom always admonished.

I always intended to put in the extra practice time, but there were many distractions. The year of "The Butterfly" was a particular challenge. I was eight years old. My teacher had pushed me to the limit and had given me a piece with lots of runs and crescendos. This meant I needed the pedals below. The music had to be memorized and played without flaws. Considering my skills and interest, I was worried.

The recital was a big deal, and everyone, including friends and relatives, assembled in the Lutheran Church basement for the performance. I could hear the wooden chairs clacking against each other and scratching the floor, and the nervous performers or parents clearing their throats. Mrs. Udahl stood at the front in her latest fancy dress and spoke words of welcome. "Thank you for the privilege of teaching your children. There will be cookies and punch after the recital. Now we must begin." Then, before each student walked onto a small platform to play, she announced his or her name and the musical selection to be performed.

It was finally my turn.

My body was sweating like a glass of ice water on a hot, August day. I approached the piano and then pulled the bench away. Taking a deep breath, I looked down and put my right foot over a pedal. Wiping my perspiring hands on my skirt, I *stood* and began to play "The Butterfly." Someone dared to chuckle loudly enough for me to hear. I imagine it did look funny. Because of my short stature, even standing, I could barely touch the pedal below, have my hands on the piano, and stand upright. Irritated that they had the nerve to laugh at me, I lifted my hands from the keys and scowled at the audience.

There was not a sound from anyone.

Turning back to the keyboard, I started again. Would you believe, Chief, I played the number perfectly? Before leaving the stage, I took a bow. The audience started clapping. As the applause got louder, my somber face broke into a smile.

At the next lesson, Mrs. Udahl placed a gold star on my sheet-music.

"The Butterfly" went down in history as my only perfect performance...

TWENTY-NINE

BLACK JACK

Living two doors apart and attending the same class in school, Tina and I remained inseparable. Both of us received the same number of marked achievements on our report cards, liked the same kids at school, and loved to ride our bicycles. We were as enthusiastic about life as two well-fed puppies romping on a lush green lawn and rolling on their backs in pure ecstasy. Neither set of parents minded our friendship, and both had two rules in common—stay out of trouble and be home for supper. Most of the time, we were outdoors or at Tina's house. She had more playthings, plus a television.

Tina's dad teased us at every opportunity. "How are my unidentical twins and my special little girl," he would add, to include Tina's sister Lizzy if she were around. Most of the time, his greeting was followed by some story or joke. That's just the way Mr. Duke was.

One afternoon, when he came home, Tina and I were sitting by the table at the breakfast nook swapping our penny candy. "I can't believe how lucky you kids are," he said, unwrapping a caramel of Tina's and popping it into his mouth. "My brothers and I had such a small allowance that we couldn't afford gum or candy. Of course, that didn't bother us. We just picked up a piece of tar off the road and chewed away, pretending we had a fresh stick of Black Jack Gum.

Sometimes our playmates offered to swap a stick of Juicy Fruit, but we just smiled, never letting anyone in on our little secret."

Tina and I groaned at his exaggeration. Unlike any parents I had ever met, Mr. and Mrs. Duke treated us more as friends than children. I figured that their liberal thinking was the result of being very young parents and not "pure-blooded" Scandinavians. Nevertheless, it was a luxury for me.

"Quit making up stories, Dad," Tina said.

"I'm not kidding," Mr. Duke took another piece of candy. "Really, my brother and I bicycled around and looked for newly paved streets. The glossy tar at the outside edge of the street was the good stuff. It tasted like wax but chewed like gum." (Have you ever heard of that?)

Tina and I challenged Mr. Duke, but he smiled and replied, "Ask Grandma at Christmas."

We forgot all about his silly story until a few weeks later when we were riding bicycles side-by-side down a street that was smelly and black and freshly paved.

"Tina, I just saw some shiny tar over by the curb like your dad told us about. Maybe it's the perfect stuff to chew."

"Yeah, let's look," she replied.

We put down our kickstands and squatted to inspect the asphalt. Cautiously, we inspected the glistening ridge of tar, poking it with our fingers to check how gooey it was.

"This is no good," said Tina. "It feels runny."

"Let's ride down the street to see if it's all the same." Following the road another few blocks, we parked our bikes and continued to check the tar alongside the curb.

"Hey, Tina, this feels like the perfect stuff," I said, holding up a wad of tar. "What do you think?"

My friend nodded in agreement. Each of us took a piece, rolled it into a little ball and popped it into our mouths. "This tastes awful," Tina said. But we kept chewing in hopes of proving Mr. Duke's story.

"This is crumbling apart," I said, grimacing. "Maybe it's not the right kind."

Tina started laughing. "Your teeth are all black. You look pretty funny."

I pointed at her. "You look like you put in licorice teeth for Halloween."

Spitting the tar out, we rubbed our teeth with our fingers, which only made matters worse. Our front teeth were now streaked black. "Oh great," I said, realizing we were in a serious predicament. "It looks like this stuff isn't too easy to get off. Let's get home and clean up before anybody sees us." Jumping on our bikes, we took off.

"Why don't you come to my house?" Tina suggested. "Lizzy would never know if you used her toothbrush."

"No, I'd better go home."

After parking my bike in the garage, I walked in the back door and saw Mom in the kitchen. I shot down the basement stairs, dumbfounded at my bad luck.

"Is that you, Judi?" Mom asked. "Would you bring me some corn from the deep freezer?"

Holy cow, I thought, *I'm in trouble this time.* Sheepishly, I walked up the steps, corn in hand. Mother turned to greet me as I stood before her, lips pulled over my teeth like an ancient old granny.

Mom looked at me. "Is there a reason you're acting so strange?"

Putting my hand over my mouth, I answered, "I forgot to brush my teeth this morning."

"Young lady, what have you been up to?"

Mom shook her head in amazement as I told the story. "Don't you have any common sense at all?" she asked.

"But Mom, Mr. Duke gave us the idea, and it would've been so nifty to fake the kids out at school."

My comment didn't impress Mother, nor did the results of my tooth brushing. Taking things into her own hands, she used a dishrag and Bon Ami and scrubbed my teeth until the black and white streaks blended into gray. During supper, Dad chuckled and said someone had told him the same thing when he was a kid. My brother Don told me I shouldn't be so trusting, and Sheryl called me a "nut-case," adding, "Don't you dare smile at any of my friends— you'll embarrass me."

Mr. Duke stopped by later that evening to apologize. Mom told him it was gracious to come over, but "Judi should have known better."

It took a few weeks for my teeth to change from grey to dirty white. I was relieved that my teeth looked better before it was time for the children's choir to sing at the Sunday morning service. With my visible position in the front row, Mom would never have forgiven me.

THIRTY

LAKE SIBLEY

Susie and I were playing in our backyard when Tina came over. "Judi, guess what?" she asked, excited. "We've rented a cabin on Lake Sibley for two whole weeks. Mom and Dad said you could come along."

We raced into the house to ask permission. Mom was kneading bread dough and talking to her sister Marion, who was drinking coffee in the breakfast nook. Tina and I patiently stood there, waiting to interrupt.

Finally, Mother turned to me. "Judi, what in the world do you want?"

Barely able to contain myself, I said, "Tina has invited me to stay with her at Lake Sibley for two whole weeks. Can I go pleeeeeeeeaase?"

"I'll talk to your father tonight, okay?" Mom replied.

As we turned to go outside, I heard Aunt Marion say, "Those two are a couple of rapscallions. It's wonderful for Judi to have such a friend."

After supper, Sheryl and I bickered, as usual, while we washed dishes. She washed, and I criticized the way she put the dishes in the rack. Sheryl complained that I wasn't drying the dishes thoroughly or fast enough.

"Girls, girls!" Mom said as she walked into the kitchen. "Can't you be friends?"

"We are," Sheryl answered. "I'm just trying to get her to shape up. How is she ever going to get good grades if she's such a slowpoke?"

I jumped in, "Just because you're a teenager, you think you're so smart."

"Enough," Mom said. "Judi, you can stay with the Dukes for three days. That's sufficient time to be away."

Sheryl turned to Mom. "Why don't you let her stay longer? Nine is old enough. When I was her age, I stayed with Aunt Dorothy for a week. Besides, I could use some peace and quiet."

Unfortunately, no begging or pleading could change Mother's mind.

I went over to Tina's house and told her the news. "Oh well," she said. "At least you can come for a while. Let's make root beer floats and start planning."

My friend found a piece of paper, and we wrote a list of stuff to bring and chatted about everything we were going to do.

The day of departure arrived. Early in the morning, I set my suitcase by the front door. It was really Mom's old suitcase and had been used so many times that one of the clasps had broken. Dad had put a strap around it before he left for work and then gave me a big hug. "Now have a good time," he said, "and don't drown because if you do, I'll never speak to you again."

Sheryl overheard his comment. "You're a real card, Dad."

Tina's father, who commuted twenty-five miles every day, picked me up after he closed his shop. He put my dilapidated suitcase in the trunk of his cream and cherry New Yorker. "Let's roll the windows down and get some air," he said as he got into the driver's seat.

This must be what a convertible feels like, I thought, as the huge windows disappeared into the doors.

Once outside the city limits, Mr. Duke stepped on the gas and drove fast. My red hair blew in the wind, masking my eyes. I imagined myself to be a rich lady in a racing stagecoach with curtains fluttering on the windows. Why was I so lucky? I smiled at my good fortune.

After a mile or so, Mr. Duke began to sing in his tenor voice. I joined in as we sang, "Row, Row, Row Your Boat." We laughed as he taught me his favorite folk song, "I love the wiener man, He drives a wiener stand, He sells everything from wieners on down. And in my future life, I'll be his wiener man, Hot dog, I love the wiener man."

After I had sung the Weiner Man song perfectly, he said, "Okay, Judi, we're almost there. Why don't you get in the back seat? When we drive up, I'll tell you to duck down. Let's pretend that you didn't come."

Mr. Duke turned off the main road and onto a rutted, lonely path. I crawled over the back of the seat.

"Out of sight… now!"

I crouched down on the floor. Tina must've been watching because she immediately ran over to the car. "Daddy, where's Judi?"

"She couldn't come."

My friend started crying.

Springing up and putting my head out the window, I yelled, "Surprise!"

Tina kept crying and sobbed, "That wasn't a nice joke."

Mr. Duke got out of the car, kneeled down in front of his daughter and started making funny faces. Tina stopped crying, took a few deep breaths and smiled. Then she laughed and turned to me, "Come on," she said, "I'll show you around."

The cabin was one room with a screened-in back porch for eating and one on the front with a set of bunks and a cot. The main room had a stove, fridge and a bed for Mr. and Mrs. Duke. Tina patted the bottom bunk in the front porch and said, "You can sleep here. My sister gets the cot."

Her mom came in with Tina's little sister, Lizzy. "Why don't we all take a swim and then roast some hot dogs and marshmallows?" she suggested.

The first evening, I drank too much Kool-Aid before we went to bed and woke up in the middle of the night needing "to go." Then I thought about the darkness and the outdoor toilet. Somehow, I held it until daylight, and then I raced out the door to the stinky outhouse.

When I came in, Tina and Lizzy were awake. "Come on," Tina said. "Let's eat and go hunting for shells."

After breakfast, we played by the lake.

With their olive skin, the Dukes all looked like Indians. But not me! Because of my fair skin and freckles, Mom had given me strict instructions to wear a large T-shirt and hat every minute I was outside. "No exceptions!" she directed.

We swam, had water fights, built sandcastles with moats, and looked on the shore for washed-up objects. "Hey, look," Tina yelled after finding an empty snakeskin. Into our satchel it went, along with clamshells and combs that Lizzy found. My treasure was a large tooth about four inches long that I found sitting on a rock as if a gremlin had put it there for me. I think I showed it to you, Chief.

"I believe it's a cow tooth," Mr. Duke said knowingly when he inspected our finds.

That night, we lay on our bunks whispering so Lizzy wouldn't know our secrets. The owls called to us. Could they hear what we were saying?

For the next few days, the warm weather and overcast skies gave us many hours to play and swim. We caught some tadpoles in one tin can and a crayfish in another. Then the sky became cloudless, and the sun started to beat down. My T-shirt was no match for its rays. Blisters popped out as fast as mosquitoes after a rain. All my flesh was bubbling and pink, even the skin on my shoulders under the shirt.

I couldn't sleep that night. Mrs. Duke pressed wet washcloths all over me to ease the pain. Tina hung down over the edge of her bunk to watch. Even upside down, she looked worried. "Judi," she whispered, "do you think your mother will ever let you come again?"

The next morning, it was time to pack up and go home, but I was still in agony. I took a few tadpoles in a jam jar to show my little sister. Tina's Dad put nail holes in the lid so they could survive the trip.

I climbed in the front seat and rolled down the window. "Thanks, Tina," I said, trying to smile even though my face was sore and stiff.

We didn't sing on the return trip—Mr. Duke played the radio instead. The cherry and cream car flew down the road, breezes blowing through its opened windows. But the cool air did little to soothe my boiling skin.

I walked up to our house red as a beet, suitcase and jar in hand. Mother opened the front door to greet me. My first words were, "I wore a hat and shirt the whole time."

She didn't say a thing.

Susie was happy to have me home and immediately wanted to play with the tadpoles. "Come on," she said. "I wanna see them swim."

Eager to get out from under Mother's gaze, I followed her upstairs and into the bathroom where I put a few inches of water in the tub. Sue dumped the tadpoles in and leaned over the edge as she tried to catch them in her hands. "I got one," she cried, but in her excitement hit the plug, and the water and tadpoles disappeared from view.

It took forever before my blisters collapsed, and my skin started to peel. Every time I looked at my splotchy face in the mirror, I envied the snake shedding his skin all at once and wondered just how long he had lain in the sun.

THIRTY-ONE

SEX EDUCATION

Tina and my bicycles had been locked up for three days. "How come we got such a mean punishment over a few lousy apples?" I asked.

"I don't know," Tina said. "Maybe because Mrs. Oakleaf buys glasses from Dad, and he wants her business."

"And also, she's a good friend of my grandma's," I added.

Suddenly we heard a shout. "Judi, Tina, wait for me!" Turning around, we saw Debby, a girl from the neighborhood, running toward us. We didn't like her, and we didn't like going to her house either. She had an obnoxious twin brother, Daryl, who saved his boogers in a glass jar and always showed his moldy specimens to gross us out. Also, Debby never rode her bicycle like a normal kid. She was a prissy little girl and acted kinda uppity, flaunting the fact that she was a year older and in the sixth grade. Tina and I thought she was a real pain.

"What are you doing without your bikes?" she asked sweetly.

"Our parents are mad at us right now," I replied. "They got a call from Mrs. Oakleaf. You know, the lady who lives across my backyard. We invented a new game. I threw a softball to Tina, who stood on her own lawn near Mrs. Oakleaf's apple tree. Pretending to be a terrible thrower, I threw the ball high into the tree over Tina's head, hoping I could knock some fruit down. When Tina ran over to get the ball, she picked up a few apples. Can you believe Mrs. Oakleaf called our moms and told them we were stealing from her? Boy, did we get in trouble. Our folks made our bikes off-limits to teach us a lesson."

Debby swung her blond ponytail as she walked. She didn't seem to be interested in our problem and changed the subject. "Do you want to come over and see my baby sister? She's a cutie. I'm going to have lots of kids when I grow up."

"Not me," I answered. "My parents said I had to marry somebody from church, and there's no boy in my class I like. Anyway, I'm going to do lots of traveling. Maybe I'll be an old maid."

"Well, silly, you could still have a baby even if you don't get married. My mom and I are best of friends, and she's explained everything." Then Debby looked at me and rolled her eyes like I was stupid or something.

I looked away, embarrassed. Tina and I had tried to get a straight answer on how babies are made but got nowhere. When I asked Mother, she said, "God plants a seed in your stomach." Tina's mom's response was, "You'll know soon enough. Why don't you go ride your bicycle?"

As we approached Debby's house, she repeated her question. "Are you coming to see my sister or what?"

Tina and I looked at each other. "Okay," we said in unison.

Debby smiled. "I'll run in and check if it's okay." She left us outside her chain-link fence, closing the gate as she went into the yard. Her big boxer, Fritz, greeted her—another reason it wasn't any fun to visit Debby. Her dog was very big and drooled all the time.

As we stood there waiting, Tina suggested, "Why don't you ask her about babies? No one else will help us."

"Okay, I'll give it a try."

Debby came back outside and walked over to us. "Mom said you can see her, but we have to be quiet. She just fell asleep." Then Debby opened the gate, and Fritz came up and nuzzled me with his slobbery mouth. I grimaced at the foamy saliva he left on my arm. *This had better be worth it*, I thought.

She led us into the kitchen, leaving Fritz on the other side. We tiptoed into the living room where her mother was sitting in a chair holding the baby. "This is my sister, Patty," Debby whispered, as we looked at a tiny face peering out.

"She sure has a little nose," I muttered, feeling I should say something.

We stood there silently for a minute and then went back outside. Fritz was waiting for us. Debby sat down on the floor and started petting her dog. Tina and I sat down too, dropping our legs over the edge of the porch and looking out over the lawn.

Taking a deep breath, I started jabbering. "My mom told me some stuff about babies being born, but you said you knew everything. Can you tell us?" It humiliated me to ask, but I really, really wanted to know.

"You don't know much, do you?" Debby asked with a tone of arrogance.

What a smarty pants, I thought. But I wanted an answer, so I sat there swinging my legs and hoping.

"So, tell us," Tina interrupted.

Debby continued to pet her drooling dog as she told us the facts of life. "Did you ever see how a boy pees?" We nodded, eager for her to continue.

Sensing our eagerness, Debby kept on with her lecture. "I've seen my brother's weenie lots of times. When we were little, he used to take it out and pee in the bushes. Well, anyway, that's not all it's used for. If a guy puts his weenie inside a lady, he can give her seeds to start a baby."

"I don't believe it!" I said. "You're making this up. How could you make a baby that way?"

Debby smugly cut off my questions. "I just know that the man pokes IT in your 'gina. Mom said that all ladies have lots of tiny eggs that can only grow into babies when the man adds his stuff. You know, kind of like making a cake? It doesn't work if you forget something in the recipe."

Tina and I were in a state of shock. Then Tina jumped to her feet. "This makes me sick. My parents wouldn't do that!"

"Mine either," I added, disgusted by the picture Debby had painted with her explanation. "Isn't there any other way to have a baby?"

"No, not unless you adopt one."

"Are you telling the truth, crisscross your heart and hope to die?"

"Cross my heart and hope to die," Debby answered with a chest-crossing gesture. "Anyway, Mom said the worst part is how stretched your stomach gets, and when the baby comes out, your 'gina gets stretched too, and sometimes it tears down there. And if the baby doesn't come out soon enough, the doctor has to cut open your stomach to get the baby."

Tina and I were speechless. This was way beyond anything we could imagine! What a crummy day this had turned out to be. First, we were without our bicycles, and now this awful information. It was too much! (It's embarrassing, Chief, for me to be telling you this story.)

"Let's go," I said to Tina. "I promised I'd be home right after school. See ya." And out the gate we went.

Slowly, my friend and I walked down the street kicking stones, mulling things over and talking. "If it's true," Tina said, "then your parents and my parents and Debby's parents did 'it' so we could be born. It sounds like such a horrible thing to do. I can't believe it, can you?"

Later that evening, desperate to know the truth, I approached my sister. "There's something that's been bugging me." Then I hesitated.

"Make it quick. I have to call Margaret."

"All right..." Taking a deep breath, I blurted out, "Is it true boys put their thing in you to make babies?"

Sheryl's eyes almost fell out of her head. "Yes. But if you tell Mother I told you, I'll make your life miserable."

That night, after I fell asleep, my dreams became nightmares. An endless parade of apples turned into people as they fell from the tree to the ground. They rolled on and over one another like tumblers before disappearing into the darkness. The parade never stopped. A peaceful slumber never came.

The next morning my family went to church. I walked down the hall to my Sunday School class and passing the door of the nursery, I saw Sally, the prettiest and youngest Sunday School teacher I ever had. There she sat, rocking her baby. My stomach did summersaults. Did Sally and her husband really do what Debby talked about? I was so confused.

Tina called when I got home. "Can you come over for a game of Parcheesi? I have to watch my sister for the afternoon." I loved board games. Also, I knew there was a bonus in store... one of my hands would be holding a root beer float while the other was rolling the dice.

As we played Parcheesi, Lizzy teased us, "You are both grouchy. It's not my fault your bicycles are locked up. Do you want to play something else?"

"Nah," Tina grunted as she looked at me. "We'll be better tomorrow when we can ride again."

It helped to get our wheels back, but our minds were still reeling from our discussion about babymaking.

"Hey, Judi," Tina said. "Let's take the long way around. I don't wanna see Debby."

"Me either," I replied.

After school, we stopped at Tina's for cookies. On the back step was a package addressed to my friend from her grandma. Mrs. Duke drove up as we were opening the box.

"Well, look at that," Mrs. Duke said, "a transistor radio."

Tina and I were ecstatic. It was red and as small as a box of Jell-O. One wire hung off each side—on the left was an antenna (a jawed-clip attached to a wire) and the other an earplug.

After deciphering the instructions, we clipped the antenna to a lamp and listened. At first, each of us tried to hear with the earphone, but we discovered that by disconnecting that wire, we both could hear the sound.

"Wow, isn't this great? Tina exclaimed. "Let's take our bikes down to Carlson's drug and get a chocolate Coke. We can take the radio with us."

At the drug store, we climbed onto stools and ordered Cokes with the radio between us so we could hear the tinny sound and be amazed at the miracle of science. The teenage soda jerk gave us a suggestion, "Why don't you clip that wire onto the malt machine? You'll get better reception."

We did… and music filled our ears as we sipped our Cokes.

Tina blew into her straw and made tons of chocolate bubbles in her glass. She lifted her head, looked over at me and whispered, "This is a lot more fun than talking about babies."

"Yep," I replied with a smile. "I'm glad we're still kids."

THIRTY-TWO

ATTEMPTING FAME

Susie and I sat on the porch swing discussing Don's job change and wondering how our brother could ever quit Town Talk Bakery. "No more smashed muffins," Susie said, referring to her favorite treat, a benefit of Don's part-time job. We had always eagerly anticipated Don bringing home broken cookies, day-old pastry or anything else with messed-up frosting.

As you know, Chief, our family had a work ethic handed down from our ancestors. After we learned to ride a bicycle, we were expected to use it productively. Mom and Dad provided the basics, such as clothing, music lessons and books, but if we wanted extras, we were on our own. Sheryl was saving for a pair of Kickerinos, a stylish shoe boot, so she wouldn't have to wear her ugly zip-up rubber boots. I was earning money for a record and a magic trick book. Susie was saving for a wagon. Now that Don was no longer working at the bakery, we'd be forced to use our own money for sweets, which created a dilemma for all of us.

When Don was thirteen, our uncle Reuben—part owner of the *Tribune*—gave him a paper route. After a few years, Don got his driver's license and started delivering for the bakery, and Sheryl inherited his newspaper route.

Even though Don no longer worked for Reuben, Don remained in his uncle's thoughts. Don was Uncle's favorite nephew, and a favorite topic for his column "Man About Town," which was a running commentary of community events. Gregarious and talented, Don had won many awards, which earned him the title of "Parker Falls Favorite Son." His musical performances earned him the most notoriety. Don played the trumpet in the band, played trumpet solos, sang in a trio and was an accompanist or soloist on the organ or piano. He loved the praise he got for his musical achievements.

In the case of his delivery job, though, his stardom became a punishment. All the aging women in town ordered bakery goods on the days my brother worked so they could see their hero and give a smile of support. Town Talk Bakery, pleased with its sales boost, gave Don a ten cent per hour raise. But that didn't elevate his spirits. Don, annoyed by the attention of his smiling patrons, announced one night at the supper table, "If I have to deliver pastries to one more old lady, I'm going to scream."

Reuben came to the rescue and offered Don a job selling ads for the *Tribune*. Then Reuben wrote in his column. "I have my nephew selling advertising now. If his sales ability is 50 percent of his musical talent, our paper will grow by leaps and bounds."

Relieved that he no longer worked at the bakery, Don enthusiastically approached his new customers and told them about his latest aspiration. "Next year is my senior year of high school. I'd like to become the first male drum major of Parker Falls. What do you think?"

The business community supported his idea. Most of them had been risk-takers, so why shouldn't Don be adventuresome too?

In the history of Parker Falls, there had only been drum majorettes. When the band had marched in other town festivals, Don noticed that some musical groups were led by drum majors wearing high fur hats strapped under their chin, whistles in their mouths and batons pointing in the air. The drum majors were directing and leading. Don imagined himself in such noble attire—a white uniform with gold braids strung across his chest.

Of course, I had a theory of my own, which I shared with Susie. "He loves the Queen and King of England. You know all those books he gets from Carlson Drug about the royalty? I bet he just wants to pretend he's one of them."

Don talked about his goal at dinner. He had asked the band director, Nick, to consider letting him try out to be drum major of the Kaffee Fest parade in June. Nick gave him a granule of hope, replying, "We'll see."

Kaffee Fest was the best festival in Parker Falls with a crowning of a queen, a parade and a carnival. And Don's dream was to lead the parade.

My brother began training privately with Cindy, the current drum majorette, who also had a dream that her baton class would march in the Kaffee Fest Parade. Cindy had already approached Nick, who was still "thinking about it." She believed it would happen, but admitted to Don, "I really should have more twirlers. Why don't your sisters take my class?"

Don used his persuasive powers on Mother, who smiled proudly and said, "I'll pay for the lessons. And I know Uncle Oscar will buy your sisters batons if you'll let them practice with you. He was very upset when he saw you twirling a baton. He phoned me, yelling, 'My nephew is a boy, why is he twirling a baton?'"

It wasn't difficult for me to imagine my brother leading the band down the street, white gloves holding a bright silver baton high in the air. He'd be a natural with his musical talent and good looks.

"What if you drop the baton?" I asked him, bringing my pleasant thoughts to a halt.

"I won't drop it," Don answered."That's why Cindy's my tutor."

"I don't get why she's teaching you. She could lose her job as the majorette."

Don ignored me and went outside to practice. Uncle Oscar fulfilled his promise, and graciously bought batons for all of us, including my friend Tina. We started Cindy's class and loved the twirling. The difficult part was acrobatics.

"Come on, everybody, I want you to run down the steps and do a cartwheel," Cindy said.

I ran down the stairs and kept right on running. But I persisted until I finally did the cartwheel, modeling myself after my brother's dedication. On many afternoons, I watched him throw the baton high into the air. Again and again, he practiced until he could throw it as high as our house. I was sure that Nick could be persuaded to give him a chance.

When Don marched down the street, Tina and I followed. Listening to his commands, we stopped and twirled while Don threw his baton high into the sky AND caught it. When our neighbor Mrs. Severson saw us, she called my mother and said, "Oh Marguerite, you have such cute children. They look so darling marching together."

Tina's parents took pictures of us when we marched by their house. Uncle Oscar saw the photo and nodded his approval, changing his mind about Don's new hobby. "That's where women should be," he said, "following behind the men." Then he looked over at Tina and me and shook his head, "You two are such hellions, it'd make me nervous to have my back to you."

I saved Tina's photo in a comic book just in case Uncle Rueben needed it for the newspaper when Don became famous. Of course, my face would be right by his side. This motivated me to feel that I, too, should do something legendary.

"Hey, Tina," I said. "Don't you think if I jumped further than any kid in Parker Falls, then Uncle Reuben would put my name in the paper too? Let's go over to the park, and I'll start to practice."

I jumped out of the swing and then off the monkey bars. My legs were short, but swinging my arms as I leapt into space gave me momentum. I was making progress. We rode our bikes over to the track where the high schoolers practiced, and I learned a few pointers from them. "Watch the guys jump, Tina. If I crouch like that and really throw my arms back, I should get somewhere. Come on, I've got an idea."

While bicycling a few blocks down the street, I asked Tina, "Remember Mr. Jacobson's pigeon house across the street from Grandma's? It'd be a perfect place to practice. He's still not home from the railroad, so he won't even know. I bet I can jump from the roof of his pigeon coop and over the picket fence at the back of his property."

"Looks pretty far to me..."

"Nah, I can do it."

Climbing up on the roof was a challenge. First, I stepped on a big overturned bucket, then the window ledge. Grabbing onto a lightning rod affixed at one end, I pulled myself up onto the roof. The small shed was covered in green rolled roofing and stood about eight feet high. The pigeons made a commotion as I landed on their roof. Standing up, I wiped the asphalt pieces off my knees and said, "Well, I made it."

"Are you sure this is a good idea?" Tina asked.

"I'm ready," I replied, ignoring her remark.

Concentrating, I hunched down and focused on jumping over the distant fence. Taking a flying leap, I made it over the hurdle with my arms swinging to the back of my body. I felt pain, though, as my left arm swung high and back into space.

"Ouch," I yelled. "Ouwee, ouwee, ouwee!" I pulled my arm to my chest then bent over, grimacing and holding my arm. Trying to be brave, I turned to Tina and said, "Let's push our bikes over to Grandma's and call Mom."

Grandma opened the door and immediately noticed my puffy arm, "My goodness, Judi," she said, "what did you do now?"

Mom drove over and took me to City Hospital.

A few hours later, Dr. Hodap set my arm in three places and said my elbow was shattered. I came home wearing a heavy plaster cast that held my arm at a right angle.

So much for my baton lessons.

Mom felt sorry for me and let me carry her best coffee pot one-handed to our neighbor, Mr. Norris, a big wheel at the Chamber of Commerce, who had called Mother to ask to borrow a pretty coffee pot that would look good on television. I know they used it because Tina and I were watching *Robin Hood* one afternoon, and there was Mom's pot, as big as you please, on an advertisement for the Kaffee Fest.

Dad felt badly that I couldn't march in the parade, "Why don't you ride on the float Lester is making to advertise my business. It's decorated in red and silver and says, 'Buy an Olds from Bob.' I'm going to pull the float with a new convertible. You and Susie can wave to everybody and have a good time."

It didn't sound that great, especially since Tina would be marching, and there I would be with my little sister. But I thought it might be better than nothing.

At Tina's next baton lesson, I sat on the steps and watched. Cindy announced that Nick had agreed to let her girls march in the parade. "The uniform will be a short white skirt with attached underpants, white blouses and white tennis shoes. Your mothers will have to get busy with their sewing machines since it's only two weeks away."

Sheryl, excited about her debut, described the costume at supper and said, "Don't worry, Mom. I'll use my paper route money to buy the material."

Mother had a conniption fit. "No daughter of mine is going to parade around like that. You can't show all that skin. Just think of what you're suggesting."

"What?" I asked.

With a dirty look, Mom continued, "You'll just have to forget it."

To make matters worse, Don came in the back door fuming, "That rotten Nick. He said that there's no way that he'll consider me as a drum major. 'You're the only good trumpeter I have,' he said. Can you believe it?"

The supper table was tense that evening with my brother and sister complaining bitterly.

I quickly ate and high-tailed it over to Tina's. "Somehow, the world isn't fair," I explained to her. "Don won't be a famous drum major, and I won't be a famous jumper. And Sheryl doesn't get to march. What a rotten deal. The only thing famous is our coffee pot."

"Hey, why don't I ride with you on the float? We can pretend we're celebrities and wave at everybody."

"Are you sure?" I asked.

It took a few days for my brother and sister to survive their disappointments, but with the Kaffee Fest such a big event, there were other things to think about.

Sheryl came up to me with her latest idea. "When the carnival comes to town, why don't I take you and Tina with me to watch them set up the rides?"

"How come you want to be with us?" I asked, suspicious of the invite. This was the first time Sheryl had asked me anywhere.

"After the carnival sets up, they always test the machines by giving free rides to a few people. I'd like a ride on the octopus, and with your broken arm, we'll definitely be chosen. Sound okay?"

"I thought you had to be a teenager to ride the octopus."

"Just stand tall," Sheryl answered. "Besides, you'll be with me."

Grinning, I ran out the door to tell Tina. Things were looking up!

THIRTY-THREE

KAFFEE FEST

We were ecstatic! It was a tradition to hold the Kaffee Fest on the last weekend of June, and it was finally time. Mom said it was held during the same time of year as Midsummer celebrations in Sweden. Before immigrating to Minnesota, the first settlers of Parker Falls had lived near the Arctic Circle in Scandinavia, a place where the winter months were cold, and daylight was as short as the eyelashes on your face. During the dark winter, residents looked forward to Midsummer in June when the sun does not set, and the summer days never end. In Parker Falls, the children and grandchildren of the Swedish immigrants looked forward to the commemorative celebration called the Kaffee Fest.

The entire community was involved in the activities. The lawn of the courthouse and four adjacent blocks became the carnival grounds. A huge booth sat at the corners of Benson Avenue and Second Street. Members of the Kiwanis Club designed the booth to have four low counters. Folding chairs crowded the booth like ants finding sugar. Hanging high on the corner posts were large banners painted in big black letters saying "Kaffee Fest." For the duration of the festival, the women of the community served all the coffee you could drink for free. All religious and secular organizations donated sweets of various shapes and tastes that could be purchased to complement the bottomless cup of coffee. The proceeds went for improvements in the community.

This was an ingenious way to make money for Parker Falls. Even though the seventeen churches were often in conflict over their specific beliefs, they were united on their priorities. Every citizen acknowledged three necessities—COFFEE, SWEETS and RELIGION.

When the Kaffee Fest opened on Friday afternoon, the mayor, escorted by the queen candidates, cut a ribbon that stretched across Benson Avenue and announced, "We're pleased to see you for this annual event. Remember, the coronation of the Kaffee Fest Queen is at 8 p.m. in the auditorium. The parade is at noon tomorrow, rain or shine. Now let the activities begin."

The men leaned on the counter, eager for their first cup of coffee. Most of the children headed for the rides. Tina and I loitered, watching the candidates and betting on who would win. With my arm in a sling, we weren't as eager to stand in line to fight for tickets on the Tilt-A-Whirl or Ferris wheel, so we decided to check out the games and carnival shows instead.

The sideshows were the most interesting. "See the world's smallest horses," one sign read. Painted on the face of a small trailer were tiny black horses. "I saw those once," Tina said. "They're just little ponies."

Next to the ponies stood a billboard: "See the two wonders of the world, Ivan the snake charmer and his brother Byron the human pin cushion." We stood, mouths agape, reading the signs and intrigued by the images that had been painted. A foreign-looking man was blowing a long skinny horn as a snake danced with his head in the air. "Do you think that it's for real?" I asked, looking toward the tent in the distance.

"Yikes, look over at the other guy. It looks like the man with millions of pins sticking in his pimples. How can he sleep at night?"

"He doesn't even have a neck," I pointed out. "He can't look like that. It's got to be a joke."

We continued to stand gawking at the picture of a squatty looking man that looked like a human frog with protruding pins.

"You know, Judi, we should go see them. It says 'two wonders—one price of forty cents.' I've never seen a snake charmer. That Byron guy looks scary with those pins sticking out of him, but I bet they're fake."

"Can't go," I replied. "Mom and Dad said that show people gamble and drink a lot, and I'm not supposed to throw my money away."

"Then we shouldn't go on any rides or buy any snow cones. All the people travel together, you know. Anyway, I'll treat. Mom is working at the coffee booth this afternoon, and she'll give us a few bucks."

I desperately wanted to see the freak show. With Tina treating, how could I pass up the opportunity?

Wandering through the game area, we watched a man leaning over a counter throwing nickels toward rows of flat dishes that sat on top of a large glass. There was a huge four-foot-tall panda hanging over the dishes, tempting the man to go on and on. The nickels kept rolling across the plates and onto the table below. The owner of the booth picked them up, yelling, "Win a bear! Win a MIGHTY big panda! Always win a prize! Step right up! Come on, folks, it's only a nickel. Oh, lookee here—we have a winner." He handed a small teddy bear to the man with the pocket of endless nickels.

"I thought you were going for the big panda," someone yelled.

"I am," the player responded. "But, it takes five of these to get one."

"We'll be here forever," said Tina. "Let's go find my mom."

Mrs. Duke was standing by one of the stainless-steel coffee urns filling cups of coffee. She smiled when she saw us. "Where have you two rascals been? I thought you'd be here ages ago."

"We were checking things out. May I have some money?" Tina asked.

"Here's three dollars. Don't spend it all today."

Tina and I walked to the ticket booth of the Two Wonders.

"Do you really think we should go?"

Both of us approached the booth window where a sweaty man in a scoop-neck T-shirt was selling tickets. Grunting, he gave us the tickets and twenty cents. We timidly walked into the tent.

"Let's sit right in the front row," Tina whispered.

"I agree. If someone sees me and squeals, I might as well have the best seat in the house."

Tina and I sat in two folding chairs right in the center. The elevated platform looked worse for wear with dirty canvas nailed onto the front as if something evil was lurking beneath the floor. We sat and whispered to each other, unsure of ourselves in this surrounding.

The tent quickly filled as Ivan, a man in a turban, ran on and off the stage with a musical instrument and a large burlap bag tied at the top with a white rope. He cleared his throat very loudly, and the tent became silent as if it were a signal to begin. Then Ivan stood behind the bag, removed the rope, leaned over and started making clucking sounds. The head of a snake rose from the burlap bag and wiggled up onto his arm and over his neck, landing on the floor in a perfect coil. I held my breath, hypnotized by Ivan—brown-skinned, hairy-chested and dressed in a velvet vest and tight black pants—who worked his magic. He looked like a man in my picture book about Morocco who sold spices and teas. And here he was at our very own Kaffee Fest.

Ivan started playing his pipe, a long hollow tube with holes that he held directly in front of him. The music drifted out in slow, melancholic rhythms that stirred the sleeping snake below. The reptile lifted its head and began to rise into the air, waving his body like a fat blade of green grass. Back and forth, it moved to the song.

Then Ivan changed the tempo and played the pipe with only one hand, holding the other toward the snake as if inviting him to perform for us. As he played single, short notes, the snake wriggled up his master's arm and around his neck. Then the two of them walked down the steps of the stage and out the tent.

The audience demanded an encore. Ivan returned with the snake draped around his neck and hanging limp onto his chest like a huge necklace. Lifting the snake's head in one hand, Ivan took a bow.

The crowd continued to clap as Ivan disappeared off the stage. The audience talked and laughed. I was giddy after viewing such an exotic performance. At the same time, I felt guilty, knowing that my parents would never approve.

Ivan returned, interrupting my thoughts. He was accompanied by another barefoot man who wore a turban and black pants but no vest because his face and body were covered in large warts.

"This is my brother, Byron," he announced.

I almost fell off my chair. "He must be adopted," I whispered to Tina. "I've never seen anyone so ugly in my whole life."

"The picture was right," she answered.

Our eyes were glued to the freakish man. His neck was non-existent and his features very enlarged. He smiled, which made him look ghoulish.

Tina and I held our breaths.

Holding out a dish of long pins, Ivan said, "See these pins? I will show you that Byron is a human pin cushion."

Nobody moved. The entire audience gasped as Ivan stuck the first pin into one of his brother's warts. Byron just smiled.

"Let's get out of here, Tina."

Jumping up from our chairs, we fled the tent.

"That was really disgusting," I remarked, taking a gulp of fresh air.

Tina nodded in agreement. "Let's get a blueberry snow cone. That should help."

"Good idea," I responded, adjusting the sling around my neck. "We should've left after the snake charmer. All those warts give me the willies."

We purchased our snow cones and sat on the courthouse steps discussing our adventure.

"You know, we'll have to keep this secret forever." Then I hesitated and looked at Tina. "You don't think tomorrow, when we ride on Dad's float, someone will yell, 'I saw you two kids at the freak show.'"

Tina laughed, "I doubt it."

After finishing our blueberry snow cones, we looked at the games and rides. It all seemed uninteresting after our experience with the "Two Wonders."

During our ride home, Mrs. Duke quizzed us about our day. Tina started asking her questions about snake charmers, but I changed the subject.

"Why don't you come to my house tomorrow at ten-thirty?" I asked her. "We'll go down to my dad's and find our place on the float."

Saturday arrived sunny and bright. Tina came over wearing a new pair of shorts and a cute top. Little sister Susie and I proudly displayed our new clothes too. Clothes new to us, that is. Sheryl let me borrow one of her outgrown, short-sleeved red blouses, which contrasted with my dirty white cast and sling. Susie borrowed my favorite horizontal striped T-shirt.

When we arrived at Dad's garage, Lester's kids were there wearing their Sunday clothes. I looked at Tina, "Oh, well, my Dad owns the place, so we don't need to dress up."

We piled on the float, and a new Oldsmobile pulled us down the street. "Let's pretend we're queens," Susie proposed.

Lester's kids liked the idea. Within one block, Tina and I lost our enthusiasm. When I waved at people, my broken arm made me feel out of balance. By the end, I was sitting with my back against

Tina's. Like two bookends, we rode in the parade, sometimes waving but always yelling when we saw our friends.

Afterward, we took Sue on the merry-go-round and the Ferris wheel. Avoiding the area of the Two Wonders, we ate miniature donuts and watched people ride the Tilt-A-Whirl. At bedtime, I told my sister the story about our Great Aunt Ida joining the circus as a snake charmer. Susie fell asleep, and I did, too, only to wake up in the early hours of the morning frightened by a nightmare. I dreamed my freckles had changed to warts, and I was working alongside Byron as "Brenda, the world's smallest pincushion."

I sat up immediately and felt my skin—nothing had changed. It was just my imagination, perhaps haunted by my guilt over sneaking into a freak show.

Tina and I kept our secret forever.

Well, ALMOST, Chief.

THIRTY-FOUR

CAMP KORONIS

My brother continued to be the favorite son of Parker Falls. His musical talents opened many doors for him. Since Don was an opportunist, he walked right through those doors, expanding his horizon.

I, too, enjoyed his fame and proudly listened to the radio when he accompanied singers on WKLM or sat in the front row (just like I did for you, Chief) whenever he performed in his vocal or instrumental quartet.

Mother, a soloist and choir director, was excited over Don's musical talent. Dad, born and bred to be academic, was proud of his son's scholastic achievements. Whenever Don competed in any contest, he won, setting the stage of expectations for the rest of us. Uncle Reuben continued to rave about him in his column.

My brother stacked his awards on a shelf in his closet. As the pile of them grew, it became as high as his collection of Archie comic books. I intuitively knew that "the pile" was the measuring stick for my future achievements. My suspicions were confirmed at the supper table when Sheryl grumbled to Don, "You're a real pain. Mom and Dad expect me to keep up with you."

I interjected, "You can do it, Sheryl. You're as smart as Don."

"Don't be such a dope," Sheryl answered. "Wait until you start junior high. You'll have to study your butt off to get As."

Mother interrupted. "That language is not used in our house."

Sheryl's comments haunted me because I already knew my talents were different from my brother's. I mean, on a nice summer day, who else read three books, practiced the piano, rode around the block on their bicycle and talked to Es, Charlie and Mrs. Swenson AND played with friends in the park? If I had to study as much as my sister said, how could I possibly find time for all the things I loved?

But getting back to Don... Between his junior and senior year he won a state piano competition. As a result, he was offered a job as the pianist—the youngest ever—of Lake Koronis Bible Camp. The auditorium held three hundred people. The piano and choir were the main musical entertainment. There was a large stage with risers for the choir and baby grand piano positioned so the pianist could have eye contact with the audience and the choir. Susie and I loved to watch our brother perform there. When he turned his head and smiled at the audience, we felt like we were watching the Liberace of religious music.

Besides wages, Don also received money for the dormitory and meals, and tickets for sweets at the concession stand. Fortunately for him, our family was renting a cabin, giving him the best of both worlds.

Even before I could walk, camp was already a tradition. I think we started going to camp because Mom was a guest soloist and when the audience heard her voice they couldn't live without her. By the time I was in grade school, she was the choir director. Every year the teachers asked, "How many years have you been at camp?" Just about everyone raised their hand at one year and two years, but by the end the only hands in the air were mine and my sister Sheryl. The teachers never believed that our attendance records were two years short of our actual ages. They challenged us by asking, "Are you sure you're telling the truth?"

I liked being a seasoned member of camp and eagerly looked forward to the experience.

***

With both cabins and dormitory rooms available, a lot of other families attended too. Actually, it was mostly the moms and kids. When everyone arrived, it looked like a parade of cars reminding me of "The Old Women and the Shoe." Considering most families had only one car and two or three children, the automobiles were totally stuffed with kids, blankets, bedding and groceries. Even the trunks were tied down, since a whole week of groceries and supplies had to be transported, along with the children. It made for a difficult drive. All my parents ever heard about it were our complaints. "Do I have to sit on so many blankets? It's hot. Can't I sit in the front seat too?"

Dad was very anxious to dump us off at camp. After emptying the car, he was ready to turn around and head back home. "Okay kids," he said, "have fun and listen to your Mother. Remember, if you need anything just holler."

Susie and I gave Dad a hug and went to buy popsicles at the canteen. We walked across the campus past the huge tabernacle, which was very impressive. It was designed to withstand the torrential summer rains and the sweltering August weather. Endless long wooden benches sat on a sloping dirt floor. The roof was built with an eight-foot overhang. To keep the mosquitoes out, screens started at the ceiling and didn't stop until two feet above the floor where short wooden splash-walls kept the rain from coming in. A sidewalk circled the building under huge eaves so mothers could walk their restless babies and little children. Anyone on the asphalt path could be included in the service by looking through the screen to the lighted stage. Large speakers carried the music and sermon to every man, woman or child within a five block radius.

After the first night in the dorm, Don was back in our cabin. He didn't like the obnoxious boys and the food in the cafeteria.

"Wait a minute," I said. "If I have to give up my bed and sleep with Susie, it seems to me we should get some of your tickets to the concession stand."

The first few days my argument worked. When we saw him at the canteen after the evening service, he bought each of us an ice cream bar. But then one night, we looked around and noticed that Don wasn't hanging out with his friends from Parker Falls. He was standing talking to a pretty blond girl.

Susie and I came running up to him eager for our evening treat. Don gave us some tickets and sent us away, saying, "Don't bother me. I'll see you later."

After getting ice cream, we found our older sister, Sheryl.

"Who's that girl Don is talking to?" I asked.

"His new girlfriend, dummy."

Our mouths fell open. Don had never been serious about anybody, but this time he really was struck by love. We found out her name was Susan Carlson. She sang in the choir, sat in the seat closest to the piano and stayed in a cabin two doors away from us. My brother couldn't resist her charms—blond hair, blue-eyes, petite figure and Scandinavian heritage. But most importantly, she was from the same church. Well, technically at least. Her father was the guest minister and they were from Los Angeles.

"If you get married, we'll never see you," I teased.

"Shut up," Don answered.

Mother interrupted, "I never thought children of mine would talk like this. Why don't you go swimming and leave your brother alone? The lifeguard is on duty. Put on your suits and find the Swenson girls, then you'll each have a swimming buddy."

We loved Lake Koronis. Camp was scheduled during the same week of July each year, and by then the sun had smiled on the water and warmed it to the perfect temperature. The beach was sandy, but the shore was steep, making it a challenge for the lifeguard to keep his eyes on the little kids so they didn't wander into the deep water. Most mothers were pretty casual, ours included, figuring that their children could swim under the watchful eyes of a teenage lifeguard and that he and God would keep their children safe from harm. It was everyone's duty to watch small children, and that if by chance some little tyke wandered into deep water, anybody could pick them up by the scruff of the neck and throw them onto the beach. This Mother's Theory apparently worked because no one ever drowned during the many years we attended camp.

Of course, the buddy system also helped.

The lifeguard blew his whistle every fifteen to twenty minutes demanding that we stop and find the hand of our friend. Looking around for our buddy, we swam toward each other and then all stood with joined hands held high in the air. After the next whistle, normal chaos resumed. For two hours, the water was alive with swimming and screaming and the interruption of whistles to reclaim our buddies. Finally, the lifeguard blew his last whistle and yelled, "Everybody out!"

"Now!" he added.

Quickly, the lake became quiet, emptied of its boisterous swimmers and all of us, dog-tired and sunburned, walked back to our cabins to change clothes. It was now time for our religious training. The scheduling was ingenious. We were all so exhausted that we sat quiet as zombies.

My favorite hour of the day was craft class. The camp hired college kids who were majoring in art. My auntie knew that I liked to make things and always gave me money to do something special. One year, I painted a plaster of Paris plaque saying, "Bless this

House." Another year, I soaked reeds in a bucket of water and then wove a small basket. The most recent challenge I presented to the teacher was this: "My Father just finished his flying lessons and got his pilot's license. He promised to take me up in his airplane real soon. Is there something I could make for his plane?"

There were very few items that could even faintly be associated with flying. My teacher offered another plaster plaque with the "The World's Greatest Dad" on it, but somehow it didn't seem appropriate. Dad couldn't hang it in the cockpit. If it came loose, it would cause brain damage.

Finally, we concluded that I could make a leather key chain. The teacher helped me cut a two-inch circle out of leather and then told me to use leather punches to create a design. I ended up using the leather tools and a hammer to imprint "Dad's Plane" in the center. Then I found a metal piece shaped like a star, which I stamped around the edges. It looked sharp with the blue paint on the lettering and yellow on the stars. We punched a hole at the top for his key. I was convinced it would be a hit! To make it even better, I found the niftiest gadget in the gift shop. It was a plastic pyramid with a small magnifying glass at the pointed end, when you held it up to the light, you could magically read the Lord's Prayer. It was attached to a gold key chain and looked great on Dad's new leather piece. I felt confident it would bring him good luck.

The last two days of camp were cold and rainy. When our cabin roof started leaking, I was ready to go home. My sisters and Mom were ready to go too. Only moonstruck Don wanted to stay behind. When Dad came to get us, we almost had to push Don into the car.

"Come on, get in. You can always write her letters," Sheryl said. "Maybe you can persuade her to come to college with you in Chicago."

With that, Susie and I started chanting, "Don loves Susan, Don loves Susan."

Mother told us to "shush."

Don just stared out the window.

Dad caused an interruption to our silence when he said, "Anybody want a ride in my plane?"

At that, Mother glared out the window. She was not enthusiastic about my Dad's new adventure. She resented that he had traded a customer a new Oldsmobile for his airplane and flying lessons and then put off the purchase of a new sofa and chair. He'd tried to soothe Mom's spirits by saying, "It's always something I wanted to do. I'm sure that I can sell it anytime and turn a profit, and then we'll get your furniture."

The day finally arrived when Dad said, "We'd better take that airplane ride. I know Don's already had a ride but I'm ready to take all of you now."

Mom stayed home, but as we got in the car she said, "Nothing had better happen to you."

As we drove off, I yelled, "Don't worry, Mom. We'll be safe. When we come back, I'll tell you what it's like to fly like a bird."

By the time we arrived at the Parker Falls Airport, we were all nervous. Even Dad seemed quiet. We walked by the hangar where two men were working on a plane. Dad said, "Let's get going. See the gold airplane on the runway? That's mine. I'll get one of the guys to help us off."

We all climbed in. It sure felt tinny and fragile. Don sat alongside Dad, holding Susie in his lap. Sheryl and I sat in back. Some man took blocks from under the wheels and Dad started the engine—using the key chain I had made for him. The propeller started turning and we crept forward.

"What's happening? Aren't we going to leave the ground?" I asked.

"Be patient!" Dad replied.

Soon, the rumbling noise subsided and the little plane started to rise. My stomach fluttered as I held my breath. The airplane kept going up like a bird, its nose in the air and its wings stretched out. For one moment, I was frightened—but the next, I felt safe remembering that my father was the pilot, so no harm could come to us. I put my forehead against the window and looked below. We flew over all the familiar places—our house, Dad's Oldsmobile business, church, Grandma's and Grandpa's, the lakes, and our schools. If the engine of the plane hadn't been so noisy, I would've thought I was flying on the back of an eagle. It was a strange sensation to be floating above the land in a little machine.

Then Dad took us back down. When the plane bumped onto the runway, exhilaration pulsed through my veins.

"How about ice cream?" Dad asked. "Let's live it up."

"I think I like flying even better than ice cream," I answered.

Dad laughed.

Sheryl seized the opportunity. "If you don't want your ice cream, I'll eat it."

We went to Gandrudts and I had my second most favorite thing called Hilda's (Mrs. Gandrudts) Special. The soda jerk put a huge dollop of peanut butter in the top of the machine and out came soft ice cream with smidgens of peanut butter mixed in. It was delicious!

When we got home, I told Mom about the wonders of the airplane ride.

Later I wrote this poem. Hope you like it, Chief.

"BETTER THAN ICE CREAM"

Above the town looking little and small,
I flew with Dad as my pilot, so strong and tall.

Don sat in the front seat with Sue on his lap.
Sheryl and I sat together on two seats in back.

It felt like we were riding high up in the sky
inside of a noisy bird with windows for eyes.

I looked down at a skinny lake shaped like a spoon
And smiled at the water tower that looked like a balloon

Soaring above the ground, I could see our house and street.
Hugging myself I laughed, thinking... This is my very
favorite treat!

THIRTY-FIVE

COLLEGE BOUND

I was excited by the good news. My brother was leaving for college and allowing me to use his bedroom. He promised to empty one of his drawers and clean off the top of the dresser, otherwise his room was to remain untouched as if it were a shrine to a dead man. I didn't mind. I'd have a room all to myself. Besides, it would feel cozy to be surrounded by bookcases filled with Don's books and ceramic dogs. And I would sleep in his big bed and listen to the radio. Of course, I'd miss the nighttime whispers and secrets shared with my sister Susie, but she could still visit or sleep over.

All of us were taking Don to Chicago. It was an eight-hour drive and the first family outing that would take us over the Minnesota line. As we were eating dinner the evening before the trip, Dad asked, "Are you taking your bicycle? When I went to North Park, that's all we used. Your mother and I went to the ice cream parlor on many a date with her riding on the handle bars. Remember dear?"

Don groaned. "Nobody takes bicycles these days, Dad. Besides my girlfriend is in California, so I'll be studying all the time."

"Hey, Mom," I interrupted. "Didn't girls have bicycles when you went to college?"

"Not any I knew. I never had one."

"You mean you don't know how to ride a bicycle?" This was totally unimaginable—I LIVED on my bicycle.

"Well, sometimes I rode my brother John's."

"I don't believe you," chided Sheryl. "Besides, you told me you've never owned a pair of pants. How could you ride Uncle John's bike in a dress."

"I did," replied Mother, feigning extreme huffiness.

"All right then, show us," my older sister replied.

This was just the comic relief we needed. None of us knew how to deal with Don leaving the family nest. We would miss his teasing but not his academic precedence—that would become our millstone for years to come.

Mother laughed. "Don, get your bicycle and I'll show you."

We all went outside and stood by the driveway. Mom grabbed the bike from Don. Scrunching her skirt on top of the saddle bar, she swung her leg over and started to pedal. At first, the bicycle wobbled like she was going to fall. We held our breaths as Mother regained her balance. Then she rode down the block and took a U-turn and ended up riding toward us and waving. We were all hooting and hollering as she rode up.

"Let that be a lesson to all of you," Mom said as she came to a stop.

Don shook his head. "I don't think I'll tell my new college buddies that my mother rides a bicycle."

Mom took the teasing well. "Just tell them you come from a family with lots of spunk!"

The next morning, the car was filled with so much stuff that the family could barely squeeze in. As we drove out of town, Mom announced, "If anyone gets hungry, let me know. There's no need to waste money at a restaurant. I brought lemonade, cookies, rice pudding, Swedish meatballs, and a fresh loaf of bread."

We stopped at a park in La Crosse, Wisconsin, to eat a picnic lunch. Before leaving, Dad said, "Be sure to use the facilities—

which in this case was an outhouse—because there will be no other stops until Chicago." True to form, he ignored all other requests for bathroom breaks. By the time we got to North Park, we all raced to the restrooms like our pants were on fire.

The best part of the trip for me was walking around campus imagining myself grown up and attending college. Sheryl walked by my side, enthusiastic about the surroundings. "Look at all the good-looking guys! I'm coming here for sure."

We slept overnight in a dorm, which was a lot nicer than the one at summer camp, except the food was worse. All of us were disappointed with the mushy spaghetti for supper and slimy oatmeal at breakfast. For a few moments, I even felt sorry for my brother.

The worst part of the trip was seeing tears run down Mother's face as we drove away. It made me sad and almost squashed my happiness at inheriting Don's room. By the time we stopped at La Crosse for our second picnic in twenty-four hours, Mom was her old self and said, "Let's write Don his first letter."

My paragraph was, "Please write us sometime. I already miss you, but thanks for your room. Mother cried a lot when we left. Maybe you could write us a letter sometimes instead of always writing to Susan in California, otherwise we'll think you're dead. Love, Judi."

I would've thought he WAS dead except for the big aluminum box tied with canvas straps that arrived on our doorstep every two weeks from Chicago. In it were Don's dirty shirts. Can you believe it, Chief? Good old Mom faithfully sent back newly starched and pressed shirts along with a few dollars, treats and a letter.

I wrote my brother often. Since Don allowed me to read all the books that filled his shelves, I told him about my activities and the latest books I'd read. Also, I requested that he buy me a college sweatshirt for Christmas, figuring that if I mentioned it weekly, my odds of receiving it were pretty good.

When we had visited the North Park campus, I noticed that the students wore navy and gold sweatshirts with the college logo. I wanted one of those. Don never responded to my request personally, but he did drop a few lines in his laundry box asking how we were and "would Mother send him stamps and chocolate chip cookies?" From all the stamps Don requested, there was no other conclusion but that he was feverishly writing a lot of letters to his girlfriend, Susan, in Los Angeles. On a letter to our whole family, my brother had sneaked in a clue to his intentions when he wrote, "I really must go out and visit Susan and her family next summer."

Mother was worried. "He's too young to be serious. Maybe we should all go. We could stay with Alice and Sid. It'd be like old times."

Mom was referring to the years Aunt and Uncle lived in Parker Falls. Before they had moved to California, our two families were inseparable. Both dads were in the car business. Both moms were sisters and best of friends, and their eight children—four from each family—were matched in age. During the summers, when the fathers were at work, the two moms and a carload of kids shared picnics and laughter.

"Come on, Bob," Mother pleaded. "We could borrow a station wagon from your business. Never have we taken a family vacation together, and now that Don is in college, this may be our last chance."

"We just took Don to Chicago. If we set a precedent by visiting his girlfriend on the other side of the world, we'll have to take a trip for each of his sisters."

Sheryl laughed. "Dad, don't worry about it. I'll try and find somebody from the Midwest."

"What if I marry a guy from another country?" I asked, having just read a book about Dr. Leakey.

"Then you're on your own, kid," Dad answered.

Nothing more was said, but I knew that once Mother got her mind on something, "watch out." So, I immediately started researching information on the states we'd be passing through. Every month I checked the advertisements at the back of the National Geographic magazine and wrote for all the free information that might be helpful for our trip, especially anything on caves—an item on my dream list. The travel packets eventually filled an entire dresser drawer.

The site I most wanted to see was Wind Cave Park. My new trombone teacher, Mr. Swenson, said those caves were unforgettable and very convenient to Mt. Rushmore, where we would be visiting.

I forgot to mention that the summer before Don went to college, I took up the trombone. I was to choose an instrument, or I should say SUPPOSEDLY was to choose an instrument. I had observed my sister playing the oboe and my brother playing the trumpet in many band concerts. Neither instrument appealed to me. But what did, was to be in the marching band carrying the largest brass instrument and blowing the rhythm-note that helped the entire band stay together. Dad went with me to see the band director of the high school. I was excited as we walked into the classroom. There stood Nick, a bald, bushy-browed and solemn man. "I want to play the tuba," I said, looking up at him confidently.

He lifted his eyebrows in disapproval. "I don't allow anyone under five feet to play the tuba. It's just too heavy."

I argued, saying my legs were strong from riding bicycles and my arms were strong from helping my sister with her paper route. I was disappointed that Dad didn't help me out, but he said nothing— probably because he was thinking about the cost of a tuba.

Nick said, "The band needs trombones. It's the largest brass instrument you can play. I know your arms will be too short, but you'll grow into it."

I was devastated when I walked out of the session carrying a trombone. At home, Mom felt my disappointment and immediately set up lessons, hoping to create some enthusiasm for my new instrument. She loved music and knew all the musicians in town. Mom's friend ran a music store and had just hired George Swenson from northern Minnesota, who had just married our doctor's daughter.

Mr. Swenson quickly convinced me that the trombone was perfect. When he demonstrated the trombone, I loved the sound, plus I noticed how handsome he was. I developed a very serious crush on him, which inspired me to practice faithfully, and also to change my hairstyle so I would not look like such a tomboy.

My hair had always been cut with square bangs and blunt straight sides. I was the "pea shooter champ" of grade school and proud that I could laugh as loud and pull the same quality pranks as the boys.

But this time I did not want to be thought of as a buddy because my feelings were different. They were feelings of admiration and idolization. I wanted Mr. Swenson to notice me as a girl. So, I started setting my hair with one huge, messy pin curl on each side of my head. Sheryl told me the hairstyle looked stupid.

Little did she know, because I never told her, how grown up I felt peddling my bicycle down the street in my favorite corduroys, T-shirt and pinch hat with my new curls flying.

After arriving at the music store, I placed my bike in the rack out front and, taking the music from my front basket and mouthpiece out of my pants pocket, I walked into the store looking for my musical knight.

Mr. Swenson seemed to be unaware that I was a bit self-conscious. Handing me a trombone, we began the lesson. When I focused on the music, I became relaxed and forgot about my infatuation. One day I decided to tell him about our possible trip. I knew it was months away, and I was already missing my music teacher.

"By the way, Mr. Swenson, we might be going to California to visit some relatives so my brother can visit the girlfriend he met last summer at camp. Do you think I'll be good enough by then to skip a few lessons?"

"Sure, just take your mouthpiece—that way you can build up your embouchure"—a big word he taught me that meant good cheek and mouth muscles. That's when my teacher proceeded to tell me about his vacation to Mt. Rushmore as a teenager.

I could hardly contain my excitement for the upcoming trip, even though neither parent had said we were going for sure. I began to get worried, though, when Mom said one night at the dinner table, "Maybe when Don comes home at Christmas he won't be serious about Susan anymore."

Immediately, I wrote Don a letter. "I admit that I don't especially like your Susan, but do you think if you decide to break up you could wait until after we visit California? I want to see the caves and Mt. Rushmore and float on the saltwater at Salt Lake City. Love, Judi. P.S. My trombone teacher says I can go. P.S.S. Why don't you buy me a North Park sweatshirt as a Christmas present?"

The holiday arrived. We picked Don up at the train station and he looked older and manly. "Are you still interested in Susan?" we all asked.

"Yes, but I could get a ride to California with the kids from college when the school year is out."

Mother, upset by his comment, replied, "You're not riding across the country with some teenagers. We'll take you!"

Dad turned in surprise. "Can't you wait another year? You're too young to get married."

The discussion continued.

When we opened our presents, I was upset that my brother didn't give me a sweatshirt—he bought me a pair of mittens. I looked over at Don with disappointment. "What happened?" I asked.

"I ran over to the bookstore before I left and they were out. I'll get you one for your birthday," he replied.

After Don went back to Chicago, I kept reminding my brother of his promise. My birthday came and went but there was no sweatshirt in the mail. Finally, Mom gave me the money from a trombone lesson that Mr. Swenson cancelled when he took his wife on a holiday.

I wrote again. "Dear Don: My trombone teacher went on vacation. Here's my lesson money. Mom said to give it to you to buy me a sweatshirt. Send it with your laundry but PLEASE put my shirt in a plastic bag. I don't want it to stink from your dirty clothes. Love, Judi."

Two weeks later the metal box arrived. In it was my sweatshirt and I was ecstatic. But when I put it on, it was HUGE. My hands were lost halfway up the sleeves, the cuffs dangled empty near my knees.

I was furious and wrote my brother again. "Dear Don: Remember I'm a kid. Didn't you look at the size? I won't be able to wear the sweatshirt until I'm in college. Your sister, Judi.

"P.S. Even then, I'd have to be a real fatso to wear it!!

"P.S.S. I'm really REALLY aggravated!!!!"

THIRTY-SIX

THE CAVES

The topic of conversation continued to be our trip to see Don's girlfriend in California. Mom had written about it to Aunt Alice in Los Angeles, who phoned her back the minute she received the letter. "Come on out," she told Mom. "The kids could play together and we could chat just like old times."

Dad visited the travel agent in Parker Falls, but he came home discouraged after adding up the cost of gasoline, food, motels and Disneyland. We all desperately wanted to go and volunteered to contribute from our savings, but Dad was still worried about the expense.

"I've never paid for a hotel except when I married your mother," he confessed. "Just the thought of paying for the six of us to sleep in someone else's bed bothers the heck out of me."

That's when Mom stepped in. "Bob, I'm not allowing Don to travel across the country with some college buddy. It'd worry me silly. I know he's serious about this girl, so we'll just have to take him out there. Alice and Sid offered to put us up once we got there. There just has to be a way we can do this."

Dad came up with a compromise. "Looks like the only way the family can do it is drive through the night, so bring extra blankets.

If we have to stop for a night, we'll get just one room. Someone will have to sleep on the floor."

"Can we go to Disneyland?" asked Susie.

"We'll see."

It seemed forever before Don came home from college, and when he did he was limping.

"What happened to you?" I asked. "We're leaving in three days, so you'd better get well."

"I stubbed my toe," he explained. "It's no big deal."

Not convinced, Mom made an appointment at the clinic. Doc Hodap diagnosed an ingrown toenail. Don returned with his toe wrapped in gauze and wearing rubber thongs. "Now I'll look like a cripple when I see Susan," he grumbled.

It seemed to me that there were advantages to being crippled. Our brother realized this too as he leisurely read the newspaper while we carried the suitcases out to the car. Don sat in the front seat, another advantage of his malady, so he could put his bandaged foot up on the dash. Mom and Sheryl got in the next seat, and the back seat was folded down and loaded with luggage. Susie and I rotated between the second seat and lying on the blankets that were wedged between the piles of luggage. I didn't complain, but since I was due to start junior high in the fall, I felt that I should have an official seat. To show my aggravation, I practiced tooting my trombone mouthpiece every time I was sitting alongside the luggage.

During the first few hours on the road, we planned all the things we'd do with our cousins in California. We had already studied the big fold-out map and measured the distance from Minnesota to Los Angeles. Using the "miles per inch" legend at the bottom of the map, we had calculated the driving time necessary to complete the trip. But none of us could really comprehend what that meant. Other than last fall, when we had driven eight hours to Chicago to take Don to college, our family had not left Minnesota. The words travel and vacation were not in our vocabulary.

After a while, we played the one and only car game we all knew—the "alphabet game." Each letter in the alphabet had to be found on the billboards or signs we passed. Sheryl was the scorekeeper and wrote the words next to the letter of the alphabet along with the initial of the person who first saw the word on a sign. No words could be saved until later, and we had to follow the order of the alphabet. At the end of the game, the person who had the highest number of words was the winner.

Mother was not a serious player, and neither was Dad. Don was usually a contestant, but on this occasion he was preoccupied with thoughts of a reunion with Susan, and also absorbed in self-pity for the ingrown toenail on his right foot. That left Susie, Sheryl and me as the participants.

On the border between Minnesota and South Dakota we stopped for a picnic. Because of the lack of space, Mother had packed a huge bag of food not needing refrigeration to save money and get us some exercise.

"All of us need to stretch and run around a bit now and then," she told us. "We surely can't do that in a restaurant. This way we can kill two birds with one stone."

Don didn't agree. "I'll just sit in the car. I don't want to get my bandage dirty."

"It's up to you," Mother replied. "There's no eating in the car, so if you prefer to diet, it makes no difference to me."

We had a selection of cheese, pickled herring and summer sausage or peanut butter sandwiches, along with homemade bread and cookies. Mom also brought Melmac bowls, plates and cups, which we washed off in the drinking fountain after we finished eating. For our first meal of the trip, none of us complained about our limited menu choices. But later that day. when we stopped for supper at a park in another town and had the same menu, we weren't quite as enthusiastic, especially when Dad announced, "We'll drive right through this evening because otherwise we won't get to see Mt.

Rushmore in the daylight. Right now, I'm going to take a snooze, so why don't you walk around and check out the town. Maybe you can find an ice cream cone." He paused for a moment, then added, "If you find anybody who makes chocolate Cokes, bring me one, will ya?"

"Me too!" said Don. "I'll stay right here and watch the fort."

"Okay, Hopalong," I teased, "but I might drink your Coke before it gets here."

"Hey Dad, does this mean we'll see the caves tomorrow?" Susie asked.

Mom whisked us away so Dad could rest. We walked all over the town but there was no soda fountain. Only ice cream sandwiches and Dixie cups were available. We wandered back with two melted cups of ice cream.

We all tried to sleep in the car, but it was impossible. Every time I opened my eyes it was still dark. I thought of you, Chief, realizing how tough it must've been to do all that traveling. I guess I must've dozed off because the slam of a car door woke me. I opened my eyes in the daylight to see Mother walking into a grocery store. Soon we were sitting around a picnic table eating Cheerios with milk and bananas and a gooey Hostess sweet roll. I sat contemplating the meaning of "vacation." Or maybe I was just realizing that "saving money" not only meant avoiding restaurants but also picnicking in a park isolated from any of the possible tourist areas that I had seen advertised along the road.

Interrupting my thoughts, Susie asked a question. "How many days do we have to eat in parks and sleep in the car before we get to Cousin Marcia's?"

Dad didn't look too alert after driving all night. He pushed his hand through his hair as if he needed a moment to think. "It takes two days and two nights. Maybe tonight we'll find a place to sleep, then we'll all feel better. Right now, I'm going to get a little shut-eye before we drive any farther."

Soon we were on the road again passing by billboards that announced the Badlands were near. As we approached the brown and gray rock formations in weird shapes and forms, I got an ominous feeling. Eager to share my knowledge about the history and geography of the area, which I had presented in a report last spring, I was pleased when Susie set me up with a question. "How come this is called the Badlands, anyway?"

Quickly I recited my knowledge. "Because no one can grow anything in this soil—so they can't live here. Even the pioneers were afraid to travel through the Badlands because the shapes of the rocks were eerie, and the wind traveling around the formations made scary sounds when they camped out. Some of the land looks like rocks, but it's really dirt, and it's so soft that when the winds blow, the shape of the terrain changes. People would get lost because their landmarks would disappear. To make matters worse, criminals were hiding in the hills to avoid the law. These guys were called the Badlands Bandits."

Mom clapped, and Sheryl and Don whistled. I think they were making fun of me, but it didn't matter. We stopped along the road by a plaque to stretch our legs and read the historical inscription. What I had just told them was written there, just like I said. Susie was impressed—she loved my stories. That's one of many reasons we were the best of friends. Don, the only family member with a camera, took a bunch of black and white photos of the landscape. Sheryl offered to take a picture of Don. "Come on," she said, "I'll take a picture of you with your bad toe in the Badlands."

"Oh, grow up," he answered. But there was a smile on Don's face, so I knew that his toe was on the mend.

I took a handful of dirt as a souvenir, wrapping it carefully in waxed paper. The ground looked the same as the valleys and peaks of the rocks on the horizon. It was cracked and dry, reminding me of a red-and-gray jigsaw puzzle. It made me wonder if some fissure way out there would open deep into the earth so I could see dinosaur bones or fossils from a very ancient time.

The scenery started to change as we entered the Black Hills. The brown turned to green and pine trees sprouted on the landscape. All of us felt a sense of relief. The emptiness of the Badlands had become monotonous. And I don't suppose it helped matters any that I was tooting on my mouthpiece. Sheryl covered her ears and said, "I forbid you to practice anymore, you're driving me nuts."

"I second that," Don added.

Fortunately, Dad started singing, "In my Merry Oldsmobile" after he saw the sign that said "Five Miles to Dakota's Famous Monument." As we approached a single-lane tunnel, Sheryl said, "Wouldn't it be something if some idiot clobbered us head-on after all the driving we've done?"

Dad assured her that the car was new, and the horn was extra loud so we could safely drive through the tunnel. As we approached Mount Rushmore, we got out of the car and looked up at the granite faces carved into the hill.

Wow," I said. "Look at that, just like the pictures in the library. There's Washington, Jefferson, Lincoln and Roosevelt." To see the huge stone faces in real life was overwhelming. I kept watching the eyes, waiting for them to blink or move. It just seemed like there had to be some magic in those life-like images.

Steps and a walkway led us closer to the gargantuan faces. A gift shop sat adjacent to the hillside. Knowing that Don's Brownie Kodak, with its black and white film, couldn't do the place justice, I went into the shop to look for postcards. After much deliberation, not only did I buy postcards, but also a letter opener with the Rushmore faces on the handle and some vanilla Turkish toffee.

Dad bought us each a Coke. "Everybody ready?" he asked. "We have miles and miles to go."

"Just think, we get to see the caves next," I said.

The whole family started playing the alphabet game, reflecting some enthusiasm after our stop at the monument. There were lots of signs, and the alphabet filled in quickly. Don said he saw a "z" on a message that "Burma Shave" had posted on the sequential red signs planted along the road.

"I didn't see any 'z'," Sheryl declared.

"Me neither," I added.

And so, a heated discussion was off and running. Sheryl called Don a bully, and Don replied, "Your eyes aren't as quick as mine."

The discussion turned into an argument, and the voices grew louder.

Dad honked the horn before announcing, "I won't put up with this. Stop your arguing."

We did, just as he drove by the exit sign for Wind Cave Park.

I started sobbing. "You said we could see the caves. And I promised my trombone teacher I would see them."

"Everyone is too wound up. We can't spare the time now," Dad replied.

The car became silent. A few hours later, we stopped for peanut butter sandwiches. I walked around the park tooting my mouthpiece until my lips were swollen and was commanded to get into the car.

As dusk arrived, we passed a hand-painted sign, "Carl's Caves, next exit. Turn right in six miles."

"I think we'll stop. I need a rest," Dad said. When he turned into the drive, it was dark, but bright lights spilled out over the lawn. A man was working on his fence. He saw us and came over to the car.

"Want to see the caves? My name's Carl. You just drive right alongside the barn and park by the lake. Meet me at the dock."

Sure enough, when Dad parked the car, we saw a small wooden boat tied to the dock. To call it a lake was really exaggerating. Turning to Don, he said, "Mother and I will stay here. Can you be the responsible one, Don?"

My brother hesitated before answering. I crossed my fingers. Maybe he would feel some guilt over the alphabet game and not worry about his darn toe.

"Sure, I'll go."

Mom stood on the shore. As Carl rowed us across the murky swamp into the black mouth of the cave, I watched her disappear. The boat suddenly hit the ground, and Carl jumped out at the bow, pulled the boat onto the rocks and helped us out. He handed us each a flashlight. "Turn on your lights and follow me single file."

We walked along the edge of a small stream. The wet and slimy rock sloped into the water, and we could neither see nor hardly keep ourselves from slipping. Carl was elated to have an audience and kept his voice loud enough to entertain us plus any nearby critters. He showed us the stalactites forming in the ceiling and a hole overhead where we could see out into the starry sky. Don followed behind Carl but was limping and bemoaning the fact that his bandage was already wet. I held Susie's hand, and Sheryl, who was at the rear of the line, kept muttering, "What a rip-off."

Turning my head, I pleaded, "Please don't tell Dad."

We continued to follow Carl. Water dripped wherever we turned. "I have to go to the bathroom," Susie whispered.

"Just hold it," I answered.

The cave became darker and wetter the farther we went until finally, we reached an impasse. "Okay, time to turn around," Carl said and then kept right on talking, his voice echoing as he told us how he found the cave on his father's land as a small boy. "And to think that I made a business from it," he added.

Sheryl whispered from behind me, "He can't really be serious."

I almost burst out laughing before I reminded myself that at least I got to see a cave.

As we climbed into the boat to row across the swamp, the sky was hazy, and the stars were hidden from view. Mother and Dad stood waiting for us on the dock. I could tell they were worried. Carl tied up the boat and shook Dad's hand, thanking him for the visit. He walked into the barn and turned off the yard lights. The shock of the sudden blackness felt invasive and cold until Dad turned on the headlights, which pierced the night and led us down the road.

Don plunked his foot up on the dash.

"How's your toe, Don?" I asked.

"Okay. It feels better than when we left home."

I breathed a sigh of relief.

"How were the caves?" Dad asked.

"Spooky," I said. "We had to watch our step on the wet rocks, but nobody fell."

"I should hope not!" Mother responded. "Anyone care for a peanut butter sandwich? We're eating in the car. Father says we'll be stopping at a motel tonight."

Eventually, we stopped at the Lakeland Motel and took a room with two double beds. Mom and Dad, Don and Susie got the beds. Sheryl and I got the linoleum floor. We piled up our blankets to sleep on, but it still felt like we were lying on cement. "Next time, we get the bed," Sheryl announced.

But she quickly fell asleep. I lay there replaying the day's events. I knew one thing for certain—if I were a bandit, I'd definitely choose the Badlands instead of Carl's Caves.

THIRTY-SEVEN

LAS VEGAS

Dad promptly woke our family at seven o'clock. "Okay, up and at 'em. We've got another full day ahead. Use the bathroom, and let's get going."

Conversation was at a minimum when we drove away from the motel. Sheryl went back to sleep. Susie and I, seasoned veterans of the road, played Tic-Tac-Toe as we waited. We knew Dad would not stop driving until he discovered a town that met our requirements for breakfast—a grocery store and a community park.

Soon we were at a picnic table eating Cheerios topped with sliced bananas and Parker House rolls spread with butter and strawberry jam.

Don cleared his throat and said, "You know, I've been thinking. Maybe I'll go into church music."

None of us bothered to comment. After all, it didn't seem too surprising. Mom had directed church choirs for years. Besides, who wanted to talk about what you were going to do for the rest of your life at eight in the morning?

"Aren't you going to ask how I made my decision?"

"Okay, why?" I asked, eternally grateful that he had accompanied us into the cave and that he had not further damaged his ingrown toenail in the process.

"I realize now that if I joined a group like the Four Freshmen, I'd be on the road all the time. And after sitting in this station wagon for two days, I know that I'd go crazy."

"Wise decision," replied Mother.

"That's not a valid reason," challenged Sheryl. "You could always take a plane. But you'd have to change your name since our family and your girlfriend would disown you. I'm sure Susan's father, Rev. Anderson, would never allow his daughter to marry a music celebrity."

"We're not getting engaged this week. I just need to see if I'm still interested in her."

Dad, who was putting more cereal into his bowl, looked over at Don. "You mean I'm driving from Minnesota to California just for the fun of it?"

Mom came to the rescue. "Now Bob, I've always wanted to visit my sister, and you've always loved to drive, so quit complaining!"

After packing up our dishes and food, we continued our marathon. The miles fell behind us, and the horizon changed as we drove. As the sun rose higher and reflected off the asphalt, it created an optical illusion that we were coming to the edge of the earth. It came as a welcome relief when Sheryl saw a sign that said "Las Vegas 300 miles."

We all knew about The City of Bright Lights and had been told tales of the show people and gambling there. We'd been forewarned by the church and community that Las Vegas was the "Cauldron of Wickedness."

Surprisingly, Mother seemed pleased with Sheryl's announcement. "Good. That means we'll be passing through before dark. Things should be reasonably quiet."

Passing through? What a disappointment, I thought. In Parker Falls, we never saw anyone famous. The closest we had come was the Bell Ringing Choir from Scotland, and Lapplisa, a singer from

Sweden and of course, you, Chief. I wanted to see somebody really famous like Dick Clark of American Bandstand, but I'd even settle for Don's favorite group, the Four Freshmen. It just didn't seem fair that we were so close to celebrities and would never see them. Of course, I already knew my parents would avoid the Stars. "Be hardworking and sensible" was the family philosophy that had been inbred for generations.

We only stopped for bathroom breaks. Dad refused to stop for lunch or supper—he was eager to get to California. We ate sandwiches in the car, our bottoms were numb from sitting, and no one was talking except me.

I pestered Dad a million times by saying, "How many miles have we gone? Please read the meter and tell me." Secretly, I kept my fingers crossed, hoping that we would see some evidence of the Vegas glitter and gambling when we drove through.

I tried not to act excited when Mother was wrong in her calculations, and it would be dark when we got to Las Vegas. Sheryl let out a whoop of excitement. "Look. The whole city is lit up!"

Mother, sitting next to Sheryl in the back seat, mumbled something about the general decadence and decline of the human race while we three girls oohed and aahed at the lit-up casino marquees. The signs held rows and rows of flashing lights in every color, making the streets look like a silent display of Fourth of July fireworks.

Susie pressed her nose to the window. I climbed from my spot among the suitcases and squeezed between my sisters to get a better view. My senses were overloaded, but I still couldn't get enough of it. When Dad stopped for a red light, we noticed a lady in a tight, blue-sequined dress walking on the sidewalk.

"Look," Sue whispered. "Isn't she pretty?" Wiggling around to get a better glimpse, my little sister caught herself on the door handle. As my father obeyed the green light, the back door opened, and she fell onto the asphalt.

"Dad, stop!" I shouted. "Susie fell out of the car!

Mother snapped into action and screamed, "She'll be kidnapped by those heathens!"

Dad slammed on the brakes with such vigor, he just about killed all of us.

The car behind us squealed to a halt. The driver laid on the horn and drove around on the right side, yelling, "You're lucky I didn't nail your ass."

"Get her, Don," Dad commanded.

My brother leapt out of the car, as though his sore toe had been miraculously healed and snatched Susie from the ground. Jumping back in and slamming the door, he hugged his little sister tightly against his chest.

I was glad my sister was safe, but at the same time, I wished that the ugly man who sped by would run into a telephone pole.

Mom leaned over the front seat and kissed Sue on the cheek. "You okay, little one?" she asked.

"Wasn't that lady pretty?" Susie replied, unphased by the commotion. "I'm hungry," she added.

"Don't you think Susie should sit in the middle from now on?" I suggested.

"She'll be all right," Dad replied. "On the way back, we'll drive through Salt Lake City. None of this will happen around the Mormons."

Having been raised in a religion that was riddled with superstition, I knew before Dad made his comment that he would blame the evil city of Las Vegas for the accident. However, I was concerned with a new question in the "what if?" category.

"Hey, Dad," I asked. "What if Susie'd been kidnapped? How much ransom money would you pay?"

Brother Don smirked before adding his two cents. "Now, that's a very interesting question."

Dad never responded. He was bailed out when my little sister repeated, "I'm hungry."

"Okay," Mother said. "At the first opportunity, let's you and me go pick out a treat."

At the edge of town, we found a grocery store. Mom and Sue splurged on something very special—huge, fancy ice cream sandwiches with nuts and marshmallows. For a second, I was glad my sister had fallen out of the car.

Susie enjoyed being the center of attention. She sat in Mom's lap while eating her ice cream and chatting away. "Do you think I'll like my cousin Marcia?" she asked. "Tell me again how we got our picture in the newspaper. Wait, I remember. You and Aunt Marion and Aunt Alice all had babies."

"That's right," Mom replied. "My sisters and I were born a year apart, and our babies were born one month a part. Uncle Reuben thought Parker Falls would find it interesting, so he wrote about it in his column and then photographed us and put the picture on the front page. It also inspired him to get a movie camera to record the babies playing together."

"Yeah, I'll never forget that camera," Sheryl said. "He took pictures of the kids climbing in and out of their toy box, and I had to help him. Those huge lights were so hot I just about sweat to death. And I had to help Uncle again when he decided to make movies of Sid and Alice's house and garden before they left for California. I held up a sign that read 'the Old Homestead on Swede Hill.'"

Mother defended her brother-in-law. "Reuben should have taken movies. Do you realize that house had been in the family for seventy-five years? When we were little and lived two blocks away, we would run up to Grandmas for 'lemonsnade,' at least that's what she called it. That was the only English word she spoke. Otherwise, we had to speak Swedish. Grandpa and Grandma kept their house on Swede Hill until fifteen years ago when they both died within months of one another. It stayed in the family until Alice and Sid moved to California."

"How come they went away?" Susie asked.

"I think Uncle Sidney has some Gypsy in his blood," Mom replied.

I would never forget how the lives of our families had been so tightly woven together. As I mentioned before, Chief, Aunt Alice had kids exactly our ages, so we each had a playmate. Mom and Alice got along so well that we were forever on outings and picnics together. Us kids were allowed to go wild as the moms shared their secrets. The families never questioned their future. We even bought lake lots side by side.

One spring day, though, after a long hard winter of waist-high snow, things changed. Uncle Sidney was drinking coffee at our kitchen table when he said, "You know, Bob, last winter was too much snow for me. I'm ready to join my brother in California. Of course, I'll have to sell the business first, and the house."

"Think about it," Dad replied. "It's easier to put a coat on than move across country and sweat."

But no one realized how serious Sidney was. Before we knew it, he'd sold the house and business and built a 20 x 20 frame cabin on his lake lot. "Now we'll have a storage place for anything we can't fit in the car and trailer," he said. "I'll send for the furniture and dishes when I find a job. If I can't find work, we'll come back and start again."

But we knew by his excitement over the move that they were gone for good.

We all waved as they drove away, not comprehending just how much we would miss them. I knew it was one of the saddest days of Mom's life. Aunt Alice was her best friend.

As Dad drove through the night, eager to make it to Los Angeles, I drifted to sleep with my thoughts.

The slam of a car door woke me up. "What's going on?" I asked groggily.

"Your father is making a phone call. He's been driving in circles and can't find Buena Vista Avenue."

"What time is it, anyway?"

"Five o'clock," Mother responded. I could tell she was miffed.

"Won't they be sleeping?"

"Not anymore."

Dad returned to the station wagon and talked to Mom through her window. "Sid offered to come and escort us to his house. He said it'd be easier than trying to explain it."

Sure enough, within twenty minutes, my uncle drove into the parking lot and stopped beside our car. "It's great to see you, Bob. The coffee's on. Just follow me."

It felt like we'd been on the road forever, but now we were behind Uncle Sidney's Volkswagen driving down the quiet, dimly lit streets. I looked out at the houses passing by and then at the taillights of the little car leading us to our destination like a tugboat brings home a ship at sea.

THIRTY-EIGHT

CALIFORNIA COUSINS

After days of driving from Minnesota to Los Angeles, it was a relief to be in a house instead of the station wagon. Uncle Sidney had gone to work, Dad was asleep, and Mom and Aunt Alice were talking in the living room as if they had just seen each other yesterday.

Sheryl, Sue and I were eating corn flakes with our cousins. They looked a lot bigger than us—but then, it'd been five years. We had a new cousin, Dean. It felt comfortable to be sitting at the same Formica table that we had laughed around at their old house on Swede Hill.

We talked among ourselves and sometimes with our moms in the adjoining room. Excited voices filled the air, like kernels bursting into popcorn.

Susie turned to Marsha and said, "I really want to go to Disneyland."

"We're going tomorrow," answered Aunt Alice, overhearing the conversation.

"Could we go to Hollywood?" Sheryl asked.

"Dad's trying to get tickets for *Truth or Consequences*," Mary replied after finishing a mouthful of cereal.

Knowing that movie stars were not on my Mother's list of best influences for young minds, I looked toward the living room, anticipating an objection. Hoping her silence meant approval of the television show, I asked, "Can we go to Chinatown? My friend Rachel told me it's like visiting another country."

Don, who had been talking to his girlfriend for the last thirty minutes, finally hung up and walked to the table. There was only one telephone on the wall by the back door. Don, who had been speaking quietly to Susan, was also eavesdropping on our conversation. "Susan agrees with you," he offered. "She said we should definitely visit Chinatown."

He walked over to Mom. "Can I use the station wagon? I'd like to visit Susan."

"Ask your Father. He's resting in the bedroom."

Don was back in a minute. "Dad said to be careful and be home by dark."

"Did you check with Susan on directions?" Mom asked. "Be sure to greet Rev. Anderson from us."

Without answering, my brother raced down the hall to change his shirt.

When he came back through the kitchen, Sheryl said, "Don't wreck the station wagon. It'd be a disaster if we had to squeeze into a regular car and drive all the way to Minnesota."

Don rolled his eyes, grabbed a cup of coffee and headed out the door.

"Hey," I asked my cousin Dave, "can I borrow one of your bicycles? I'd like to see what your town looks like."

"I'll go with you. Come on, you can ride Mary's bike."

We went out to the garage and pulled up the door. "Do you think your brother will marry this gal?" he asked.

"I just can't imagine it. He practices the piano so much I don't know why anyone would want to marry him."

Side by side, we rode up and down the streets of Dave's neighborhood. The houses were flat-roofed and small. It felt very different from Parker Falls, especially when my cousin waved at some of the kids and stopped to introduce me.

"Aren't there any Swedes around here? Everyone is dark-haired and dark-skinned."

My cousin said I was funny. "It's all the hot sun. Most people are a blend of nationalities—my dad calls them 'Heinz 57.' There's a lot of Mexicans here too—the hard-working good ones," he added.

When Uncle Sidney came home, he was ready for some action. "You've been lounging while I've been working," he said. "I need some exercise. How about going to the ocean?"

Aunt Alice and Mom decided to stay home and make supper. Mary and Sheryl were excited about checking out the boys. And the rest of us? We just wanted adventure.

It was warm and sultry at the beach. Dave and I hiked along the water's edge, watching the huge, foamy waves turn over and disappear into the sand. My cousin challenged me to ride the waves. "Not me!" I replied. "I'll watch."

Dave swam for a few minutes, and then, to impress me, bravely rode a wave onto the beach, almost killing himself in the process. The way his body flew off the wave and splattered on the beach looked pretty painful.

I ran over to see if he was hurt. "Are you okay?"

He got up, grinning. "Yeah, I'm fine. Guess I was trying to show off."

In the distance, we noticed a crowd gathering. We walked over to see what was going on and found Uncle Sidney working on a life-size sand sculpture. He seemed oblivious to the audience.

I said to Dave, "Wow, it's a girl lying with her face to the side and arms by her head, just like she's sleeping—or sunbathing."

The viewers muttered approval as the sculpture's limbs became defined. Then Sidney created a facial expression and sculpted the girl's hair long and flowing to one side. If she'd worn a cloth swimsuit instead of one of sand, I would have mistaken her for a real person.

Susie asked, "How do you do that, Uncle Sidney?"

"I've taken some drawing lessons and made figures in clay. Now I'm taking Spanish classes, and soon I'll teach art to some of the Spanish kids in the area. It's something I've always wanted to do."

It seemed like a really bizarre thing to me, having a Spanish-speaking Swedish uncle. I knew no one who spoke Spanish until now. In fact, the only languages taught in school were Latin or German. Swedish was the language spoken by the adult community to discuss things that children were not supposed to hear. By repetition of "those conversations," many Swedish words were absorbed by the younger generation so they also would pass on the language. I overheard one classmate say that she thought Swedish was a necessity for raising children.

Anyway, I looked down admiringly at this human figure in the sand. My only regret was that Don had taken our only camera and now I wouldn't have a photo to show my friends.

Later that evening, Don came into the house with the desired camera in hand, his face aglow. Immediately, we started teasing him, "Don's got a crush on Susan. Don's got a crush on Susan…" When he came back to earth, he bellowed, "Stop!"

Then he turned and said, "Hey Dad, I know we're all going to Disneyland tomorrow, but Wednesday, I need the car. Susan wants to show me Chinatown."

"Not unless you take us along," I interrupted. "It'd be good if we got to know your girlfriend. Don't you agree, Dad?"

Suddenly, everyone wanted to go. It was finally decided that Don would take his cousins and sisters to meet Susan. Don didn't like the plan, but we pressed our demands relentlessly and promised we'd stay out of his way. Our parents agreed that the sixteen-year-olds, Mary and Sheryl, could be the guardians for Sue, Marcia, Dave and me—but little Dean, age 3, would have to stay home.

No one complained about going to bed that night, aside from Don, who protested sleeping in the living room on a roll-a-way near the sofa bed where Aunt Alice and Uncle Sid slept. The rest of us doubled up in single beds, but we really didn't mind. We were exhausted.

Little Dean woke us up the next morning. "Let's go, let's go! I wanna see Dopey."

Marsha explained Dean's excitement as we ate our breakfast. "Last month, when we took Dean to Disneyland for his birthday, the Seven Dwarves were his favorites."

Our cousins' vivid description, however, could not prepare us for the visual treat that we would experience. Disney's world of storybook characters was beyond our comprehension. We had been raised not to believe in Santa Claus—only in the Star of Bethlehem. Yet, here were the figures from our fairytales and fantasies standing right in front of us talking and smiling as if they were real. We met Alice in Wonderland and Mickey Mouse. Then Dean insisted we visit the Seven Dwarves.

I could tell that my parents' imaginations were ignited too because when we took a jungle ride, I saw Dad jump, and Mom let out a cry when the lion growled at us from the bush. Of course, when we stopped to eat our peanut butter sandwiches and drink our Kool-Aid, they wouldn't admit they had been fooled.

We felt surrounded by magic until Dave persuaded us to visit a whale at the aquarium. The tanks had excellent lighting that showed off the creatures. We were enjoying ourselves until we saw a huge whale swimming back and forth, its jaws opening and closing as if it were aggravated with its watery cage. I guess the younger kids and I knew the whale wanted out, and immediately we all grew somber. I think we wanted the whale to be in Fantasyland too.

I turned to my cousins and said, "Let's get out of here."

Eager to escape the unhappy beast, we hurried out of the building into the bright sunshine. A ski lift-like contraption was gliding over our heads.

"I've got an idea," Dad said. "Why don't we take a break and see what everything looks like from above?"

We waited in line until it was our turn. Susie sat between Dad and me. Finally, we were viewing Disneyland from an open lift suspended on a high wire. I felt giddy. I felt breathless. Disneyland had stretched my imagination to greater limits. Yes, I would continue to read adventure stories, but I wanted more of this. I knew for sure that I wanted to visit places and see things for myself...maybe become a nomad like you, Chief.

Excited, I turned to Dad and Susie. "When I get older, I'm going to travel all over the world."

"Fine idea," Dad said, nodding. "Just make sure you find a boyfriend in the Midwest. I'm not driving across country again."

THIRTY-NINE

CHINA TOWN

Sitting around the kitchen table, my cousins and I jabbered about our visit to Disneyland. Sheryl and Mary were not part of the conversation because they were studying the new issue of *Seventeen* magazine on a table between them. My brother sauntered in wearing a robe over his striped pajamas.

"Whose robe is that?" I asked.

"It was hanging on the back of the door," Don answered. "Before I shower, I want to remind everyone that I'm leaving pronto at noon. If you aren't in the car, you'll be history."

I looked over at my cousin Dave and grinned. "We were wondering—are you going to ask Susan to marry you this afternoon?"

Mom and Alice, who were sitting in the living room, could hear the bantering. "Judi!" Mother yelled, "Quit making your brother's life difficult."

I could tell our mothers were counting the minutes before we left. Nine children and four adults in a small bungalow made for a lot of commotion. We kids were doing fine—it was Mom and Aunt Alice who were wearing out.

"Do we have to pack a picnic lunch?" Sheryl interrupted.

"No, I'm sending money with Mary to buy a snack from one of the street vendors," Aunt Alice replied.

We went back to our conversations. Suddenly, little Dean started burping to demonstrate his latest talent. Of course, we started laughing, egging him on.

Aunt Alice came into the kitchen. "Okay, everybody, you're too wound up. Why don't you put your swimsuits on and run through the sprinkler—get rid of some of that energy."

Sheryl and Mary were still engrossed in their magazine, but the rest of us changed and ran outside. We hollered and screamed as we squirted each other.

Mom came out to stop the hubbub. "Get in the house right now!" she demanded. "The neighbors will think we have a house full of hoodlums."

After changing back into our clothes, we settled down to watch *Robin Hood*. We were enjoying the adventures of the charitable men of the forest when Sheryl came over and turned off the TV. "Move it! Don's honking the horn and ready to leave."

At last, four wet-headed kids and three dry-headed teenagers were on their way to Chinatown, elated at the prospect of being without adult supervision for an entire afternoon. My brother immediately tried to take charge. "Judi," he said, "if you don't keep your voice down, I'm going to put you in the trunk."

That was entirely the wrong thing to say. We booed and hissed and gave him such a hard time that he turned up the radio. Don didn't talk to us until he needed help to find a parking spot on the congested streets of Chinatown.

We followed Don to Sam Choy's, the restaurant where his girlfriend had agreed to meet us. "There she is," he said, blushing.

After an awkward hug, Don quickly introduced Susan and said, "Let's check back here in two hours." Mary and he synchronized their watches, and we were suddenly on our own.

Mary was very serious about her responsibility. She took Susie's hand, and Sheryl took Marcia's. Dave and I were to watch out for each other.

I couldn't believe all the new things I was seeing. Just yesterday, we were roaming around a fantasy world of life-like figures from our books, and today we were in the foreign land of Chinatown. It felt overcrowded and strange like we'd traveled across the universe. There were unusual aromas everywhere and signs in oriental hieroglyphics. Our fellow pedestrians were short, small people walking briskly and chatting in Chinese, a musical, sing-songy sound. Not having any real goal, we were swept along with them as if we were in a school of fish. We walked two blocks this way, then that way, our enthusiasm fading with each step.

Suddenly, Mary stopped. "Can't we think of a better way to spend our time? Let's go over to that hot dog stand and plan our strategy."

We bought Cokes and sat on a bench to discuss our next moves. "I don't feel safe here," Sheryl said. "What if they kidnap my little sister?"

The man who ran the hot dog stand overheard our comments. "I know these folks look different," he told us, "but they are fine people," he added. "My kids come with me on weekends, and they've made some good friends. I've got an idea. Why don't you go and look one of them up? See that sign right up the street, 'Tan's'? Just walk in there and say 'Charlie sent us.' They'll show you around."

I looked up at him. "Do they speak English?"

"His daughter does. Just go over and introduce yourselves."

We followed his advice and walked into the store, a quaint little shop with clothes and trinkets plus a few groceries. The six of us were silent. Sheryl cleared her throat. "Hello," she said, "Charlie sent us to see your store."

The man nodded and then called out something in Chinese. A girl walked out through a beaded curtain. In broken English, the man said, "Here's daughter Ping Ping." The curtain beads danced and settled into place. "She schools in America and helps you." He bowed and walked away.

Ping Ping knew English well. She was nine years old and showed us the Chinese toys and candy. The shop had a lot of school supplies—notebooks with dragons on the covers, pencils in bright red and green, and exotic-looking kites hanging from the ceiling.

Sheryl and Susie bought candy, and Mary got some fortune cookies. Dave purchased a kite. I spent the most and bought some red slippers like Ping Ping wore. They looked like a cloth boot to wear over a pig's foot because they only had two toes. When I pulled them on, my big toe went in one spot and all the others in the remaining section. The slippers had thin rubber soles and two silver flaps that folded into loops at my ankles and made the slippers fit snuggly. "Every time I wear these, I'll think about you," I said to Ping Ping.

We left the store and went to thank Charlie, the hot dog man, but he had locked up his stand.

"Oh well," said Mary. "Let's explore some other shops, okay?"

We looked in store windows and felt brave enough to walk into a large indoor market. We saw octopuses hanging over counters and unusual vegetables that were fresh or marinating in pots. The people were bargaining and laughing. Some were in a hurry and quickly made their purchases. The shy children didn't speak to us, just gave us a smile.

"Hey, look over there," I said to Dave as we walked outside. "Those boys are playing softball."

"Quit gawking," Sheryl said. "Sometimes you are so stupid. Remember, they're Americans."

I was just about to smart back to my sister when I noticed Don across the street by our station wagon. His head was down, and he was kicking the tire. "Look, Don's already back at the car," I said, "but something's wrong."

We all raced over.

"What happened?" Sheryl asked. "Did you and Susan have a fight?"

Don was very upset. "You know why Susan wanted to meet me here?"

We all stood there looking at him.

"Well, I'll tell you why… because she felt the calling to be a missionary in China. Since I'm majoring in religious music, she assumed our future together was 'meant to be.' And she couldn't comprehend why I wasn't interested in teaching and performing music in China."

"I can't believe you'd even think of going," Sheryl said. "You're still sending Mom your dirty shirts from college. You could bring them to a Chinese laundry, I suppose."

"Bad joke, Sheryl," Don replied. "Can't you ever shut up? Susan and I are finished. I need a large choir and a pipe organ to play my kind of music. I care about her but not enough to compromise my music."

We got into the car.

Don turned on the radio and cranked the volume up. The noise was too much. Mary, sitting in the front seat next to my brother, turned the radio down and tried to be cheerful. "Okay, it's time for a cookie."

Mary opened the bag she'd purchased at Tan's. Handing us each a cookie, she said, "Crack it in half, and a little paper inside will tell you a fortune. You can eat the cookie too—it tastes pretty good."

We all stared at our fortune cookies.

"I'll go first," Mary said. "Let's see…" After breaking her cookie, she read the message out loud. "'Many doors will open for you.'" Then she laughed, "I guess that could mean a lot of things."

"Me next," Susie said. "'I am pretty,'" she read, giggling.

"You made that up," said Sheryl. Grabbing her fortune, she read, "'Your wit will bring you wealth.'"

Dave didn't like his and crumpled it up.

Marsha was disappointed because hers ambiguously read, "'Your fortune is going to change.'"

"Hey, Don, why don't you read yours?" I asked.

"You read it," he grumbled.

"Okay, I will."

I uncrumpled his fortune and read, "'You will have many children.'"

We all laughed.

Don didn't crack a smile.

"Here is mine," Sheryl said. "'Good advice is beyond price.' What a lousy fortune! I hope the cookie is good." She popped it into her mouth.

I was lucky. I thought my fortune was better than the cookie. It read, "Your imagination will bring joy to others." Is that true, Chief?

FORTY

TRUTH OR CONSEQUENCES

When we arrived back from Chinatown, our parents listened to our tales of the day's adventure. Don never came into the house; he sat in a lawn chair in the backyard, looking out into space as if rigor mortis had set in.

"Come on," I coaxed. "Aunt Alice and Mom made meatballs and scalloped potatoes. It's your favorite."

"Just leave me alone. I can't believe I wasted an entire year thinking Susan and I were something special."

"You were. Maybe you liked her because she was the prettiest Swede you'd ever met. Anyway, look on the bright side. We got a trip to California."

"Go eat, okay? But save some for me."

In the kitchen, everyone was discussing Don's issue. Dad rolled his eyes and said, "That'll be the day when my son leads church music in the middle of some strange country."

"Now, Robert," Mom gently chided. "You have lots of ministers in your family."

"A clergy I could see. But playing some out-of-tune piano on the other side of the universe?"

"He'll get over it," Uncle Sidney said. "By the way, does anyone want to go with me to Spanish class? It's over at the high school. There's a field and a playground and lots of kids. My class lasts about an hour, and then I can take everyone over to our favorite pizza place. We could save our dinner here for tomorrow."

With incentive like that, we all decided to go. Even though Don came along, he remained antisocial and stoically read a book. As Sidney practiced his Spanish, Mom and Aunt Alice gabbed on a bench while Mary and Sheryl played tennis, and the rest of us helped Dave fly his kite. My uncle was right. There were lots of kids at the playground, and most of them gathered around Dave and his lime-green triangular kite—which was supposed to look like a dragon. The kite floated high in the sky, its long white tail dangling.

My cousin let me hold the string. I felt the kite strain to be free as if it were a big bird, eager to pick up the currents and fly away.

"Okay, Judi, give it more string," Dave told me.

As I followed his instructions, I could feel the envy of the other kids who were watching. Dave proudly introduced me to his friends. "This is my cousin, Judi, from Minnesota."

I said, "Hello," but felt timid comparing my almost-teenage, freckled self in a white blouse and pedal pushers with their tanned faces, T-shirts and shorts. As we joined in chatter, though, while watching the kite fluttering in the sky, I lost my shyness.

After a while, Dave decided to haul the kite in, but the spirited paper monster did not want to come down. The winds began to tease until a large gust blew the kite into a tree. The string caught on a limb where the green paper form hung lifeless.

"I'll get it," Dave said, and then shimmied up the tree. He managed to get it down just as Sidney said, "Time for pizza. Put your kite in the trunk, and let's get moving."

Sidney greeted the owner when we walked in. "Hi, Al, these are my relatives from Minnesota. Can you believe they came all this way to see us? Give us two of my favorites and let them taste the best pizza in California. We'll choose our pop from the cooler."

Uncle held up the lid as we read the caps of the bottles in the racks—Coke, Squirt, 7up and Orange Crush. After choosing one, he slid the pop bottle down the channel, pulled it up and out, and removed the cap. I tried to be casual, but this was an adventure for me. Our family often went out for ice cream cones or sodas but never for anything else. Even on our trek across the states to visit our cousins, we had eaten only picnics in the park or sandwiches in the car.

We all sat around a Formica table drinking pop and anticipating our treat. Soon the pizza arrived, hot and spicy. I tasted one bite and almost spit it out.

"How do you like it?" asked Aunt Alice. "It's 'anchovy,' our family favorite."

Somehow, I finished my piece. My sisters did too. We were all raised to be polite, but the pizza tasted awful. My taste buds and stomach were not ready for anything that strange. I didn't feel good until the next morning when two bowls of Cheerios helped me feel better.

Or maybe it was Mary's announcement. "Guess what?" she said. "Mom called, and there are tickets available for *Truth or Consequences*. Do you want to go?"

Everyone did. Don was even willing to go. We knew we'd get a few laughs.

The show proved to be more entertaining than we'd anticipated. When we arrived, the auditorium was packed, so we could not all sit together. Dad, Uncle Sidney and little Dean ended up in the second row. The rest of us split into two groups and sat toward the back or in the middle.

The cameras focused on one area of the stage at a time. There was an invisible wall between the areas being filmed and "behind the scenes." It was like seeing two plays or movies at once.

One of the crew members stood on the right end of the stage and held up signs like "LAUGH," "GROAN," or "SILENCE." He also gave us a countdown for when the show was to begin.

Bob Barker, in his slicked black hair and plaid sport coat, appeared on the stage. He greeted the audience, walked down the steps with a microphone and asked questions like, "Where are you from?" "What's your dog's name?" or "Do you have a favorite comic book character?" He kept everyone laughing while he fished for contestants that he chose based on their responses.

Dave and I, Sheryl and Mary were sitting toward the back of the auditorium watching Mr. Barker interview people in the front rows. We gasped as he started talking to Uncle Sidney. When he asked the question, "Who is the president of Tasmania?" Sidney laughed and gave him a name. Bob Barker chuckled and said, "Go up on stage. We need you."

My uncle got to be a star for one day, along with three other men. Three of them were blindfolded and given a cookie by look-alike girls in swimsuits and spike heels. The fourth contestant sat ten feet away from the others. His assignment was to talk while each blindfolded contestant, one at a time, walked toward the sound of his voice and put a cookie in his mouth before returning to his chair. It all had to be done as quickly as possible. The fastest participant would be rewarded with gift certificates and two hundred dollars.

After Mr. Barker gave out the instructions and the contestants were blindfolded, a commercial for Tide detergent played on the other end of the stage. Meanwhile, a chimpanzee was brought in to replace the contestant who was supposed to eat the cookies. The audience began to snicker and immediately, the sign "SILENCE" appeared.

Sidney was the first blindfolded participant to be called. Uncle walked toward the chair, following the sound of the voice. He held his hand out with the cookie in it. When Sidney approached the chair, the chimp grabbed his wrist. Except for little Dean, Sidney's son, we all laughed so hard we almost peed our pants. When the chimp grabbed Sidney's wrist, Dean yelled, "Dad watch out." As the chimp brought my uncle's hand up to his mouth and ate the cookie, Uncle Sidney pulled off his mask to see what was happening. "Hey!" he said, laughing.

The audience was in hysterics.

Uncle didn't win any prizes, but he stole the show.

After *Truth or Consequences* was over, we all clustered together laughing about Uncle Sidney's acting debut. Dad was chuckling as Sidney walked up. "Sid, you are a brave man," he said, shaking Uncle's hand. "I think it's only appropriate that I buy a treat for everyone. I noticed an ice cream store across the street. Anybody object to double-dip cones?"

"Wow," I said. "I wish this vacation would never end!"

FORTY-ONE

BUSTER'S MOTEL

It seemed impossible that our time in Los Angeles was coming to an end. While Don bemoaned the fact that he no longer had a girlfriend, the rest of us were grateful that his short-lived romance included our trek across the country.

Uncle Sidney insisted that we visit another tourist attraction before we left. "Forest Lawn Cemetery is a must," he said. "There's no place like it in the world."

"What's the big deal?" I asked my cousin Dave.

"You'll see."

The cemetery parking lot was as big as the one for the Minnesota State Fair. It was surrounded by acres of tombstones and sculptures, and small stone houses called mausoleums that Uncle said were for rich or famous people.

Sidney became our tour guide. We followed him across the green carpet of grass. "I'll show you the best sculptures here," he said.

Uncle's favorite was a life-size granite figure of Neptune standing on top of a chest engraved with the words: "To my husband Alfred and son Danny who died at sea."

We stopped to read various gravestones and then sauntered over to a garden surrounded by trees that were trimmed and sculpted to look like green hourglasses and isosceles triangles. It was like we'd been transported to Alice's Wonderland. "This entire plot belongs to the Hannibal Family," Uncle said. "They were the ones who purchased the original acreage that now is the area of Los Angeles."

After admiring the fountains and flowers amidst the sculpted trees, we walked over to a gargantuan public mausoleum. Stone statues, like figures at Mount Vesuvius, stood there with eyes open and arms extended as if frozen in time and place. Sidney pointed to some large, marble-faced drawers. "Embalmed bodies are placed in here," he said. "The smaller drawers contain the ashes after cremation."

Dave turned to me, grinning. "Can you imagine having the job of pushing a dead body into the furnace? You'd have to be a weirdo to do something like that."

Knowing that he was trying to be funny, I meekly smiled in return, but my thoughts lingered on the idea of cremation. The Scandinavians of Parker Falls did not have such a word in their vocabulary. Our lineage dictated that the deceased be buried in a quiet and grassy cemetery in their best Sunday clothes next to the rest of their departed kin. It was imperative that there be present a large, upright tombstone and fresh flowers to show eternal respect.

We wandered into a wing of the mausoleum that was reserved for children. The urns and statues there were cherubic or childlike. The marble-faced vaults were smaller than those for adult bodies. My stomach heaved thinking of all the little kids represented.

"Come on," Uncle said. "Let's go to the chapel to view the portrayal of the Lord's Supper. The figures are life-size and made in wax. It's beautiful."

We walked into a room where we could see the thirteen men sitting around a long table depicting the historical night when their Leader was betrayed, and the calendar of history was forever changed from B.C. to A.D.

I was still thinking about all the dead children when I turned to my cousin Dave and blurted out, "What if someone cremated these guys by mistake?" We started giggling hysterically, and when Dave snorted, all hell broke loose. We exploded with laughter at a decibel level that brought Mom and Aunt Alice to our sides. They immediately hustled us out of the chapel, flinging adjectives at us like "sacrilegious," "disrespectful," and "embarrassing." We stood outside trying to regain our composure, but that ended the visit to the cemetery. Walking through the gift shop on the way to the parking lot, I quickly bought a souvenir—an expandable silver ring embossed with the words Forest Lawn Cemetery.

"Why did you have to act up?" Sheryl asked. "We drove all this way, and now we have to turn right around and go back home."

I ignored my sister. It didn't bother me to leave. The place gave me the creeps. I turned to Dave and said, "How many people are dead in Forest Lawn Cemetery?"

"I dunno."

"All of them," I said.

We reverted to laughter again. Marsha and Sue joined in. Boy, I was going to miss my cousins. They were so much fun. Maybe I could persuade Don to make up with Susan so we would visit again. I had to admit that it was a lot more interesting to visit Disneyland and *Truth or Consequences* than to be riding my bike or delivering newspapers in Parker Falls.

Since this was our last evening in Los Angeles, Mom and Aunt Alice were very lenient with the curfew. Dave, Sue, Marsha and I put on our pajamas and sat around the kitchen table eating popcorn and playing Parcheesi until, finally, my brother insisted that we go to bed because he was condemned to a cot in the living room and couldn't sleep with the ruckus.

The next morning, Dad woke us up early. "Let's get moving. We have a long drive ahead of us."

None of us wanted to say good-bye. Teary-eyed, we drove away. Don sat in the front seat reading the map and calculating the miles and hours before he would see the famous pipe organ at the Mormon Tabernacle.

I was not interested in visiting the Mormons, but I wanted to swim in the celebrated Salt Lake. "Come on, Dad. It'd be really neat to float on the water and not sink. Can't we stop for just a quick dip? It's one of the wonders of the world."

I kept pleading with the hope that we could make two stops. "Just think," I said, "we could lay on our back with our hands behind our head and just look around. We could pretend we were magicians." Dad decided there was only time for one "tourist trap," as he called it. And since Don was majoring in religious music, neither parent would give my suggestion a second thought. The subject was closed.

Those first hours in the car were truly an endurance test. When we stopped for a snack in the park, I was already questioning the reality of the visit with our cousins. "I'm taking a survey," I said at the picnic table as we were eating cookies. "Did Don really break up with Susan, or did I dream it? Have we really gone to California already?"

"Will you quit bringing up her name?" Don complained. "Just wait until you find a boyfriend."

Mother frowned. "We'll have no teasing, Judi. I thought you had practicing to do."

I wandered off, tooting on my trombone mouthpiece. My brother and sisters refused to allow any practice except when we were out of the car. There was one consolation in returning to Parker Falls. I would be continuing my trombone lessons and see my handsome teacher, Mr. Swenson. I hoped he wouldn't be disappointed that I hadn't made any real progress since we had left Minnesota.

After we resumed driving, Susie and I pretended that we were riding the Greyhound bus, touring the country and playing the game, "What am I thinking of?" We tried to figure out the answers from the fewest questions or clues. After our visit with our cousins, the list of ideas was endless and kept us occupied until we stopped at a gas station. He paid the attendant, and after returning to the car, he muttered, "Seems like we're not getting as good a mileage as the trip out."

About four hours later, a trucker pulled up alongside of us and yelled through his open window, "Hey buddy, I think your gas tank has a hole in it. I've been following you for thirty miles, and something's leaking from your car."

Dad stopped and saw gasoline dripping out of the tank. The trucker was right.

"It's a new car!" Dad said, angrily. "It shouldn't be leaking! Now we'll have to stay overnight and get it fixed."

Sue and I smiled at one another. Of course, we were thinking of something more luxurious than Buster's Overnight Motel, where we rented a room. Dad gave Mom the room keys and said, "I'm going to look for a mechanic."

Wow, I thought, *this place is something out of the movie Psycho*. Rusting metal lawn chairs sat on the adobe-dirt drive that serviced the chipped and peeling six-unit structure. We all hesitated before walking through the door. The room smelled of mildew and had two double beds, two kitchen chairs and a TV on a small dresser. It was a real dump! Here's hoping you never had to sleep in a place like this, Chief.

Mom took command. "I'm opening some windows. Make yourselves useful."

We did an about face and walked back outside. Sheryl and I swiped other metal chairs from the uninhabited rooms, and the four of us sat side by side watching traffic.

I looked over at my brother. "I'd say this is a taste of what might've been if you'd decided to be a missionary in China."

"Sometimes your humor leaves a bit to be desired," Don replied.

"Well, then I might as well remind you that Sheryl and I get the bed tonight, and you get the floor."

Mom walked through the door, shaking her head as she heard the last words. "Can't you children get along? Why don't you read for a while?"

I went inside and checked out the TV. One channel was visible through snow and static. There was nothing of interest on, so I returned to my rusty chair just as Sheryl grumbled to Don, "I can't believe we're staying at a place like this. It's a real pit."

Don ignored her and continued to read.

When Dad drove up, Susie and I were counting cars. Mom came out of the room to shake one of the bedspreads.

"I was lucky to find a mechanic. First thing tomorrow, he'll put in a new tank. These vacations can sure get expensive."

Mom stared at him. "Bob, this is the very first vacation we've ever had, and I want you to know how much we appreciate it." She took the bedspread back into the motel and left Dad standing speechless by the car.

After sitting on our rusty lawn chairs and eating a supper of sandwiches, Kool-Aid and potato chips, my family adjourned to the room, hoping that a television program would come to our rescue. Then we could avoid listening to Dad groan about the financial inconveniences of traveling or about cars breaking down.

Dad did get his comments in during the advertisements, but he had some competition because Don kept saying, "I'm not sleeping on the floor. It's filthy and sticky, and I'll end up with pneumonia or tuberculosis."

Finally, Don settled on using the two chairs and sleeping in a sitting-up-position. Naturally, we found it humorous. But Don did get even the next day by being a real grouch. I suffered too. A spider bit me on the neck when I was sleeping. My face got so swollen I couldn't practice on my mouthpiece. Sheryl was pleased when she heard about it. Folding her hands, she looked to the heavens. "There really is a God!" she said.

Dad returned to the motel to find us in our outside chairs reading. He was in pretty good spirits, relieved that the mechanic didn't overcharge him. "Okay, everyone, let's hit the road. There are a lot of miles to get under our belt."

We loaded the car and headed for Salt Lake City, and Mom started talking about the Mormon Tabernacle Choir. It was one of her favorite singing groups, and she was anxious to see where all the recordings were made.

Hours later, when we arrived, she and Don were disappointed because only Mormons were allowed in the sanctuary. The organ had to be viewed from the back vestibule. "We might as well visit the museum now that we're here," Mom said.

The museum was one large room in the Education Building filled with old photos and artifacts. I was most intrigued by two mummies in showcases. It felt strange to me that during the past couple of days, I'd been introduced to cremation and mummification. As I thought about it, I decided that I'd rather be wrapped in rags and lie above ground than to be burned or buried in the earth. Then relatives and friends could see me if they wanted to. But somehow, I didn't think that the folks of Parker Falls would consider this an option.

Even more interesting than the burial practices of the Mormons were the marrying rituals. The men could have a hundred wives. I remembered Aunt Ida, a branch on my father's family tree who was spoken about in hushed voices. She had left her town and joined the circus, then later became a Mormon. I turned to Mom and asked, "Did Aunt Ida's husband have a bunch of wives?"

"Judith, you know he didn't. You love to bring that woman up."

"Aunt Marion says it's not true, anyway," Sheryl said.

"What does she know?" I said. "Aunt Jenny was the only one who kept in touch. Ida sent her lots of postcards from the cities she visited. A few years ago, Aunt Jenny showed them to Dad. Right, Dad?"

He nodded.

Susie turned to me, saying, "What happened?"

"When Aunt Ida joined the circus, her parents disowned her. She wrote Jenny that she had become a snake charmer. Of course, it was even crazier that when she traveled through Salt Lake City, she met some Mormon guy and fell in love. He persuaded Ida to leave the circus and marry him. When her parents found out that she'd settled down, they wrote, saying, 'Welcome back into the family.' Ida sent them a letter and said, 'Good riddance to you. If I wasn't good enough for you before, then I'm not good enough for you now.'"

"Did she ever bring her husband to visit her mom?" Susie asked.

"Nope, Aunt Jenny said that Ida's folks came out to visit, but they never really made up."

We rode through the night and the next day. Sometimes Dad took a catnap while Don or Mom drove. Since we were behind schedule, all available drivers were needed to put the miles behind us.

It felt like my butt was glued to the car seat and that I might never be able to ride a bicycle again. For a moment, I even thought that the night before, with its lumpy beds and rusty lawn chairs, had been a treat.

Finally, we crossed the border into Minnesota. "Hey, Dad, I've got an idea. Maybe next year we could take another vacation—not as far as California, but just someplace different. What do you think?"

"I can tell you now that it won't happen. And if you girls want to traipse across the country after some guy, I'll give you the money for a Greyhound ticket."

"Good," Sheryl replied. "I'd rather sleep on the bus than at Buster's Motel."

Mom started to laugh, then we all joined in—even Don.

FORTY-TWO

GROWING PAINS

The trip to California had expanded my world. Until then, my only contact with unusual people and places had been through reading. Well, I guess there were three exceptions—you, Chief, plus I'd met a singer from Sweden who gave a concert in Parker Falls. Oh, and then there was the Italian who cleaned our furnace.

Even though books continued to be my friends, my travel experience was way better than any stories. Now that I'd seen all kinds of geography and observed the different shades, sizes and sounds of people between Minnesota and California, my life had gained another dimension, making me feel smarter and older.

It was a comfortable coincidence that I was going to be attending Parker Falls High School, which was for grades 7 through 12. My one concern was that I would be in the same school as my sister Sheryl. Don had preceded her. Both earned the nickname "genius." I tried not to think about the bombardment of verbal comparisons that would come my way.

I knew my life would never be the same. I also knew that Sheryl was extremely worried that I would embarrass her in high school. One day she gave me a few pointers. She and her friend Margaret cornered me in the kitchen as I was making a peanut butter and brown sugar sandwich. I felt like a mouse trapped by two big Cheshire cats.

At that stage of my life, Sheryl and I didn't hang out together much. We ate meals at the same table and, on rare occasions, did the dishes together, but that was the extent of our camaraderie. Our tastes in clothes and books were totally different. I wore comfortable clothes and read biographies and adventure stories. Sheryl was interested in fashion and liked a juicy love story.

Anyway, my sister and her friend Margaret plunked themselves down on our red vinyl kitchen chairs. Sheryl leaned over the table and glared at me. "Sit down, Judi. We need to talk." Then she grimaced and added, "How can you eat that stuff anyway?"

"You don't have to eat it, so what's it to you?"

"Margaret and I have decided that you need to know the scoop. You're too young to date, but I don't want you grinning at the wrong times and looking stupid." They were right. I wasn't interested in dating. I was just starting to put a few curls in my hair and noticing my chest was changing shape. Boys were not of great interest to me unless I wanted to challenge their wit or strength.

"Now look," Sheryl continued, "if a guy comes up to you and says, 'I'm a giraffe,' that means he wants to pet heavy and give you hickeys."

Margaret could tell I wasn't catching on, so she explained. "Hickeys are the spots that girls get from the guys sucking on their neck and making a red mark. The nice girls wear turtlenecks to cover them up, and the 'sluts' wear low blouses to show them off."

I finished chewing a bite of my sandwich before responding, "Sounds really uncomfortable to have some guy biting your neck. Why don't they call it a Dracula? Anything else you want to tell me?"

Margaret took a deep breath and continued. "Never kiss a guy on the first date. He'll get the wrong idea."

"Thanks for the pointer, Margaret, but you don't need to worry. Remember, the only choices I have are Jerry Sandstrom and Ronnie Swanson." These were the only available boys at our church.

Sheryl groaned and said, "Don't be such a smart aleck. Knowing you, you'll probably date a Presbyterian. And one more thing, if a guy asks you to French kiss, he wants to put his tongue in your mouth."

"Yuk! Great stuff you're telling me. Can I go now?"

They seemed relieved. I think they were more embarrassed than I was. The slang words must've come from some teen magazine that was printed in another country. Nevertheless, I knew they were trying to help me out.

School began, and I thought it was great. Changing classes seven times a day really made the hours evaporate. My favorite classes were English and band. The worst were physical education and home economics.

It was the beginning of the separation of the sexes. The boys took a shop class to train in the manly skills necessary for marriage while we girls were required to take sewing and cooking to prepare us for household chores. The menu choices in home economics were peculiar. One assignment was to make peanut butter and mashed raisin sandwiches. After doing this, one classmate ran to the sink and threw up. I never attempted to eat mine, but instead slipped it into my zippered notebook. It finally hit me that by choosing such strange recipes, Mrs. Johnson was subtly trying to give us a menu to support the Scandinavian philosophy of home management: "Rebel in subtle ways or you will acquire more domestic tasks."

My gym class was almost as strange as home economics. The teacher, Heloise Trader, came right out of a science fiction comic book. With her dark hair and skin, I knew she wasn't a Scandinavian, which already made me suspicious, but that was the least of my worries. I couldn't figure out if she was a man or a woman.

Most of the time, I didn't discuss my teenage life with Mom. First, we had always been raised to fend for ourselves. Second, we were always told never to complain. And third, we had been warned not to gossip.

This time, though, I just had to talk to Mom. "This teacher dresses in khaki shirts and the pants of a man. Her voice is low. She has no chest and takes our towels when we go into the shower. Don't you find that a bit strange? Everyone in my class is afraid of her. I think she must be some kind of a pervert."

"Judi, Heloise didn't always look like that."

"What are you talking about?"

Boy, did Mom squirm. She had to define hysterectomy for me, and explain what happens if a person doesn't take the hormones they're supposed to. *Wow*, I thought, *this is much more interesting than Sheryl's slang words about dating.*

My talk with Mom helped me understand Heloise's condition, but it still didn't make me like her. Nor did it make sense that we had to put on gym uniforms, exercise a little, and take a shower all in fifty-five minutes.

It was because of the gym class that I realized that I was one of the few girls wearing a camisole—the top half of a slip—and that maybe I should buy a bra. Usually, I shopped by myself for clothes at one of two stores in town and charged it to our family account. But selecting a bra sounded very complicated, so I decided to ask Mom for assistance.

We hardly ever went clothes shopping together. She raised us to be independent at a very young age, and I had learned how to shop the hard way. When I was eight years old and was shopping for a pair of shoes, the clerk talked me into boy's oxfords—and I'm still mad at him. (Remember, I already told you this, Chief?)

Anyway, one afternoon, when Mom was ready to buy groceries at Piggly Wiggly, I asked, "Can I come along? Maybe we could run across the street to Penny's first, and you could help me buy a bra."

"Let's get going then," Mom replied nonchalantly.

Edna, a Penney's clerk and family friend, cheerfully greeted us. "What's the special occasion?"

"Judi wants a brassiere. I guess all the girls at school are wearing them."

Edna walked us over to the bras, which happened to be near the front of the store. Anyone who walked through the door could see us looking at the lingerie. I was petrified. What if someone walked in and saw me?

Mother didn't seem to mind. As Edna and she were discussing the new fall Bible School program, and I was watching the door, Mom grabbed a bra and pulled it around my midriff right over my T-shirt. My face turned red as I quickly pulled the bra away. "Mother, I can't believe you did that."

"Don't be silly. There's nobody in the store."

Then she handed it to Edna and said, "We'll take it."

As we shopped for groceries, I kept muttering to myself— repeatedly and loudly enough so Mother could hear—"If I find out that someone saw me, I'll die."

"Oh, Judi," Mom replied. "I'm sorry. I guess that at my age, I forget what it was like being a teenager."

Shocked by her admission, I quit complaining. And when she bought a half-gallon of my favorite ice cream, I almost forgave her.

Later that evening, I came downstairs wearing the new bra under a blouse. Walking into the kitchen, I pointed to my chest. "Look, Mom. My classmates will think I have a smashed newspaper under my shirt."

Sheryl, hearing my statement, quit studying and joined us. "Holy cow, what size did you buy? It's huge."

I related the disastrous shopping incident at Penny's.

My sister was very sympathetic. "Hey, why don't we go to Roswell's Department Store this Saturday? The lingerie department is in the back of the store, and nobody will see you."

Selecting a bra didn't end up being as complicated as I had thought. At Roswell's, Sheryl chose a bunch of styles and sizes and handed them to me. "Go into the dressing room and try these on. I'll watch so nobody opens the curtain."

Afterward, we went to the drug store and had chocolate Cokes. I was so grateful for Sheryl's help that I didn't argue with her about anything. We just sat and talked. "You know," she told me, "I saw a picture of Heloise in Margaret's mother's yearbook. Trader used to look like a woman. Maybe I should put a note in her mailbox and say, 'Shape up. Stuff your bra with stockings or socks and dress like a lady.'"

We started to laugh together, hysterically.

Wow, I thought, *life really is changing. Maybe being in high school with my sister won't be so bad, after all.*

FORTY-THREE

THE CATASTROPHE

During my first year in high school, I never learned to appreciate home economics or gym, but otherwise, I loved my seventh-grade classes. A real bonus was the extracurricular activities.

After school on Tuesdays and Thursdays, I went to junior band practice. I was pretty good on the trombone and was given the last chair on the second part. I was flattered, knowing that the band was made up of seventh, eighth and ninth graders, making me one of the youngest members. The band director, Nick Olsson, was very somber—kinda grouchy, actually—but he was good at his job. Or so my brother said.

English was my favorite subject. Miss Abramson, the teacher, gave us extra points for the books we read (I read a lot of books) and for joining her speech club (which I had to join since it was a family tradition). When Miss Abramson suggested I try out for the annual speech contest held every February in Parker Falls, she assigned me the poem "Casey at the Bat." The club members helped me with the diction as I rehearsed the words: "The outlook wasn't brilliant for the Mudville nine that day, the score was four to two with one inning more to play…"

My brother coached me when he was home from college for the holidays. And my mother, a singer and speaker for many years, threw in her suggestions as well. "Lift your head," she said. "Speak loudly and exaggerate your sounds. And please look at the audience."

To memorize the poem, I recited it out loud as I performed my daily activities. My older sister Sheryl would scream, "You're driving me crazy," and then started singing "Bringing in the Sheaves" at the top of her lungs to cover up my reciting. But I persevered.

To begin, there was a local competition in February, which meant all the students of our high school were judged before they went to the county level, and the finalists would go to the state. I was confident that I would go all the way to the top. After all, I had practiced, and I was good, and that's what it was all about.

But my wishes were not granted. I was the youngest to try out, but since there were no handicaps given for age differences, I placed fifth out of six. Miss Abramson gave me A+ in English, but I was still devastated.

Nobody in my family gave me any sympathy. I think they were relieved that I struck out. Feeling sorry for myself, I thought, *Well, I'll fix them. I'll practice my trombone all the time, and they'll beg me to do more with speech club.*

Unfortunately, no one complained or covered their ears, so I practiced even more. Would you believe I became a good trombonist? I guess the joke was on me. I don't know if you remember, Chief, that all of us had been given piano lessons starting at the age of five, and we were strongly encouraged to take up a band instrument in the last years of grade school even though we were not allowed to stop taking piano. We were also strongly encouraged to use our voices in song. Since our mother was the choir director at church, we went to every choir practice and sang our part. We all had some kind of talent. I've always wondered if Mother mystically altered our brains when she sang us to sleep as babies because none of us ever declared musical mutiny.

The sound from my trombone became so much better that one day Mom asked me to play a solo at the Sunday evening church service. Nick, the band director, who could hear pitch like a fly senses movement, noticed my progress and announced one day at rehearsal, "Judi, move up to first chair on the second part." So, I began moving up the line until I was the first chair on the first part. The other trombonists called me "teacher's pet," even though they knew I practiced harder and played better than they did.

Every spring, our band had a concert on the same evening as the senior band. This was a fundraiser and a very special occasion because it was held in the large auditorium. It seemed that everyone in Parker Falls knew somebody who played an instrument, and the community showed up in droves. It was inexpensive entertainment with cheap seats in the balcony. The main floor was reserved for high-priced ticket holders who sat at tables. Refreshments and sweets were served during intermission by the band mothers who donated their time and food so all money could be used for new band equipment. At the front of the auditorium, the band was elevated above the main floor audience using special bleachers.

The junior band played for the first half, the senior band the second half. During intermission, everyone drank coffee and ate sweets as they took a break from the music. The band director always stepped up to the mic and said a few words. Mother worked in the kitchen, and Dad sat in the balcony. This year, since I would be in the band, Susie brought her friend Nora along.

The day before the concert, we had a dress rehearsal in the auditorium. I sat on the top tier on the very end, facing the audience. I told Sue and Dad to make sure they sat in the balcony on my side of the auditorium so they could see me well.

The night arrived, and Sheryl and I dressed in our respective outfits. The juniors wore dark skirts or pants and white tops. The seniors wore their red and gray marching uniforms. Sheryl and I left early since we were part of the program. Mom drove us since she was responsible for cleaning silver and cutting up the cakes and pies.

I shined up my trombone and pressed my navy skirt. My hair had finally grown long enough, and I wore it in a ponytail pulled tightly to the back of my head. I felt "spiffy," as Dad would say, and ready to perform.

The last number of our program was a Sousa march. Mr. Olsson had a brainstorm that if auditorium lights were turned off and there were only lights on our music stands and his baton, it would be a nice optical effect. Since I did not want to take a chance of losing my place, I memorized my part.

Nick primed us before the concert. "Keep your eyes on me. I don't want anyone making an entrance at the wrong time."

During the first two numbers, there were some fuzzy-burpy horn entrances, a clarinet made a terrible squeak, and somebody in the audience had a coughing fit. Our director seemed oblivious. My fellow band members couldn't believe how serious he was and wondered just how Nick managed to find such a pretty wife who always smiled. Mrs. Olsson wore her long blond hair in braids that were wound into buns over her ears. She looked like a Swedish version of Heidi. Maybe because she was so beautiful, her husband was worried that she would run away. Anyway, he surely didn't seem to have a sense of humor.

Finally, it was time for the last number. Before the lights went out, I looked to the balcony and smiled at Dad and Susie. My sister waved. I felt proud and confident. Then the band members turned on their lights and the overhead auditorium lights switched off. Suddenly, it was dark.

We all sat up in our chairs and looked at Mr. Olsson's illuminated baton. He tapped his baton on the stand, lifted his arms, and we began the Sousa number. It was difficult to see the lighted baton because the girl in front of me had teased and sprayed her hair.

I crouched forward on my feet, lifting my behind and grabbing the seat of the chair to adjust its location so that I could see Nick better.

Unknowingly, I pushed the rear left leg of the chair over the edge of the platform. When I sat back down, I flew off the back of the bleachers into outer space. My hands relinquished the trombone to the gods as my chair and I hit the floor.

Rolling over onto my stomach, I sat back on my haunches. Dumbfounded, I looked out at the audience. It was dark, so I couldn't see a thing.

Maybe nobody noticed—that march by Sousa is so loud, I thought.

I stood up and retrieved the two pieces of my trombone (their size and brassiness had cast visible shadows), then reassembled them and walked over to the bleachers. I put my instrument onto the platform and opened the collapsed metal chair. Standing on the floor behind the bleachers, I reached up and poked the guy who sat in the seat next to me. "Take my chair," I whispered as I lifted it up to him.

Then, hoisting myself up onto the bleachers, I rolled from my stomach onto my feet, grabbed my trombone and joined in for the last measures of the piece.

It's a good thing I know this by heart, I thought.

The applause was great. Nick turned around and bowed.

"Nice going," the guy next to me said to me.

The band filed out. Everyone burst into gales of laughter. Comments floated around my head, as I tried to hold it high. When I put my trombone away, I noticed its bell was no longer round but seriously flattened. "What a disaster," I muttered, "and my career hasn't even started."

The junior band filed into the balcony to hear the rest of the concert. I listened to the senior band, looking so smart in their uniforms. None of them fell off the bleachers. I hoped that my sister didn't screw up on her oboe playing because I knew she'd hold me responsible if she did.

When the audience was applauding the evening's last number, I sneaked out of the balcony and left the auditorium. Susie, Nora and Dad found me sitting in the car. The girls immediately burst out laughing. "That was the funniest thing I've ever seen," Susie said. "Nora and I were watching when all of a sudden over you went."

"Did you see my trombone hit the floor? The bell's a mess!" I replied, not seeing any humor in the situation.

Dad leaned over the back seat, eyes twinkling. He bit his lip to hold back his laughter. "Don't worry, Judi. My friend Nordie at the music store can fix it. Come on, I'll take you for ice cream."

We all went to Gandrudt's Dairy. They made their own ice cream, and one of Mrs. Gandrudt's creations, a peanut butter whirl-and-whip—remember their specialty, Chief?—brought folks in from miles around.

We all chose peanut butter cones and then sat in old school chairs with wooden backs and arms that were lined up against the wall. After eating and hearing my sister repeat the story of me flying over the edge, I joined in the laughter.

"I didn't think anyone noticed me—it was so dark."

Even Dad admitted it was pretty funny. His friend Nordie attempted to fix my trombone, but it was never the same.

Neither was I.

FORTY-FOUR

BAD NEWS

My career as a professional trombone player was off to a very bad start. How could I make such a mess of things? The bell of my trombone was dented, along with my ego. Worse yet, Susie kept repeating the story, which became ever more embellished.

"The crash of your chair hitting the floor was so loud," she would say, "Grandpa probably turned in his grave. Nora and I burst out laughing. You got up off the floor and tiptoed around to find the pieces of your trombone. You were so funny! You acted like nobody could see you. We watched as you put your trombone up, your chair up, and then belly-flopped yourself up too. I laughed so hard I almost wet my pants. Then you sat down and finished the piece with the band like nothing happened." When she finished, Susie would laugh all over again.

I had to admit that the more she told it, the funnier it sounded. Eventually, I began to laugh with her. Sheryl, however, was very upset with me. "Mr. Olsson says I can go to St. Olaf on an oboe scholarship. If your antics screw it up, I don't know what I'll do."

"You have to go to the college to try out," I reminded her. "I doubt my fame has spread that far. Of course, I could come along, and we could play a duet."

"You're such an idiot," Sheryl replied.

"Girls, can't you be kind to one another?" said Mother.

My falling off the bleachers was like one raindrop compared to the storm that followed.

One evening at supper, Dad put down his coffee cup, cleared his throat and said, "I have an announcement to make."

Immediately there was quiet. Our Father NEVER made an announcement, so we knew something major was up. He looked at us with a very serious expression. "Mother and I have decided that we're moving to the Twin Cities. I have an opportunity to work for Remington Rand, and I've sold my share of the car business to Red. We'll move in the fall, in time for school."

My sisters and I were in shock. We knew that Mom and Dad made all the big decisions for us, and we got to make the little ones for ourselves. But this was too unbelievable for words. I felt like a little Indian who had been ambushed on his own reservation.

Sheryl turned to Dad, "What about my scholarship to St. Olaf? Can I stay with my friend Margaret and finish high school?"

"No," answered Mother. "You're coming with us."

My eyes turned watery as I spoke to Dad. "Can't you find another job here? I've lived here forever."

"We're only moving a hundred miles away. We'll keep our lake cabin. Don't worry, we'll be back to visit."

Mother spoke up. "Missionaries go to Africa, and they adjust, so I'm sure you'll do just fine too."

I knew better than to smart back. The discussion was over. I left the table and headed out the door for my bicycle. Susie followed saying, "Can I come?"

She sat on the carrier over the back fender, and we took off. I pedaled up and down the street before deciding to take a right turn and head away from home. "Where are we going?" Susie asked.

"To the Dairy Queen on Litchfield Avenue."

"That's pretty far away."

"If you want to come with, then be quiet."

Susie clung to me as we rode. We passed the cemetery, then my Great Uncle Emil's house, and finally arrived at our destination. We bought vanilla and chocolate swirls and sat by the picnic table. I was feeling very sorry for myself and sorry that I'd snapped at my sister. My vision was fuzzy, and I felt the tears sitting on the edges of my eyes, ready to drip down.

Susie turned to me as she was licking her cone. "Do you think we'll be able to find some friends?"

"It's such a big city—it sounds horrible! Everybody knows us here. I just can't imagine living anywhere else."

Susie tried to cheer me up. "Remember, there's a zoo, and a place with rides that we visited with Aunt Dorothy. Maybe we'll live around there."

I felt numb and didn't even reply. I couldn't believe we were moving! The school year was ending, and so was my life at Parker Falls. I was already looking forward to the next year of high school when I would no longer be the youngest. What a bad deal!

I wrote Don at college, but he wasn't upset over the news. "Good, I can stay at home, go to the University of Minnesota and save on room and board."

So much for his help, I thought.

Sheryl immediately accepted her fate and found another part-time job to save for college. "I'll need more money now that I've lost my oboe scholarship," she complained.

It wasn't easy telling my friends "I'm moving away, but I'll come back to visit."

Each time I said it, the lump in my throat grew like bread dough on a radiator. Oh, I got some sympathy, but not enough to feel the least bit better.

It was coincidental that I began stopping at Es's on the way home from school. I hadn't seen much of her recently, but it seemed appropriate to visit her now. As she painted at her easel, I knew she'd give me just what I needed—endless glasses of milk and sweet vanilla cream cookies—plus her undivided attention.

"How old is your canary anyway?" I asked as I looked out the window. The bird was singing and spitting seeds onto the table.

"I don't know," she said. "I think I got her when you were little and used to ride your tricycle to see me."

"I guess if I'm thirteen, so she would be nine," I said. "See, that's just what I'm talking about. I won't be able to come over anymore. When I was a kid, your house was my favorite place. It was extra special when Chief White Feather was visiting."

Suddenly, I felt as if my little-girl days were gone forever. I used to live in this kitchen, watching Es paint her mystical paintings. Angels and cherubs with halos and trumpets came to life on her ceilings and walls. Plus, we'd had so many good discussions.

My thoughts were interrupted by Es as she continued to paint. "Don't worry, Judi. You've read so many books about pioneers, now you get to be one. I'm sure you'll come back to Parker Falls often with your grandparents and cousins here."

"I guess you're right," I answered. "There's no other choice but to go with my family, but it sounds awful."

My friends tried to make me feel better. At school the next week, when the gym teacher asked for volunteers to be on the girls traveling softball team, Tina asked me to sign up with her. Tina had heard that there were lots of cute guys in the surrounding towns, and this would give her a chance to check them out. "At least you'd be doing something so you won't mope so much," she added.

Dad bought me a glove to encourage my new interest in softball, and I started practicing with the boys across the street. They really didn't want to include a girl in their games, but when they were desperate, I got to play.

I gained confidence on the ball field. Our traveling girls team placed third out of twelve in the junior varsity league consisting of seventh and eighth-graders. I knew that next year the team would probably be champs and I wouldn't be there.

Tina's wish came true. She met a cute guy in Raymond, and they began to write letters. I benefited from joining the team too. My throwing arm became much stronger, and when I played outfield, I could toss the ball most of the way to the catcher. In fact, the boys at the park were so impressed with my improvement they allowed me to play second base.

"It's mine," I yelled as Randy hit a fly ball. I caught it right in the nose. It hurt so much I thought I was going to die. Somehow, I finished the game. Under no circumstance would I leave my position at second base.

Mom jumped when she saw me at home. "What happened to you?"

Even though I put ice on it, my nose remained huge and blue. When we visited Dr. Hodap, he gently wiggled it around and said, "You'll be okay. Stay with the ice if it makes you feel better."

Sheryl was furious when she saw my appearance. "We're getting our last family photo taken for the church booklet. You're a mess—a real embarrassment!"

"Don't worry about it," I shot back. "I'll stand with the Stenburg family. They always liked me. Besides, they have ten kids and won't know the difference."

"You're such a moron," Sheryl said.

"Girls, will you cut it out? I can't stand your bickering," Mom said. "Let's go get our photo taken and get it over with."

That Wednesday, we all dressed up and went down to church to get our family picture taken. I had a brainstorm and decided to cup my hand over my nose like I was sneezing.

Sheryl groaned when she saw the picture. "Great pose. It looks like you're blowing your nose in your hand."

"Look on the bright side," I said. "We'll be in different schools next year, and I bet a dollar you'll miss me because I make you look so good."

FORTY-FIVE

HARD LABOR

My black-and-blue nose took forever to return to normal. The boys at the park nicknamed me Bruiser and allowed me to keep my position on second base. Each time a batter came up, I crossed my fingers and wished, "Please don't hit to me."

Finally, the day came when a fly ball went over the pitcher's head. "Take it, Bruiser!" an outfielder yelled.

I ran forward and held up my glove. My queasy insides whispered, "Concentrate, you can do it."

"Out!" I screamed, as I caught the ball in my mitt.

Grinning, I ran in to hit. The guys didn't tease me half as much as my sister did. Sheryl was relentless in her harassment. "Are you sure you're not adopted?" she'd ask. "It's hard to believe that a sister of MINE could fall off the bleachers and get hit in the nose in a matter of weeks."

"I think YOU'RE adopted," I said. "I'm smart AND athletic. You're so clumsy that you couldn't catch a ball or fall off bleachers without killing yourself."

"Girls, girls," Mother interrupted. "If you don't quit arguing, I'm going to make you clean every window of this house. I'll put you on opposite sides of the same window, and you'll work together until all the windows are spotless."

That quieted us down. We hated to clean. It wasn't worth smarting off and having to do all that work. Both of us knew that when Mom said something, she meant business.

Turning to my sister, I smiled and sarcastically said, "Let's hug and make up."

"Get away from me," Sheryl said, running up the stairs.

I left and went to the park, where I found Susie climbing the steps on the big slide. Her friend Nora was at the bottom, laughing.

Susie put some waxed paper under her butt and shot down the slide. She barely caught herself. I was impressed that she didn't hit the ground.

"Can I take a turn?" I asked.

At the top, I sat on Nora's waxed paper. "Here goes!" I yelled. I flew down fast, and my feet miraculously caught my fall. "Thanks. I'm going over to Es's. See ya later." Suddenly, I was feeling too old for that kind of activity.

I found Es painting at her easel. It seemed like she was expecting me. I noticed a new package of vanilla cream cookies and a shoebox on the table. "What're you up to?" I asked.

Es lifted her head from her palette. "I looked through some old photographs and found a couple I want you to have. Open the box."

"Wow," I said, "is that the Chief when he was young? He's sure handsome."

"Yes, he is. That was taken in our studio."

"And where did this come from?" I asked, holding up a hand-colored picture of an angel with rosy cheeks, golden hair, and bright blue eyes riding a reindeer. The angel and the reindeer both looked out at me with trusting expressions.

"That's a photo of a painting I did many years ago," Es explained. "It's called 'Guardian Angel.' I thought maybe they could watch over you. Would you like that?"

"Yes." I ran over and gave her a hug. "Thank you."

Es squeezed me extra hard. "I just received a letter from the Chief," she said. "All those years of traveling and singing must have caught up with him. He told me his heart is causing problems, and he's got to stay home."

To cheer her up, I repeated my favorite memory of the three of us. "I'll never forget when you became blood brother and sister by piercing each other's ears. I still have the photo. Remember how you set up the tripod and then took a picture of us, all in smiles, sitting on the sofa?"

We continued to reminisce about those times, Chief. It seemed like ages ago since you had come to visit, yet the time had passed like clouds in the wind. And here I was talking to Es as a teenager.

Our conversation was interrupted by a call from Mom. "Is Judi there? We're having supper early. I've got choir practice tonight. Please send her home."

When I walked into our kitchen, Sheryl was setting the table. "I found you a job."

"What are you talking about?" I asked.

"Margaret and I have jobs detasseling corn and picking strawberries for Mr. Severson. When we signed up at the town hall, I noticed that Gustafson's needed one more kid to pick mustard from his bean fields. Why don't you try it? You'll be close to the ground and shouldn't hurt yourself." She laughed at her own joke, then continued. "He'll pay fifty cents an hour and give you lunch."

The following morning, I rode down to read the notice on the bulletin board by the mayor's office. "Help needed for one or two weeks (depending on the weather). Six people age 13-16. Meet out in front at 8 a.m. and I'll take you to my farm and return you by 3 p.m. Water and lunch furnished. Wage 50 cents per hour. Pickers must furnish large brimmed hats and long-sleeved shirts. Leave phone numbers by name," signed Gus Gustafson.

I was the last one to sign up. It sounded like hard work to me, but I knew that I could live through two weeks of most anything. Plus, I could use the money.

There were only two days of freedom before my job started. Mom gave me an advance on my wages, and I went down to Woolworth's to look for a hat. All the teenage farm helpers must've been there before me as they were almost out. I found a clerk who said, "Just follow me. I have a honey of a hat."

I could tell by the tone of her voice that I was in trouble. She picked up a flat oval piece of woven straw and demonstrated it. "Just snap this end and tie it under your chin and look out Mr. Sun. Of course, that doesn't mean you won't get more freckles." Like my sister, she laughed at her own joke.

I paid the woman and went home with my purchase. When I checked the mirror, I looked really stupid! The huge brim stuck out a foot in front, and the back fit snuggly to my head like a baby's bonnet. My enthusiasm over my new opportunity was rapidly fading.

At eight the next morning, my five picking mates and I piled in the back of Gus's pick-up and rode out to his farm. The ground there was so dry that in order to pull the mustard plant out by the roots, I had to be on my knees. Within a few hours, the sun glared down from overhead, feeling like a hot iron skillet resting on my back. By noon, I had sweat so much I didn't even have to go to the bathroom—which was good since we had to use the bushes.

The ham sandwiches for lunch were skimpy. When we climbed in the back of the truck at two-thirty with only three one-dollar bills in our pocket, all of us agreed that the job was a rip-off and that the next year he'd have to ask for ten-year-olds in order to find someone who would think it was fun. We were sure going to put the word out.

That night I dreamed of wrestling humongous mustard plants and woke up exhausted, wondering how I could get out of my commitment. Lucky for me, when I looked outside, it was pouring.

After a day of recovery, only four of us showed up to fulfill our obligations. It took us eight days to clean the mustard out of Gus's bean field. One sixteen-year-old boy admitted that after the grueling job of picking mustard, he was no longer interested in joining the army.

I learned an important lesson: "To think first before signing up."

The last day in the field, I had to "go" before we left Mr. Gustafson's, so I sneaked over to the neighbor's woods to take a pee. As I was walking back to the field, I noticed some pretty red branches loaded with red leaves and yellow berries. I picked a bouquet for Mom. It seemed a perfect way to show her how much I appreciated the fact she had told me to forget about the money I owed her for the hat. I think she felt sorry that I was working so hard.

I climbed into the back of the pick-up and sat down. Holding the bouquet in my lap, I joined in the chatter on the ride back to Parker Falls. We were all relieved to be through with our horrendous job.

At city hall, I jumped on my bike and rode down the street with my gift for Mom. She said it was beautiful and put the branches in water.

The next morning, I woke up scratching. A rash had broken out all over my hands and arms. It felt like a million mosquitoes had bitten me. Mother took me to Dr. Hodap, who quickly made the diagnosis. Handing me a jar of salve, he said, "Judi, I guess you didn't know that there are two kinds of sumac, one with green and one with red branches. The one with red branches is poisonous, causing irritation to the skin. Don't worry, it will go away. Put this salve on every morning and evening until the jar is empty. And keep your hands out of water for two weeks."

I bought rubber gloves with some of my mustard money so I could do my share of the dishes. After all, it wasn't Sheryl's fault that my hands were all blistered. I knew if she did all the dishes for two weeks, I'd owe her for the rest of my life!

As I clumsily washed the dishes in my oversized gloves, I was hit with a comforting thought, "I bet when we move to the Twin Cities, there won't be ANY sumac for miles around."

FORTY-SIX

ROBIN'S ISLAND

My world was upside down. How could we be moving from Parker Falls?

"Come on, Judi," Mother said. "It'll be just fine. South Minneapolis is like a small town, and you'll love our new house. I bet you didn't know that your Dad lived in the very same neighborhood we're moving to when he went to the Academy. And it's just one street away from where we lived when you were a baby."

"But Mom, I was only three months old when we left. I wanna stay here."

It was no use. Nobody would give me any sympathy. Even Sheryl became enthusiastic about the move. She had been accepted in the private school that my father had attended. When she sent in her application and mentioned that she was an oboe player, the director had called long distance to personally welcome her to the band and orchestra. Sheryl strutted around, saying, "Maybe I'll get an oboe scholarship to St. Olaf after all."

Don was pleased because he could finish his college at the University of Minnesota, stay at home and get free room and board. Plus, Dad was giving him a car. Why wouldn't he be happy?

Everyone was excited but me. Mother had found a job so they could buy a nice house (instead of the handyman special that Dad wanted). And Susie's grade school was just three blocks down our street. My junior high was eleven blocks away. How could I not feel sorry for myself?

I didn't care about a new house—I enjoyed the one we already had across from the park with its double lot and swing in the yard. Granted, the place was a hundred years old with sloping linoleum floors and cold drafts in the winter, but I was used to it and didn't want change. Maybe I would've felt better if I had been old enough to go to the Academy with Sheryl, but her school started with the ninth grade, and I'd be starting the eighth.

"Can't I live here with Tina or Rachel for one year until I'm old enough to go to the Academy?" I pleaded. "My new school is so big nobody will ever know who I am. Besides, I have to walk so far just to get there. It's just not fair."

Mother tried to cheer me up by telling stories about people who had been separated from their families in the war. She emphasized how fortunate we were to all be together. Her favorite argument was that this move wasn't far away. What if we were going to Africa to the mission-field?

Realizing that my idea of staying behind in Parker Falls was not going to happen, and Mom really didn't understand my feelings, I rode my bike to the library. I felt sad and abandoned just thinking about leaving my town and figured maybe I could find a few books about orphans that would comfort me.

When I walked in the door, Mrs. Peterson, the librarian, welcomed me with sympathetic eyes. I was one of her favorite customers, and she knew exactly how I felt about leaving Parker Falls. She suggested *Anne of Green Gables*, *Tom Sawyer*, *Tarzan of the Apes*, *Annie Oakley of the Frontier*, and *Kim*.

I had read the first four, but *Kim* by Rudyard Kipling was a new discovery. Kim became my inspiration and hero. I reread the story three times and concluded that if Kim could survive by his wit and travel across the country without family or friends, then I could too.

When I returned my book, Mrs. Peterson rose to greet me. "Judi, I was hoping you would come in today. My sister just called and wondered if I knew anyone to help her with the two-week kindergarten camp at Robin's Island. Would you like the job? It doesn't pay anything, but you'd have fun. Ask your Mother, and then call Mrs. Sorenson and give her an answer. Here's the phone number." She wrote the number on a piece of paper.

After inquiring about the details, I decided that I was interested. It would give me a chance to pretend I was Rudyard Kipling's Kim. Mother encouraged me to take the job. I think she was relieved that I'd found something else to do other than pester her.

That first morning, it was hard to get up so early. Mrs. Sorenson wanted me there at eight-thirty for instructions. I hoped that I wouldn't get stuck with another helper that was a real dud, or it would be an awfully long two weeks. The kindergarten camp ran from ten o'clock to two-clock, which included lunch and a snack. I put a half-dozen of Mom's home-baked cookies in a brown lunch bag, just in case I needed additional nourishment. Then I quickly ate my Rice Krispies and peanut butter toast and ran out the door. I rode my bike at top speed through uptown and over the bridge toward Robin's Island, a park that had been created on a small island connected by a man-made road. As I charged up the road, I noticed a girl ahead of me on a bicycle. I didn't recognize her, but I figured she had to be a helper because both of us were too old to be going to the camp. "Hey, wait up," I yelled.

The girl stopped and got off her bike. "Oh, it's you."

"Hi, Martha," I said, grinning because it was somebody I knew. She was a year older and played the clarinet in the band. "I can't believe you got talked into working here."

Martha leaned her bike on a tree. "My sister, Mickey, is one of the teachers, so I didn't have a choice. What's your job here?

You gonna teach them how to play the trombone and fall out of a tree?" She laughed at her own joke, a behavior that was becoming tiresome.

"Nope, I came here because Mrs. Peterson, the librarian, said they needed me. Anyway, we're moving in a few weeks, and I've been driving my mother nuts."

As we walked toward the pavilion, Mickey yelled out, "Come on. I need to show you how to make a sit-upon. The campers will be arriving any minute."

I never got to pretend I was Kim because I was so busy helping. First, we had to tear up newspapers into one-inch strips and then weave them into cushions. It was a pretty bad design because the outside edges were fixed with masking tape that immediately got damp and fell off when we sat in the grass. I don't think the little kids were too impressed either because, on the second day after we roasted our marshmallows, we had a huge bonfire burning the sit-upons.

I admit it was nice to be a big kid instead of a little one.

For another project, Marsha and I used pocketknives to strip twigs of bark so the campers could print their name on the twig, paint the stick in clear nail polish, and glue a little gold pin on the back. It was supposed to be a name tag, but that didn't work very well because it was difficult to print legible letters on a twig.

The best parts of the day's events were lunch and the half-hour when we sang camp songs because those were the only times the kids sat still. They especially enjoyed when Martha's sister gave them a comb wrapped in wax paper so they could put their lips on the paper and hum, making a fuzzy sound like a kazoo.

On Thursday, Mickey brought over a few long cane poles. We all searched for worms so everybody could try fishing. A boy named Stanley actually caught a fish. He was so excited he ran into the water with the pole and got his tennis shoes wet. When we roasted our hot dogs at lunch, he put his shoes on a rock near the fire to dry. Unfortunately, he forgot about them, and when he went to put his shoes back on, he found them curled up, heel towards toe, like a clenched fist—the result of sitting too near the fire. The kid was upset. Martha and I thought it was funny, but I don't think his mom did because Stanley never returned.

Most of the campers were okay. Besides, it was fun to work and laugh with Martha. We became best of friends. After the first few mornings at Robin's Island, I began spending afternoons at her house. We just rode our bikes around and talked. She lived a half-block from the Dairy Queen, so if either of us had money, we'd buy ourselves a treat. It was nice to have a new confidante. I told her how sad I was to be moving and how I didn't want to leave our big old house and familiar neighborhood. Martha's dog, Ginger, had recently died, so she understood exactly how I felt.

I told Martha how Es had encouraged me to write to you, Chief, and how special you were to me. And I was telling the story of me witnessing you and Es becoming blood brother and sister when suddenly Martha interrupted.

"Hey," she said. "Why don't we become blood sisters too? We'll write letters, share secrets and be friends until we're really old."

We each heated a sewing needle in the flame of a candle, poked our fingers with it and squeezed a drop of blood onto a piece of paper that said, "Sisters forever, enemies never." After tearing the paper in half, we taped it to the back of a charm, tied on a string and wore it like a locket.

Even though Martha was from another church, Mom and Dad were okay with my new friendship, maybe because my parents were distracted. Dad was already working in the Twin Cities, and Mom was trying to get everything ready to move while trying to be patient with me. She repeatedly gave the same response to my complaining. "Judi, you will have to get used to the idea. You are moving with the family, whether you want to or not. I need your help with this, not your hindrance."

At supper one day, she gave Sheryl and me an assignment. "Go down to Penny's and choose some fabric." Then she turned to Sheryl and said, "Since you're such a good seamstress, you can make some new skirts for Judi before she starts school."

My sister wasn't interested because she was frantically sewing things for her debut at the Academy. "Can't you just buy her a few things? I'm trying to get my own wardrobe together."

Mother, exasperated with our bad attitudes, tried to persuade us. "If you girls cooperate and get the material picked out and sewn, we'll send you to Camp Jim with the church league."

Both of us immediately agreed. Camp Jim was a special place that the Lutheran churches (like ours) within a hundred-mile radius of Parker Falls (which included about six towns) rented once a year with the goal of getting to know more teenagers. I think it was really for the junior-senior girls to meet a larger selection of boys so they wouldn't marry into other denominations.

Agreeing to Mom's request didn't make the trip to Penny's any less of a nightmare. We didn't shop well together—the only successful time was when Sheryl took me to buy a bra. Anyway, when I selected blue corduroy, my sister said she would only sew on gray. When I chose a plaid, she disagreed and thought stripes would be better. Her response was always, "I've got the permission to charge your clothes to the family account. If you don't like my choices, you can go bare-naked."

When we arrived home fiercely arguing with one another, Mom ignored our bickering and told Sheryl to start sewing.

"Come on," Sheryl grumbled. "Let me get your waist size." She took the tape measure and yanked it around my middle. "I can't believe that you get to go to Camp Jim. Thirteen years old is way too young for this group. You'll probably stub your toe or do something else stupid."

"Tough beanie-weenies, (this was a new expression that I learned from my friend Martha), I'm coming, and you'd better quit being so rough on me or I'll put cornflakes in your bed."

Just the thought of doing that made me smile. I was really looking forward to the experience of Camp Jim.

I wished I felt the same way about moving.

FORTY-SEVEN

THE ENGLISH BOY

Sheryl sat in the front seat, and I sat in the back with our luggage, sweating in the muggy August heat but not daring to complain. I was going to Camp Jim. As we rode uptown, Mother gave us instructions as usual. "Sheryl, I want you to keep your eyes on your sister. I know she's thirteen, but make sure she doesn't get lost in the woods or do something foolish."

"Right, Mom. Why didn't you buy her a compass? Judi's old enough to take care of herself. Maybe I'll luck out, and she'll get eaten by a bear."

Demonstrating my thirteen-year-old maturity, I responded, "Maybe Paul Bunyan will come by with his ox and step on your head."

"I don't know what I'm going to do with you," Mom said. "You'd better start getting along because you're going to be sharing a room in our new house."

Sheryl looked over her shoulder at me. "I think I'll get a cot and sleep in the basement."

"Good idea," I answered as the car slowed to a stop in front of the church.

We jumped out and grabbed our suitcases.

"Bye, Mom," I said, kissing her cheek through the open window. "I already know it'll be fun."

There was quite an assortment of kids and baggage waiting to leave for Camp Jim. It was a miracle when all twenty-five people plus their suitcases fit into seven cars, most of which were driven by teenagers. Only the lead and rear cars were driven by counselors. I was in a car with my friend, Dianna. We were going to bunk together for the weekend.

The camp was three hours away in northern Minnesota and involved a drive through Indian country and near the spring-fed waters of the Mississippi. I was excited since I'd never been that far north before.

As the road wound through the countryside, the trees became bigger and closer together, the houses fewer and smaller. As we sped along, I felt as if civilization was vanishing in our wake.

"Look over there at the cemetery," our driver said, noting a break in the trees and slowing down. "See those wooden structures over the graves? They're built so an Indian's spirit can come out and look around."

I studied the constructions over the graves. They were A-shaped, not cone-shaped like tepees. *I wish the Chief were here to tell me about this*, I thought, as we continued to drive through endless acres of uninhabited land. It felt like we'd never get there.

What a relief to finally see the sign for Camp Jim.

We stopped at the dining hall to get the number of our assigned cabin. The girls stayed on the east side of the hall and the boys on the west. We were told that our cabin each had four sets of bunks, two that were assigned to older girls and two for younger girls with the idea of having big sisters.

Dianna and I carried our suitcases over and found our new roommates unpacking their stuff. We got the bottom two bunks closest to the door. After introductions, my friend and I left to explore the campground.

"Wow," Dianna whispered. "Did you see the tight shirt and lipstick on that girl Sally? Do you think she's a slut?"

"Who cares?" I answered. "Do you want to check out the lake?"

The beach was beautiful. The opposing shoreline was sparsely populated with cottages. The rest was densely wooded in tall, dark trees. I could understand why Mom was worried about me getting lost in the woods and wondered if she had come to Camp Jim as a teenager.

Sitting on the sand was a sky-high, humongous water slide with a rope across the steps and a sign attached that said, "Only to be used with supervision of lifeguard."

"Wow, I can hardly wait to try this. Come on, Dianna. Let's go up and look around."

We crawled under the sign and climbed to the top, which was probably three times the height of the large slides found in our neighborhood park.

"Hey, look over there."

Turning away from the water and looking towards the woods, we saw a couple kissing. "Do we know them?" I whispered to Dianna.

"No, but don't forget it's a blond with a blue blouse and some guy with a red and white striped T-shirt. Maybe we'll recognize them at supper."

"Yeah, we'll be the detectives of Camp Jim."

We watched as they continued to kiss. Dianna and I stood hypnotized and speechless as we watched their passion increase. I couldn't keep quiet when I saw them grabbing each other as if they were fighting to stand upright. "Look, they're panting."

Suddenly, we heard a loud voice. "Hey, what are you doing up there?" It was a guy we didn't know, an older teenager looking authoritative in a turned-down sailor hat and a whistle that hung from his neck.

"Get down, or you'll be doing K.P."

The couple heard the commotion and unglued themselves from each other. They looked rather frustrated—the blonde's hair was messed up, and the guy's shirt was partially out. They grabbed hands and fled into the woods.

I backed down the steps. Half-way down, I loudly whispered into Dianna's heels, "I wish we could follow that couple. By the way, what's K.P.?"

"Kitchen patrol," the guy answered, trying to look tough.

"What was so interesting up there?" he inquired.

"That's for us to know and you to find out," I answered as Dianna and I walked down the beach.

Our two younger roommates were coming toward us. They were from Cokato and reintroduced themselves as Anita and Joyce. We told them what we'd seen and that we were determined to identify the couple.

Dianna switched the subject and started to ask questions about Cokato High School. She'd always attended a country school that had just closed its doors. Dianna was overwhelmed by the thought of coming to Parker Falls with a hundred other students in her class when she was used to having a total of fifty kids ages six to fifteen in a one-room schoolhouse.

After hearing that there were only thirty in each grade, my friend teased that maybe she would move to Cokato and live with Anita. I told them I knew Cokato since I'd visited my Aunt Martha and Aunt Viola there—they were the matrons of a Cokato old people's home.

Dianna rolled her eyes at my not-so-interesting news. All four of us burst out laughing.

We chummed around until the bell rang for supper. The sound came from a three-foot brass bell suspended over the chapel roof that could be heard for miles around.

Anita wanted to go back to the cabin before dinner, so we picked up our sweaters and ambled over to the dining hall, a screened-in building attached to the kitchen. There were roll-down tarps inside in case it was raining or cold. The kids sitting in the hall were younger teenagers like us.

Because we were the last to sit down, we had no choice but to sit across from some boys. Catty-corner from me sat a ruddy-faced kid who was around fourteen or fifteen and had a strange accent. I'd never heard anyone talk like him. "Where's he from, anyway," I asked no one in particular. My voice apparently carried farther than I expected because the boy piped up, "I'm from England—my name is Brent."

Most of the girls giggled and acted self-conscious when he spoke, but the conversation proceeded. Someone asked Brent how he had arrived at Camp Jim.

"Well, you see, I applied through the American Field Service for the exchange program in the US. My dad's in the British Army and wanted me to see a piece of America. My parents and I have traveled around Europe a fair amount but never across the Atlantic. The A.F.S. didn't have any openings, so Dad wrote to a friend he'd kept in touch with from the War. It was great when Nat's dad said, 'Come on over and spend the school year with my boy.' So here I am in New London, Minnesota. When I saw the town, I was very surprised. I thought it would have a castle or something British. But there's nothing British about it but Queen Street. Nat's dad said that the town was named by a Norwegian to entice an English girl he'd met during the First World War to cross the ocean and marry him. I guess it didn't help because she never came."

All of us who were listening were intrigued by his storytelling and funny accent.

"Hey, Brent," I said, "what's it like where you live? Is your town big or little?"

"Oh, I come from the metropolis of Liverpool. Lots of things to do there, but neither me nor my friends have cars. But here in New London, Nat needs his car. That's how we find the girls. I enjoy his Ford convertible and really like the A&W Drive Ins, which don't exist in Liverpool."

"I have to move to a huge city," I said, "and I'm not looking forward to it. I like knowing most everybody I see."

"Oh, I suspect you'll get used to it," Brent answered sympathetically.

When we left the dining hall, Joyce poked me. "Look over there, a red and white striped shirt. Geeze Louise, it's our minister's son."

"That figures," Dianna answered. "There's the old saying, 'Preachers' kids have the initials P.K.' which stands for Preachers' Kids or Petters and Kissers."

I laughed along with our new friends. Maybe it was no coincidence the talk that evening was a reminder that our bodies were sacred, and we should not give in to longing or persuasion. We suddenly figured out the "big sister" thing. The counselors really put us with the older girls in hopes we would tattle about any of *their* shenanigans with the boys. But we weren't squealers—even if somebody did wear heavy lipstick and tight blouses or pet in the woods.

My favorite activities of the weekend were the water slide and the lake football game. The huge slide was one of the niftiest things I'd ever seen. Instead of the typical metal slide, there were two rails that fit the wheels of a toboggan that we had to carry up the ladder and place into the tracks. This was no minor feat but worth every struggling minute. After positioning the toboggan in the track, somebody gave us a push, and we would shoot at sixty miles per hour—or so it felt like—down the slide and then skim the surface of the lake until we started to sink. Then we had to swim back, pulling the toboggan behind us. It was hard work, but I repeated the magical experience until my arms and legs were like rubber. Once, when I came down the slide, a creepy boy stood at the bottom and threw a coffee can of water into my face. The lifeguard yelled at him and sent him off the beach to do K.P. I think the staff depended on the free help.

The last day, we divided up into teams and played a game called "football on the lake." Don't ask me why somebody named it that, but we played it with watermelons. Someone had donated three watermelons for the game.

We divided into four teams, and then a counselor blew a whistle. "Okay," he yelled, "listen up. This is similar to football but played on top of the water. The goalposts are the imaginary extensions from the pine tree down on the south end and the big elm tree on the north end. The teams will line up opposing each other at a center point, and one member of the team who has won the coin-flip will receive the watermelon, which he is to pass to his teammates and move toward the goal. The first team to cross their finish line wins. Then the next two teams will play, and there will be playoffs between the two winning teams. The only other differences between this game and football are that you play the game in chest-high water, and the watermelon is coated with Vaseline."

A groan went through the group, as well as lots of joking and talking.

The greased watermelon was given to the first teams. The coach blew his whistle, and the game began. The campers on shore laughed or hollered as the person carrying the watermelon either squeezed too hard, causing the slippery melon to shoot into the air, or it was pushed through the arms of the team member from behind. Either way made the game very difficult. One of the watermelons hit the water so hard it split. The biggest piece that crossed the finish line won.

I was one of the lucky members of the champion team. Our prize was the honor of eating the watermelon—which none of us did. But we did all pose for Brent, who wanted to document the event with a photograph.

"My friends back home will never believe this otherwise," he said. "I regret I don't have a movie camera to show them how the ridiculous game was played."

We all knelt on each other to form a pyramid. The watermelon sections lay in front of us on the sand. One boy held a piece of watermelon in his teeth.

I never saw the photo, but I remember that I smiled in the picture and felt a little bit better about leaving Parker Falls. I figured if Brent could leave his country and make new friends, maybe I could too.

The five carloads of teenagers arrived safely back at church. Sheryl found me standing by my suitcase in the front narthex. "Go into the office and phone Mom to pick us up."

It rang repeatedly. Finally, Mom answered, "Can't somebody else bring you home?" she begged. "I have my hands full."

Mr. Jacobs, one of the counselors, offered to take us.

Mom was carrying a wrapped casserole out to the car when we drove up. "Thanks, Lester," she said. "It's bedlam around here. Half our family has already moved to Minneapolis. Bob is working, and Don is going to the university. They came home for the weekend and want to leave within the hour. I'm running around packing up their food and ironing their clothes so they can get on the road."

Turning to us, she added, "How did you girls do? I'm glad you're home."

Susie came out of the house. "Come on. We need to go through the trash. Mom's been throwing away all our stuff."

It seemed that was becoming our family's motto: "Dispose of the old. On to the new."

During the next two weeks, Mom and Sheryl sorted, packed and labeled umpteen boxes. We had lived in the house forever, and every nook and cranny had to be cleaned. I spent more time checking the garbage than I did packing, just to make sure that none of my "good stuff" was tossed out. The rest of the time I spent riding around on my bike viewing my old stomping grounds for the last time.

Mother was irritated by my moaning. "Judi, don't feel so sorry for yourself. We'll come back often to see your cousins and grandma. I'm sure you'll get used to the new neighborhood. Don't forget that my dad came over from Sweden when he was seventeen, only four years older than you. And your Grandfather Nat sold his father's Swedish newspaper by hitching rides and staying with folks when he was fourteen."

"That's a long time ago, Mom. What's that got to do with me, anyway?"

It did get me thinking about Grandpa Oskar, though, and feeling sorry that he never went back to Sweden to visit his family. But I also felt sorry for myself, and even sorrier that Grandpa was dead and unable to hear my woes.

I rode my bike around thinking and feeling great comfort in the similarity of Grandpa's and my dilemmas. I decided it might be a good idea to write Grandpa a letter and bury it by his tombstone. Of all the people I knew, Grandpa certainly would understand, even though he was lying silent in his grave.

I spent the next few days writing down my thoughts and finally decided that poetry was the easiest way to speak to Grandpa.

After copying the poem onto a piece of paper, I biked to the cemetery and tucked it next to his large granite stone. It made me feel a lot better. I spent so much time on it that I didn't even keep a copy because it was permanently carved into my memory.

On the way home, I stopped by Es's and recited the poem.

"It's good to know how you feel," she said. "But maybe now you should write to somebody who's alive. Why not send your poem to the Chief? At least he might answer you. We know he's under the weather, and it might be just what he needs. It just so happened I bought you some stationery and a journal to record your new adventures."

Es handed me a red leather diary with a little gold key attached and a box of stationery.

That night when Susie and I were putting on our nightgowns, I showed her my new diary. "Why don't you write something in it?" she suggested.

"Okay, how about this?"

Two young Swedish sisters getting ready for bed,
One has dark curly hair and the other one has red.

Susie laughed, and then we lay there talking about the big move. It just didn't seem possible that we would be leaving Parker Falls, but we knew that no matter how much we talked about it, neither one of us could do anything to stop the inevitable. Our few remaining days were disappearing as quickly as snowflakes in the desert.

FORTY-EIGHT

MURPHY-MEN ARRIVE

Sheryl's friends had a farewell cook-out at Swenson's on Green Lake. Susie's friends had ice cream and cookies during her last Sunday school class. I hadn't heard any rumors of a party for me or even seen anyone whispering or looking suspicious. I was very disappointed when Dianna asked me out to the farm for my last Sunday dinner in Parker Falls. I tried to be grateful for the invitation but didn't recover my good spirits until they served my favorite brown sugar cake for dessert.

Dianna insisted we help her mother with the dishes. "Come on," she said after we finished. "I'll show you the baby kittens in the barn."

When we came back into the house, Dianna's mom called from the living room. "Girls, come here for a minute. I want to show you something."

As we walked into the room, a half-dozen kids appeared yelling, "Surprise!" It seemed that Dianna's cousin Ronnie, who lived down the road, had asked everyone to meet at his house. While I was playing with the kittens, his father brought the group over in the back of his pick-up.

I felt so happy that I got choked up. One of the boys stopped my tears by saying, "You're such a goofball. Open your presents."

My gifts were a rabbit's foot, a pair of red MukLuks and the comic book version of *The Hunchback of Notre Dame*.

"Okay," Ronnie said, "enough of this. How about a game of volleyball?"

We played ball until we were exhausted and happy to stop for a bowl of brown sugar cake smothered in vanilla ice cream. I had seconds.

When I arrived back home, I made another entry in my diary: "It's Sunday after my farewell party. Only two more nights in our house. I'm very sad, not glad. I think I will follow Es's suggestion and start writing to the Chief after we get settled."

Monday, Mom and Sheryl were still not finished packing. When we came into the kitchen for supper, I overheard Mom talking on the phone. I figured it must be Murphy, the mover they had hired.

"Can you take Sheryl and Judi with you in the truck? They have to start school on Wednesday, and I still need to clean the house. The Iversons have rented the place and want the keys right away."

Sheryl was outraged. "I can't believe you asked *him*. Now I have to ride with that ugly son of his. I hope we don't see any of my friends. I'll die if I'm seen with him."

"Sheryl, we're moving away, so who cares?" I asked.

"Why don't you go stick your head in the toilet," my sister replied.

I guess we were all edgy and weren't feeling much better the next morning when a big Murphy's Movers truck showed up.

Susie and I watched the men load. Next to me was my small blue suitcase containing some special things—a joke book, a spool of fishing line from Grandpa Oscar, the rabbit's foot and comic book, my diary from Es (the picture of the three of us tucked between the pages), my trombone mouthpiece, a notebook and pencils for

school, plus some Jujy Fruits and Milk Duds in case I got hungry. I
guess my collection was a life jacket for stormy seas.

As Mr. Murphy was closing the rear doors, he said, "Okay,
we're ready to roll."

Solemnly, I climbed up into the front seat. "Bye," I whispered.
My heart ached, and I felt as empty as the old house.

The cab of the truck was crowded. Cliff sat next to his dad. I
was squeezed between Sheryl and Cliff with the blue suitcase under
my legs. The pressure of it gave me comfort. I crossed my arms and
placed them on the dashboard, resting my chin on my wrists.

Blocking out the awkward conversation of Cliff and Sheryl,
I looked straight ahead through the window. *We were leaving my
town*!

I thought of all my bicycle rides, my friends. How was I going
to survive? My eyes swelled up with tears. I was afraid of breaking
down and sobbing my guts out, so I started to count the houses on
the street—one, two, three, four, five, six… But it didn't help me
feel any better.

Then I silently recited the poem I had written for Grandpa.

I know Grandpa this poem is kinda late
since you died and left me when I was eight.

But today, I'm especially lonesome for you
'cause I know long ago you felt like me too.

You must've been sad when you left Sweden's shore
and came to this country to look for more.

Your cousins welcomed and took you right in
but you wondered if you'd ever see Home again.

Grandpa, you worked and fished and loved this land
pleased that you had found a future, you were glad.

But I'm only thirteen years old and don't want to move
I wish we could go fishing—it might change my mood.

Please smile down from above and help me to be brave
Stop my tears. Make me cheerful again... and always.

THE END

EPILOGUE

Over the years, many friends and family members have read the letters and stories and encouraged me to publish them. After organizing the correspondence into a book, I sent a rough draft to many of the people represented in these pages. Most approved. Some gave suggestions. Others requested I used fictitious names to protect their identity. However, the final impetus to publish was the death of my lifetime friend, sister Sue.

My hope is that as you will read *Letters to the Chief*, the pages come alive and you enjoy the experience of my small town life.

ACKNOWLEDGEMENTS

My family of friends needs to be thanked for their support. Mother, my most avid fan, read the chapters in their infant stage and thought "they were wonderful." My memoir has been an ongoing process. I wrote new stories, rewrote the old, put them away for a few years, then took them out and put them away for a few more years... Maybe it was the tough love of my sister Sheryl and her influence that caused me to be brave and persevere. Anyway, I couldn't leave my memoir alone. However, the final push came when my sister Sue was on her deathbed in September of 2018 and wanted to hear my stories, asking for more. I reorganized and rewrote them for the last time and then seriously approached the publishing market.

So here I am thanking the Northeast Ohio Writers group—their enthusiasm for the letters was never-ending. Also my friend, Beth Bracale, who edited and supported my endeavor, pushing and prodding, always answering my grammatical questions and still remaining a friend. And to Ian Graham Leask at Calumet Editions for wanting to publish *Letters to the Chief* and Gary Lindberg, his partner and my editor, who answered questions, calls and texts ad infinitum, plus did a good job of editing and believing in the book.

The North Kingsville Library gets top ratings for technical help and general support as does their fellow-library in Ashtabula called the Harbor-Topky Memorial Library.

Thanks to Peg Asensio for her rendering of the photo of the chief and me, Michael Anne Johnson for my personal photo and Wendy Walton Mishne for assistance with the graphics.

The Cleveland Museum of Natural History clarified some info on Chief White Feather. My brother Don made connections with the news media and helped me with some editing conundrums.

I thank you all. I couldn't have done it without you.

ABOUT THE AUTHOR

A native of Minnesota and granddaughter of Swedish immigrants, Judi's childhood in Willmar is the focus of her autobiographical book, *Letters to the Chief*. As a young teen, the life-altering move with her family to Minneapolis was the impetus for writing her book. Even after years of living in Ohio, she remains a diehard "nostalgian" for her days spent at Eagle Lake near Willmar. Until its recent sale, Judi returned every year to spend the last week in June at the cabin with family to reclaim the joys of summer.

Literary endeavors have always played a large part in Judi's life. Born a Franklin, three generations of published writers among her ancestors were a significant influence. Two of them are published in Swedish. The memoir of her great grandmother, Sofia, was translated into English. During her childhood, Judi started to write and has never stopped. Journaling and writing poems and stories became a way of life.

Judi earned a degree from the University of Iowa with the support of a university grant and a National Institutes of Health (NIH) grant. Her work in radio-chemistry at Washington University followed by research in immunology at the University of Minnesota and the Minneapolis VA Health Care System resulted in co-authoring a number of scientific papers.

Relocating to further her career in science, Judi moved to Cleveland, Ohio to take a lab management position. She became a member of Northeast Ohio Writers. A few years later, restless with her life in a large corporation, she felt inspired to shift into creative pursuits. Judi opened an art gallery, which became her passion for twenty-five years until Leland Emerson, her life-partner of thirty years and the love of her life, developed cancer. She sold the business and became his medical advocate until he died.

Judi is forever grateful to Lee for encouraging her to spend sequestered hours writing, both at home and at their cabin on the Lake Erie shoreline. Today, Judi still travels between her home in Cleveland and North Kingsville On-the-Lake. She continues to write, work as a medical advocate, visit with family and friends, and dream. *Letters to the Chief* is her first book.